The _____
QUOTABLE CONSERVATIVE

The
QUOTABLE CONSERVATIVE

The Giants of Conservatism on Liberty,
Freedom, Individual Responsibility,
and Traditional Virtues

With an Introduction by WILLIAM F. BUCKLEY, JR.
Foreword by WILLIAM E. SIMON
Compiled by ROD L. EVANS and IRWIN M. BERENT

Adams Publishing
Holbrook, Massachusetts

Published by Adams Media Corporation
260 Center Street, Holbrook, MA 02343

ISBN: 1-58062-056-6

Printed in Canada.

J   I   H   G   F   E   D   C   B   A

Library of Congress Cataloging-in-Publication Data
Evans, Rod L.
The quotable conservative : the giants of conservatism on liberty, freedom, individual
responsibility, and traditional virtues / with an introduction by William F. Buckley, Jr. ;
foreword by William E. Simon ; compiled by Rod L. Evans and Irwin M. Berent.
p.   cm.
Includes index.
ISBN 1-58062-056-6 (pbk.)
1. Conservatism—Quotations, maxims, etc. 2. Liberty—Quotations, maxims, etc. 3. Individualism—
Quotations, maxims, etc. 4. Authority—Quotations, maxims, etc. I. Berent, Irwin M. II. Title.
JC573.E95   1998
320.52—dc21   98–8593
CIP

Jacket design by Ed Atkeson/Berg Design

Cover art: John Trumbull
Signing of Declaration of Independence
Courtesy Wood River Gallery, Mill Valley, CA

This book is available at quantity discounts for bulk purchases.
For information, call 1-800-872-5627 (in Massachusetts, 781-767-8100).

Visit our home page at http://www.adamsmedia.com

Dedication

This book is dedicated to Rush Limbaugh, who
pointed out the need for a book of quotations
that includes great conservative thinkers.

Table of Contents

Freedom Isn't Everything ... It's the Only Thing

From Aristotle to Adam Smith, Ronald Reagan, Alexander Solzhenitsyn, and Walter Williams, *The Quotable Conservative* presents a treasure chest of words and wisdom from leading thinkers across the ages.

Peruse these pages and you will find John Locke affirming the natural rights of man, Abraham Lincoln extolling the bulwarks of individual liberty and independence, and Rush Limbaugh demolishing the mindless cant of liberal politicians. They are among the 200 stars featured in this splendid book, which illustrates so convincingly why freedom remains not only the most exciting and powerful idea in human history but also the most successful.

Thomas Jefferson's philosophy of limited government has outperformed Karl Marx's vision of statism everywhere it has been tried. And today, the concept of freedom is winning out everywhere in the world. Indeed, its principles remain as timeless and timely as ever.

Whether it is the historic political realignment in America, the drive to lower tariffs and open markets across the globe, or the courage of a lone, Chinese citizen to block the path of a government tank in Tienanmen Square, the desire for freedom—personal, political, and economic—remains humankind's greatest and deepest longing.

Here in the United States, the American people have made clear their rising distrust, and even disgust, with Big Government spending, taxing, and regulation. They no longer see government as the solution, but as the problem.

At the same time, there is a renewed appreciation for free enterprise and free markets as the indispensable wellsprings of our national vitality and prosperity, and an essential basis for our hopes to give a better life to our children.

And so, we are being challenged to put into practice the same conservative principles that have won such overwhelming support at the polls. But are we prepared to accept the consequences of our professed beliefs? Do the American people truly understand that freedom is not free—even when that means demanding less from government? Above all, do we understand that our personal, political, and economic freedoms are inextricably linked, and that once we allow our economic freedom to be taken from us, our personal and political freedoms will not survive?

The answer to these questions will determine the future of our country and our ability to remain a strong, free, and thriving nation. As we wrestle with these questions, we can draw inspiration and guidance from this magnificent source of wisdom, *The Quotable Conservative*. No other book, to my knowledge, contains such a rich variety of quotations. And, while Evans's and Berent's masterly compilation will appeal enormously to conservatives, it will appeal, as well, to anyone genuinely interested in understanding America's founding principles.

William E. Simon

Preface

To the indignation of liberals, the most popular radio talk show hosts in America today are Rush Limbaugh and G. Gordon Liddy, who are also two of the most popular Americans, period. But why? We suggest that, although their manifest wit and nimbleness have been essential conditions for their success, those qualities aren't, by themselves, the key to their popularity. After all, there are many witty and adroit people, including political satirists such as Mark Russell, who aren't nearly as popular as Limbaugh or Liddy. We suggest that their popularity stems from not only their skills but also their *values*. For they emphasize in particular the importance of self-reliance and self-responsibility, as well as small government and the dangers inherent in the negation of those values. And those values, though generally labeled "conservative," are accepted by many people of almost every political affiliation.

Even many people who disagree with Limbaugh over abortion or with Liddy over some other social issue can agree with their defense of personal responsibility and arguments against one of its biggest enemies: expanding government. For many people—not just those who identify themselves as "conservatives," but also libertarians, moderate Democrats, and others—can see that tax increases hurt our economy, that welfare programs have discouraged the formation of stable families, and that governmental growth has resulted in the diminution of our economic and other liberties. And even the *Atlantic Monthly*, which is hardly a conservative magazine, has featured a cover story in which Dan Quayle's views about the evils of single-parent families are defended (April 1993).

What's more, a large number of the most influential columnists—William F. Buckley, Jr., James J. Kilpatrick, Jean Kirkpatrick, John Leo, William Safire, Thomas Sowell, George Will, Walter Williams, and others—reflect conservative thought on many issues. And some of the most highly respected political reporters in Washington—such as Bob Novak, Rowland Evans, and others—are conservatives. Still further, the highly respected editorial page of the *Wall Street Journal* is generally conservative. And conservative views are defended in a large number of respected periodicals, including *National Review, American Spectator, Public Interest, Policy Review, Commentary, Human Events, First Things,* and *National Interest.* Finally, while some liberals may make fun of *Reader's Digest,* this decidedly conservative periodical is the most widely circulated magazine in the world, and it was this periodical that recognized and condemned tyrannical communist regimes, including that of the Soviet Union, long before many liberals did so.

In short, conservatism has become a widely accepted way of thinking. No longer, to use Charles Kesler's phrase, "an unsteady dissenting faith," conservatism has come of age and is now a dominant political force.

The Purpose of this Book

We have compiled this collection of excerpts because we believe that the time is ripe for a book that distills the best conservative thought into easily digested chunks from a wide variety of sources. We are also aware that mainline quotation books—most notably *Bartlett's*—have essentially ignored conservative thought in their selections. In the latest edition of *Bartlett's* (16th ed., 1992), for instance, more quotations are presented from "silent" Cal Coolidge than from the great communicator Ronald Reagan. In fact, as a critical *Policy Review* article ("Mr. Kaplan, Tear Down This Wall: Bartlett's Missing Quotations," Adam Meyerson, Fall 1993) has noted, the Reaganisms cited in *Bartlett's* "aren't even memorable; instead they are intended to make

Mr. Reagan look ridiculous." Of the three cited, "one suggests there is no shortage of food in America. In another, Mr. Reagan says Republicans want 'an America in which people can still get rich.' The third compares government to a baby—'an alimentary canal with a big appetite at one end and no responsibility at the other.'" The slight to Reagan, however, is, to use Meyerson's cliché, "just the tip of the iceberg." For example, there are fully eleven quotations from economist John Kenneth Galbraith, a self-acknowledged socialist, against a combined total of merely five from the free-market economists Milton Friedman (3) and Friedrich von Hayek (2). And there are no quotations from the likes of Whittaker Chambers, William F. Buckley, Jr., Russell Kirk, Irving Kristol, George Will, George Gilder, Jeane Kirkpatrick, Rush Limbaugh, and a host of others.

What we have attempted to do is to pick those conservative ideas that resonate with most Americans and to avoid those few areas that divide even conservatives. For example, we have included quotations expressing the importance of self-responsibility, but we have omitted quotations on abortion. We realize that there are domestic issues, such as abortion and flag-burning, about which conservatives disagree, just as there are foreign policies, such as President Bush's invasion of Panama, over which conservatives disagree. Nonetheless, we believe that there is a core of conservative thought, a core that emphasizes individual responsibility and liberty; and it is to that core that this book is devoted.

The Diversity of Conservative Thought

Even though we have, in large part, avoided quotations that relate to highly controversial social issues, readers of this volume might observe that it contains the thoughts of at least a few persons who would find some of the others' ideas offensive, if not revolting. *Some* degree of pluralism, after all, is inevitable among reflective people, a fact that often goes unacknowledged by those liberals who regard conservatives as "narrow-minded." We submit, in fact, that every quotation in this volume is, in a legitimate sense, conservative.

While acknowledging the diversity of conservative thought, one can, nonetheless, identify some general and important threads that run through conservatism. Broadly speaking, conservatism refers to people's attachment to long-established customs, traditions, and institutions and to the doctrines by which people explain and defend that attachment. The remainder of this Preface examines the foundations of conservatism. It is to be hoped that, with this background, the reader will then be better prepared to absorb fully the conservative wisdom embedded within the quotations, however diverse they may seem.

The Foundations of Conservatism

Although the name "conservatism" developed in London and Paris about 1830 and was adopted after 1835 by a number of British Tories, conservatism, as a fully self-conscious philosophy, is regarded primarily as the offspring of the eighteenth-century English statesman and political philosopher Edmund Burke (1729–1797). And American conservatism, it is fairly safe to say, is heir to both Burke's thought and that of Thomas Jefferson (1743–1826). This discussion, therefore, will focus primarily on the thought of those two men.

The Father of Conservatism

While there have always been persons advocating reforms and others resisting those reforms, and while conservatives have, by their very nature, appealed to the thought of previous generations, including even that of the ancient philosophers Plato and Aristotle, it is often said that conservatism did not fully develop into self-conscious philosophical maturity until the French Revolution

(1789); in fact, conservative philosophy is conventionally dated from the publication of Burke's *Reflections on the Revolution in France* (1790). In that work the Irish-born English thinker opposed the sweeping social, political, and economic changes desired by many French revolutionaries. Regarded by many as the greatest conservative thinker, Burke saw the French Revolution as calling for the complete upheaval of long-established customs and traditions in favor of untried, vaguely defined, and unrealistic abstract ideals, whose attempt at fulfillment would destroy what is good along with what is bad.

Burke was not, however, an uncritical supporter of all tradition and monarchy. Indeed, he was a moderate member of the English Whig party and an outstanding Parliamentarian who was sympathetic to the Irish movement for independence and American grievances against England. What's more, Burke approved of the English Revolution of 1688 because he saw it as aimed at restoring rights to English citizens and securing succession to the throne. Similarly, he regarded the American Revolution and the Irish freedom movement as attempts to secure traditional rights and liberties recognized by English law. Burke saw the French revolutionaries, though, not as claiming traditional rights but as seeking to remake society at the expense of attacking personal property, religion, and the traditional class structure of a Christian kingdom. (Doubtless he would have viewed the Russian Revolution in 1917 in the same light.) Burke opposed the French Revolution because he believed that social and political affairs are so complicated as to defy any rationalistic blueprints based not on custom and tradition and the world as it is (including inequalities in natural abilities) but on ill-defined and unrealistic ideals.

Burke's convictions may be summarized as follows: That governance is extremely complex, requiring special abilities not evenly distributed throughout the populace; that social and political reforms can be desirable but usually only when they are gradual and evolutionary rather than comprehensive and rapid; that differences among people in intelligence, ability, industry, and achievement-oriented values are inevitable, and attempts to neutralize them or their effects will probably produce more harm than good; that attempts fundamentally to remake society according to some idealistic vision, imposed on all members, will predictably lead to disaster; that this world is highly imperfect, good being often if not usually mixed with evil, and it is usually better to accept some degree of that mixture than to risk producing what could easily be intolerably worse—in short, that advantages often lie in compromises between good and evil, or even among evils; and, finally, that it is dangerously naive—Burke would say "heretical"—to think that people are perfectible given the imposition of some "ideal" social and political system.

Thomas Jefferson

There are, to be sure, differences between Edmund Burke and Thomas Jefferson (Jefferson, for example, spoke more highly of reason); yet there are also important similarities. Both Jefferson and Burke saw the American Revolution as prompted by a demand for established constitutional rights; both accepted differences in social and economic classes as inevitable, given differences in abilities and achievement-oriented values. What's more, even though Burke accepted the institution of hereditary aristocracy, he, like Jefferson, believed that talented people who work hard ought to be able to advance socially, economically, and politically. But since Jefferson wanted people's stations in life to be determined as much as possible by their abilities, character, and choices, he opposed hereditary aristocracies and tried to minimize the role of government in people's lives. Indeed, the aim of minimizing the role of government in people's lives is at the heart of Jefferson's political philosophy.

Yes, Jefferson owned slaves; yes, he accepted without question the nearly universal conviction that women ought not to participate in politics. Nonetheless, Jefferson supported extending the political franchise to *unlanded* white males; and that support, at that time, was considered support for universal suffrage. What's more, Jefferson believed that America's laws and

Constitution should evolve with the evolution of thoughts, values, and knowledge. In short, he was in favor of a socially, economically, and politically fluid nation that protects people's rights while requiring individuals to take responsibility for their own lives.

Jefferson was deeply influenced by the political writings of English philosopher John Locke (1632–1704). For Locke, as for Jefferson, the authority of government is derived from the consent of the governed, who have inherent rights (i.e., natural rights) that governments are instituted to protect. Those rights include the right to life, liberty, and property, protected from majoritarian tyranny by America's Bill of Rights.

Although Jefferson was by definition a revolutionary, his convictions were in many ways conservative and have influenced most American conservatives. As has been mentioned, he believed in minimal government and in social and political arrangements that would foster an "aristocracy of talent and virtue." Because he knew that the free exercise of people's talents can exist only if government respects economic freedom, he opposed progressive taxation as an illegitimate effort to equalize social and economic classes. He wrote:

> To take from one, because it is thought that his own industry and that of his fathers has acquired too much in order to spare to others, who, or whose fathers[,] have not exercised equal industry and skill, is to violate arbitrarily the first principle of association, "the *guarantee* to every one of a free exercise of his industry, and the fruits acquired by it."
>
> LETTER TO JOSEPH MILLIGAN, APRIL 6, 1816

A firm defender of economic freedom, Jefferson was no socialist or liberal Democrat. Unlike most American politicians and policy makers today, he knew the difference between charity and coercion. He also knew that the more centralized a government becomes, the more likely it is to impose the will of the few on that of the many and the more likely it is to violate the rights it was instituted to protect.

Jefferson accepted authority in government, *provided that* the authority was restricted to government's fundamental duties to protect individual rights and that it was dispersed by the exercise of state and local governments and by the placement of constitutional checks and balances. He often warned against centralizing power in the federal government.

> [W]hen all government, domestic and foreign, in little as in great things, shall be drawn to Washington as the centre of all power, it will render powerless the checks provided of one government on another, and will become as venal and oppressive as the government from which we separated. It will be as in Europe, where every man must be either pike or gudgeon, hammer or anvil.
>
> LETTER TO C. HAMMOND, AUG. 18, 1821

Jefferson warned states to be "independent as to everything within themselves, and united as to everything respecting foreign nations" (Letter to Gideon Granger, Aug. 13, 1800). He warned that, if the states were not vigilant about their authority to govern internal affairs, their yielding power to the federal government would, by degrees, lead to "the most corrupt government on the earth" (same letter to Granger).

Unfortunately, most Americans, including their state representatives, have disregarded Jefferson's conservative principles. Degree by liberty-destroying degree, the federal government has been empowered—one might say enthroned—to such an extent that it is now intimately involved in the daily functioning of every state and in the daily lives of every American. Layers and layers of federal regulations and laws prevent countless capitalist actions among consenting adults (as when people are forbidden to work for below minimum wage); citizen A is forced to subsidize citizen B, who lives thousands of miles away, in the production of art that A regards as obscene and blasphemous; citizen B must give money to citizen C *not* to grow certain crops that C may have no intention of growing anyway; and citizen C in California must give money for citizen D's New York subway car. Americans, whose freedom and values are daily flouted by the government, have become involuntarily wedded to one big, unhappy extended family.

Jefferson feared that if citizens became lazy, apathetic, and irresponsible, government would gain ground and become tyrannical and corrupt, plundering taxpayers for special interests and violating property rights and other freedoms. His fears have come to pass as the federal government has become America's monarchy or Politburo.

Jefferson, like many conservatives, was also worried about public debt, which he believed must be minimized and paid off completely within a fixed period. He believed that a "wise and frugal government" would protect the economic freedom of not only contemporary citizens but also future generations. He wrote:

> [W]e must not let our rulers load us with perpetual debt. We must make our election between *economy and liberty*, or *profusion and servitude*. If we run into such debts, as that we must be taxed in our meat and in our drink, in our necessaries and our comforts, in our labors and our amusements, for our callings and our creeds, as the people of England are, our people, like them, must come to labor sixteen hours in the twenty-four, give the earnings of fifteen of these to the government for their debts and daily expenses; and the sixteenth being insufficient to afford us bread, we must live, as they now do, on oatmeal and potatoes; have no time to think, no means of calling the mismanagers to account; but be glad to obtain subsistence by hiring ourselves to rivet their chains on the necks of our fellow-sufferers .... [P]rivate fortunes are destroyed by public as well as private extravagance. And this is the tendency of all human governments. A departure from principle in one instance becomes a precedent for a second; that second for a third; and so on, till the bulk of the society is reduced to be mere automatons of misery .... Then begins, indeed, the *bellum omnium in omnia* [war of all against all] .... And the fore horse of this frightful team is public debt. Taxation follows that, and in its train wretchedness and oppression.
>
> LETTER TO SAMUEL KERCHIVAL, JULY 12, 1816

Jefferson's conservative convictions, then, may be summarized as follows: He was a strong advocate of the states' rights to disperse power and thereby allow for greater individual freedom. He was a strong believer in economic freedom (including property rights) and opposed the forced redistribution of wealth, as through progressive income taxation. He was in favor of minimizing the public debt, which he thought should be fully paid—interest and principal—within a fixed period; he believed that it was profoundly irresponsible, unfair, and just plain immoral for one generation to saddle another with debt. He also believed that people can have good government only to the degree that they are vigilant in keeping government within its properly limited sphere and only to the degree that they take responsibility for their lives. For Jefferson, as for many conservatives, government is an umpire, a police officer, a soldier but not an indulgent parent-substitute, a permissive nanny. In short, Jefferson was in many ways the antithesis of the liberal Democrat.

The Burkean and Jeffersonian Traditions

American conservatism may be said to be a product of both Burkean and Jeffersonian traditions. Reflecting the Burkean tradition, American conservatives have at times emphasized duties more than rights, discipline more than individual expression (which can lead to permissiveness), the public good more than individual liberty, and evolutionary and gradual change more than rapid and sweeping change. Reflecting the Jeffersonian tradition, many conservatives have argued for states' rights and property rights and a limited government with minimal debt and minimal taxes. As suggested earlier, the two traditions have much in common, including esteem for property rights and an acceptance of social and economic classes.

It might be said—though this is somewhat oversimplified—that the Burkean and Jeffersonian traditions diverge somewhat over the relative emphasis given to order and liberty. The truth is, most conservatives, like most people, want order *and* liberty, but they can and sometimes do disagree over the relative extent to which the order must be imposed from without (as from the government) and from within (as from the free decisions of individuals). While Burke emphasized order somewhat more than liberty, Jefferson emphasized liberty more than order, though like Burke, he believed that liberty cannot exist without order.

A Final Word

Every quotation in this volume is to some degree Burkean or Jeffersonian or a combination of both. Every quotation has either something positive to say about liberty, personal responsibility, or excellence, or something negative to say about slavery, irresponsibility, or mediocrity. A key theme throughout the book is that liberty (including economic freedom) and personal responsibility are indivisible and that a proper esteem for them will lead to social and economic inequalities that cannot be removed without governmental tyranny and a relentless assault on liberty, responsibility, and achievement.

Rod L. Evans
Irwin M. Berent

Acknowledgments

We want to thank William F. Buckley, Jr., and William E. Simon for contributing the Introduction and Foreword, respectively. Their kind words and impressive defenses of liberty are much appreciated. We also thank David Mayer, Professor of Law and History at Capital University, for his invaluable assistance, especially in offering his interpretation of Thomas Jefferson's thoughts. We also wish to thank Susan Phalen for her invaluable assistance at the press office of the Republican National Committee.

Our editors Brandon Toropov and Ed Walters warrant a special thanks for believing in us and our work. Thanks to Brandon and Ed. And to Jeff Herman, our literary agent, we extend thanks as well.

We want finally to thank Daryl Bank for his invaluable collection of the *Conservative Chronicle*, Chuck Hanretty for the newsletters of Rush Limbaugh and G. Gordon Liddy, Steve Morgan for his useful advice, and James Piereson, executive director of the John M. Olin Foundation, for his advice and assistance.

Introduction

The collection here given us by the industry of Messrs. Evans and Berent isn't of quotations by conservatives (or, here and there, non-conservatives who have nevertheless voiced a conservative thought or two). It is more properly excerpts from their work. They are meaty and heuristic, and useful hours can be spent surveying the work.

The market is a wonderful tease, when you think about it. A year or so back the gentleman in charge of updating *Bartlett's Quotations* heaved in with only a line or two from Ronald Reagan (contrasted with a shopping mall from such as JFK). There is evidence of some public protest over the tendentiousness of that collection. Messrs. Evans and Berent don't have that problem: they prowled about only for material that can be thought of as expressing conservative conclusions and intimations.

The first warning to the reader, especially given the protest involving Mr. Reagan, should focus on the undesirability of deducing from acreage given over, to any sense of ranking. It is embarrassing enough to appear on any roster in the company of, oh, Edmund Burke, let alone Aristotle. The only way men and women living and included in this collection can stand it is to think of ourselves as closer to being listed in a telephone book, than in a Who's Who. Absolutely nothing is to be deduced from idle speculation that Mr. Jones got 20 inches of space while Mr. Smith got only 10. Maybe the conclusion is merely that Jones is wordy.

The compilers have in their preface advised the reader of the reasons why some material was not included, specifically, material focused on issues in matters where there is a sharp division of sentiment. They are wise in these omissions. They are also wise in declining to give the impression that all, or for that matter many, of the excerpts contain epigrammatic material. In fact some of them do, but it is not the purpose of this volume to search out belletristic analysis. Instead, it is a keenness of perception that is evident in the works singled out.

I need to close with a brief personal observation. I think I once recorded that Sergei Rachmaninoff developed a loathing for his C sharp minor Prelude. He was 19 years old when he wrote it and it became so popular that audiences regularly insisted that he play it as an encore to his performances. On his 65th birthday a special concert was given in Carnegie Hall and Arthur Rubenstein performed as soloist in a concerto commissioned to celebrate the occasion. All eyes were trained on Rachmaninoff when Rubenstein struck the first chords. He went pale with horror when Rubenstein struck the familiar TAH, TAH, THUMMMMM—and was elated that from that moment on the score bore no resemblance to the famous Prelude. … All of which is by way of extending my gratitude to Messrs. Evans and Berent for declining to record that, once upon a time, in my youth, I replied to the question, what would I do if elected, "Demand a recount."

William F. Buckley, Jr.

Lord Acton *(1834–1902)*

(John Emerich Edward Dalberg-Acton)

Lord Acton was an English historian who served as Regius professor of modern history at Cambridge (1895–1902). He edited *Cambridge Modern History* and wrote on the French Revolution and modern history. One of his most noteworthy addresses is *The History of Freedom in Antiquity* (1877).

Liberty and good government do not exclude each other; and there are excellent reasons why they should go together. Liberty is not a means to a higher political end. It is itself the highest political end.

THE HISTORY OF FREEDOM IN ANTIQUITY, 1877

The great question is to discover, not what governments prescribe, but what they ought to prescribe; for no prescription is valid against the conscience of mankind.

IBID.

Increase of freedom in the State may sometimes promote mediocrity, and give vitality to prejudice; it may even retard useful legislation, diminish the capacity for war, and restrict the boundaries of Empire . . . . A generous spirit prefers that his country should be poor, and weak, and of no account, but free, rather than powerful, prosperous, and enslaved.

IBID.

Liberty alone demands for its realization the limitation of the public authority, for liberty is the only object which benefits all alike, and provokes no sincere opposition.

THE HOME AND FOREIGN REVIEW, 1862

The man who prefers his country before any other duty shows the same spirit as the man who surrenders every right to the state. They both deny that right is superior to authority.

IBID.

Whenever a single definite object is made the supreme end of the State, be it the advantage of a class, the safety or the power of the country, the greatest happiness of the greatest number, or the support of any speculative idea, the State becomes for the time inevitably absolute.

IBID.

Power tends to corrupt, and absolute power corrupts absolutely.

LETTER TO MANDELL CREIGHTON, APRIL 5, 1887

The danger is not that a particular class is unfit to govern. Every class is unfit to govern.

LETTER TO MARY GLADSTONE, APRIL 24, 1881

The law of liberty tends to abolish the reign of race over race, of faith over faith, of class over class. It is not the realisation of a political ideal: it is the discharge of a moral obligation.

IBID.

John Adams (1735–1826)

*J*ohn Adams was elected as a delegate to the First Continental Congress in 1774, serving until his appointment as commissioner to France (1777–1778). He served as vice president for two terms (1788–1796) and in 1796 was elected the second president of the United States. The views of Adams, a signer of the Declaration of Independence, on human nature, on the need for government, and on the causes of political conflict are significant contributions to conservative social, political, and economic thought. His *A Defence of the Constitutions of Government of the United States of America* (3 volumes, 1787–1788) is a classic.

The judicial power ought to be distinct from both the legislative and executive, and independent upon both, so that it may be a check upon both.

"THOUGHTS ON GOVERNMENT," 1776

Let us dare to read, think, speak and write.

"DISSERTATION ON THE CANON AND THE FEUDAL LAW," 1765

That all men are born to equal rights is true. Every being has a right to his own, as clear, as moral, as sacred, as any other being has. This is as indubitable as a moral government in the universe. But to teach that all men are born with equal powers and faculties, to equal influence in society, to equal property and advantages through life, is as gross a fraud, as glaring an imposition on the credulity of the people, as ever was practiced by monks, by Druids, by Brahmins, by priests of the immortal Lama, or by the self-styled philosophers of the French revolution.

LETTER TO JOHN TAYLOR OF CAROLINE, 1814

Property is surely a right of mankind as real as liberty. Perhaps, at first, prejudice, habit, shame or fear, principle or religion would restrain the poor from attacking the rich, and the idle from usurping on the industrious; but the time would not be long before courage and enterprise would come and pretexts be invented by degrees to countenance the majority in dividing all the property among them, or at least in sharing it equally with its present possessors. Debts would be abolished first; taxes laid heavy on the rich, and not at all on the others; and at last a downright equal division of everything be demanded, and voted. What would be the consequence of this? The idle, the vicious, the intemperate would rush into the utmost extravagance of debauchery, sell and spend all their share, and then demand a new division of those who purchased from them.

A Defence of the Constitution of the United States Against the Attacks of M. Turgot, 1787–1788

The moment the idea is admitted into society that property is not as sacred as the laws of God, and that there is not a force of law and public justice to protect it, anarchy and tyranny commence. If "Thou shalt not covet" and "Thou shalt not steal" were not commandments from Heaven, they must be made inviolable precepts in every society before it can be civilized or made free.

Ibid.

The way to secure Liberty is to place it in the people's hands, that is, to give them a power at all times to defend it in the legislature and in the courts of justice . . . .

Ibid.

It is agreed that "the end of all government is the good and ease of the people, in a secure enjoyment of their rights without oppression"; but it must be remembered that the rich are *people* as well as the poor; that they have rights as well as others; that they have as clear and as sacred a right to their large property as others have to theirs which is smaller; that oppression of them is as possible and as wicked as to others.

Ibid.

Samuel Adams *(1722–1803)*

*A*merican Revolutionary leader and member of the Massachusetts legislature (1765–1774), Samuel Adams was instrumental in maintaining activities of the Committees of Correspondence among American colonies and was a leader in the agitation that led to the Boston Tea Party. He was also a delegate to the First and Second Continental Congresses and a signer of the Declaration of Independence.

What a man has honestly acquired is absolutely his own, which he may freely give, but cannot be taken from him without his consent.

MASSACHUSETTS CIRCULAR LETTER, FEB. 11, 1768

Among the natural rights of the colonists are these: first, a right to *life*; secondly, to *liberty*; thirdly, to *property*; together with the right to support and defend them in the best manner they can. Those are evident branches of, rather than deductions from, the duty of self-preservation, commonly called the first law of nature.

"THE RIGHTS OF THE COLONISTS," 1772

William Barclay Allen *(1944–)*

A black political scientist, William Allen is a former director of the

U.S. Commission on Civil Rights. He emphasizes the importance of avoiding race consciousness and its divisive force.

This is a way of proceeding in our country which leads to disaster . . . . [P]eople are in the habit of thinking in terms of race, or gender—anything except of being an American. Until we learn once again to use the language of American freedom in an appropriate way that embraces all of us, we're going to continue to harm this country.

"C-SPAN," MAY 23, 1992

It is misleading to call affirmative action reverse discrimination, as we often do. There is no such thing, any more than the opposite of injustice, for example, is reverse injustice.

AMERICAN ENTERPRISE INSTITUTE, MAY 21, 1985

James Madison thought that the most important test of American freedom would be the ability of our political system to guarantee the rights of minorities without exceptional provisions for their protection. Affirmative action is incompatible with that constitutional design. Whoever calls for affirmative action declares at the same time that constitutional design has failed and that we can no longer live with our Constitution.

IBID.

I want to emphasize that while it is true that the objective for contemporary policy is a colorblind society, a more important objective is a free society.

IBID.

To argue that the Constitution established and perpetuated slavery is a fundamental mistake. When one pulls the Constitution away, one pulls away the structures that through the years gave us our only opportunity to abolish slavery.

IBID.

The end of slavery, the Civil War, [and] the Reconstruction amendments did not come about simply because at a certain moment in history there was a fantastic revelation and what was all dark suddenly turned bright and shiny. It came about because the educative effect of these [Constitutional] principles was there working, fermenting to produce the reason that not only would abolish slavery but would lead us all ultimately to adopt the principles of the American founding as our own and make possible a

genuine national life in which we forget about group rights and instead talk about the rights of individual human beings.

IBID.

Aristotle *(384–322 B.C.)*

*A*ristotle was Plato's most outstanding pupil (367–347 B.C.), a tutor of Alexander the Great (c.342–335), and a teacher in Athens (335–322). He wrote and lectured on logic, metaphysics, natural science, ethics and politics, and rhetoric and poetics. Aristotle's great philosophical work is *Metaphysics* (13 books), but he is also famous for many other works, including *Nicomachean Ethics*, *Politics*, *Rhetoric*, and *Poetics*.

It is best that laws should be so constructed as to leave as little as possible to the decision of those who judge.

RHETORIC, 1

Good laws, if they are not obeyed, do not constitute good government.

POLITICS

Those who think that all virtue is to be found in their own party principles push matters to extremes; they do not consider that disproportion destroys a state.

IBID.

[S]ometimes the demagogues, in order to curry favor with the people, wrong the notables and so force them to combine;—either they make a division of their property, or diminish their incomes by the imposition of public services, and sometimes they bring accusations against the rich that they may have their wealth to confiscate.

IBID.

But he who is unable to live in society, or who has no need because he is sufficient for himself, must be either a beast or a god.

IBID.

Democracy [*absolute* majority rule] . . . arises out of the notion that those who are equal in any respect are equal in all respects; because men are equally free, they claim to be absolutely equal.

IBID.

Virtue, like art, constantly deals with what is hard to do, and the harder the task the better the success.

NICOMACHEAN ETHICS, BK. II

Raymond Claude Ferdinand Aron *(1905–1983)*

*F*rench sociologist, philosopher, and political scientist, Raymond Aron was a lecturer at the University of Cologne (1930–1931) and taught at various institutions, including the University of Toulouse, where he taught sociology. He received many honorary degrees and wrote many papers and books, but is especially well known for *L'Opium des Intellectuels* (1955) [*The Opium of the Intellectuals*]. He also wrote *Main Currents in Sociological Thought* (1961).

The intellectual who no longer feels attached to anything is not satisfied with opinions merely; he wants certainty, he wants a system. The Revolution provides him with his opium.

THE OPIUM OF THE INTELLECTUALS, 1955

Communist faith justifies the means. Communist faith forbids the fact that there are many roads towards the Kingdom of God.

IBID.

[F]ar from being the . . . philosophy of the Proletariat, Communism merely makes use of . . . pseudo-science in order to attain its own end, the seizure of power.

IBID.

Douglas Bandow *(1957–)*

*A*former aid to President Ronald Reagan and special assistant to the president for policy development under Reagan, Douglas Bandow is a nationally syndicated columnist and has been a senior fellow at the Cato Institute since 1984. Bandow, who holds a law degree from Stanford, was an editor at *Inquiry Magazine* and a deputy representative to the United Nations Conference on the Law of the Sea. He edited *U.S. Aid to the Developing World* (1985).

[T]he conventional wisdom is that the only alternative to a government-run, taxpayer-financed system is private charity, which would inevitably allow millions of needy to "fall through the cracks." Thus, the question in the minds of most public officials is, what kind of public system should we use? . . .

In the early years of the American republic, people created an effective, community-based safety net, one that relied on personal involvement rather than bureaucratic action.

In fact, many different forms of social organization have been used by different societies at different times to provide what is today called "welfare." In some societies, the extended family or kin group is the primary locus of providing a "safety net."

In other cases it comes through the church—the Mormons, for instance. Similarly, in Islamic society welfare is financed by alms-giving, mandatory for Muslims, but the program is only organized rather than run by the state.

Perhaps the most interesting form of welfare institution in the West, at least to those concerned about individual liberty and personal independence, is collective self-help, or mutual aid as it is more commonly called. Coexisting with traditional charity, mutual aid was the dominant form of welfare up into the 1920s . . . .

. . . History provides us with numerous effective and voluntary alternatives to today's public system, but, unfortunately, it gives us few lessons on how to convince policy-makers . . . to begin shifting the responsibility from the public to the private sector.

"WELFARE REFORM HAS BECOME A FORGOTTEN ISSUE," OCT. 21, 1992

Edward Christie Banfield

(1916–)

*E*dward Banfield's best-known and perhaps most influential work is *The Unheavenly City: The Nature and Future of Our Urban Crisis* (1970). He is also the author of such works as *Government Project* (1951), *Politics, Planning and the Public Interest: The Case for Public Housing in Chicago* (with Martin Meyerson, 1955), *The Moral Basis of a Backward Society* (with Laura Banfield, 1958), *Political Influence* (1961), *City Politics* (with James Q. Wilson, 1963), *The Unheavenly City Revisited* (1974), and *Here the People Rule* (1985).

So long as the city contains a sizable lower class, nothing basic can be done about its most serious problems. Good jobs may be offered to all, but some will remain chronically unemployed. Slums may be demolished, but if the housing that replaces them is occupied by the lower class it will shortly be turned into new slums. Welfare payments may be doubled or tripled and a negative income tax instituted, but some persons will continue to live in squalor and misery.

THE UNHEAVENLY CITY, 1970

The lower-class forms of all problems are at bottom a single problem: the existence of an outlook and style of life which is radically present-oriented and which attaches no value to work, sacrifice, self-improvement, or service to family, friends, or community.

IBID.

New schools may be built, new curricula devised, and the teacher-pupil ratio cut in half, but if the children who attend these schools come from lower-class homes, the schools will be turned into blackboard jungles, and those who graduate or drop out from them will, in most cases, be functionally illiterate. The streets may be filled with armies of policemen, but violent crime and civil disorder will decrease very little. If, however, the lower class were to disappear—

if, say, its members were overnight to acquire the attitudes, motivations, and habits of the working class—the most serious and intractable problems of the city would all disappear with it.

THE UNHEAVENLY CITY REVISITED, 1974

I was born at night, but it wasn't last night.

IBID.

Isn't it great to have people in Congress that sign the front of the paycheck?

IBID.

Haley Barbour *(1947–)*

*H*aley Barbour, who has a law degree from the University of Mississippi, has held numerous positions within the Republican Party, including executive director of the Mississippi Republican Party (1973–1976) and most recently chair of the Republican National Committee (1994–). He is on the board of directors of a number of corporations, including Deposit Guaranty National Bank, Amtrak, National Railroad Passenger Corporation, and Mobil Telecommunications Technologies, Inc. Barbour currently hosts *The Rising Tide on GOP TV.*

Bill Clinton shares with the hummingbird the ability to turn 180 degrees in a split second.

THE RISING TIDE

Claude Frédéric Bastiat

(1801–1850)

A French economist, statesman, and author, Frédéric Bastiat was a firm believer in free enterprise and an opponent of socialism. Near the end of his life, he criticized the socialistic direction in which France was headed. A believer in private charity but not in the forced redistribution of wealth, Bastiat held that socialism violates property rights and leads to conflict and economic stagnation as the ratio of producers to consumers narrows.

Whenever a portion of wealth is transferred from the person who owns it—without his consent and without compensation, and whether by force or by fraud—to anyone who does not own it, then I say that property is violated; that an act of plunder is committed.

I say that this act is exactly what the law is supposed to suppress, always and everywhere. When the law itself commits this act that it is supposed to suppress, I say that plunder is still committed, and I add that from the point of view of society and welfare, this aggression against rights is even worse.

THE LAW, 1850

Try to imagine a regulation of labor imposed by force that is not a violation of liberty; a transfer of wealth imposed by force that is not a violation of property. If you cannot reconcile these contradictions, then you must conclude that the law cannot organize labor and industry without organizing injustice.

IBID.

Daniel Bell *(1919-)*

A prominent sociologist, Daniel Bell has written a number of books, including *The Coming of Post-Industrial Society* (1973), *The Cultural Contradictions of Capitalism* (1976), *The Winding Passage: Essays and Sociological Journeys* (1980), and

The Budget Deficits (with Lester Thurow, 1986).

The presumed failure of the idea of equality of opportunity has shifted the definition of that value to equality of result, and by fiat if necessary. The increasing thrust by disadvantaged groups, or their ideological mentors, has been for direct redistributive policies in order to equalize incomes, living conditions, and the like, and on a group basis. In the shorthand of game theory, equality of opportunity is a non–zero-sum game in which individuals can win in differential ways. But equality of result, or redistributive policies, essentially is a zero-sum game, in which there are distinct losers and winners. And inevitably these conditions lead to more open political competition and conflict.

THE WINDING PASSAGE, 1980

If one moves to Western society, generally, we find a subtle but pervasive change, namely, that the revolution of rising expectations, which has been even more tangible in the advanced industrial societies than in the underdeveloped countries, has become a sustained demand for entitlement. To be a "citizen" has usually meant to share fully in the life of the society. In the earliest years, this meant the claim to liberty and the full protection of the law. In the late nineteenth and early twentieth centuries, this was defined as political rights, principally the full right to vote or hold office by all adult citizens, a status which was achieved only fifty years ago in most Western societies. But the major claim in recent decades has been for social rights: the right to a job, insurance against unemployment and old age indigence, adequate health care, and a minimum, decent standard of living. And these are now demanded from the community as entitlement.

IBID.

Distributive justice is one of the oldest and thorniest problems for political theory. What has been happening in recent years is that entitlement, equity, and equality have become confused with one another, and the source of rancorous political debate. Yet they are also the central value issues of the time.

IBID.

William John Bennett *(1943–)*

A former secretary of education and director of the White House Office of National Drug Control Policy, William Bennett is a senior editor of *National Review.* He has a doctorate in political philosophy, and is the author of *The De-Valuing of America: The Fight for Our Culture and Our Children* (1992), *Our Children and Our Country: Improving America's Schools and Affirming the Common Culture* (1988), and *Counting by Race* (with Terry Eastland, 1979). He is also the editor of *The Book of Virtues* (1993).

[The shortage of student loans] may require . . . divestiture of certain sorts—stereo divestiture, automobile divestiture, three-weeks-at-the-beach divestiture.

NEW YORK TIMES, FEB. 12, 1985

If we believe that good art, good music, and good books will elevate taste and improve the sensibilities of the young—which they certainly do—then we must also believe that bad music, bad art, and bad books will degrade. As a society, as communities, as policymakers, we must come to grips with that truth.

THE DE-VALUING OF AMERICA, 1992

The battle over culture reaches beyond art, music, poetry, photography, literature, cinema, and drama. The broader issue has to do with a growing realization that over the last twenty years or so the traditional values of the American people have come under steady fire . . . .

. . . In this period, many of us lost confidence in our right and our duty to affirm publicly the desirability of what most of us believe privately. We allow[ed] our social and cultural institutions to drift away from their moorings; we allowed the public square to become, in Richard John Neuhaus's term, "naked." We ceased being clear about the standards which we hold and the principles by which we judge, or, if we were clear in our own minds, we somehow abdicated the area of public discussion and institutional decision making to those who challenged our traditional values. As a result, we suffered a cultural breakdown of sorts—in areas like education, family life, crime, and drug use, as well as in our attitudes toward sex, individual responsibility, civic duty, and public service.

IBID.

In our time, too many Americans became either embarrassed, unwilling, or unable to explain with assurance to our children and to one another the difference between right and wrong, between what is helpful and what is destructive, what is ennobling and what is degrading. The fabric of support that the American people—families especially—could traditionally find in the culture at large became worn, torn, and unraveled.

IBID.

Conservatism as I understand it is not essentially theoretical or ideological, but rather a practical matter of experience. It seeks to conserve the best elements of the past. ("What is conservatism?" Lincoln once asked. "Is it not adherence to the old and tried, against the new and untried?") It understands the important role that traditions, institutions, habits, and authority have in our social life together, and recognizes many of our national institutions as products of principles developed over time by custom, the lessons of experience, and consensus. Conservatives are interested in pursuing policies that will better reinforce and encourage the best of our people's common culture, habits, and beliefs. Conservatism, too, is based on the belief that the social order rests upon a moral base, and that what ties us together as a people—the *unum* in *e pluribus unum*—is in constant need of support.

IBID.

Is anyone going to argue seriously that a life of cheating and swindling is as worthy as a life of honest, hard work? Is anyone (with the exception of some literature professors at our elite universities) going to argue seriously the intellectual corollary, that a Marvel comic book is as good as *Macbeth*? Unless we are willing to embrace some pretty silly positions, we've got to admit the need for moral and intellectual standards.

IBID.

The problem is that some people tend to regard anyone who would pronounce a definitive judgment as an unsophisticated Philistine or a closed-minded "elitist" trying to impose his view on everyone else.

The truth of the real world is that without standards and judgments, there can be no progress. Unless we are prepared to say irrational things—that nothing can be proven more valuable than anything else or that everything is equally worthless—we *must* ask the normative question. This may come as a surprise to those who feel that to be "progressive" is to be value-neutral. But as Matthew Arnold said, "The world is forwarded by having its attention fixed on the best things." And if the world can't decide what the best things are, at least to some degree, then it follows that progress, and character, are in trouble. We shouldn't be reluctant to declare that some things— some lives, books, ideas, and values—are

better than others. It is the responsibility of the schools to teach these better things.

IBID.

Brigitte Berger (1928–)

A professor of sociology at Wellesley College, Brigitte Berger has written *The War Over the Family* (with Peter Berger, 1983) and edited *Child Care and Mediating Structures* (with Sidney Callahan, 1979).

[T]he family, and specifically the bourgeois family, is the necessary social context for the emergence of the autonomous individuals who are the empirical foundation of political democracy. This has been so historically. There is every reason to think that it continues to be so today.

THE WAR OVER THE FAMILY, 1983

Where, then, are the institutions that instill basic moral values in individuals? . . . [T]he school as an institution appears to be quite ineffective in instilling basic moral values—*unless* it serves to reinforce values already instilled in the individual by his home life. Very much the same is true of the churches. The law, which in America has arrogated to itself (or, more likely, been saddled with by others) the role of moral source or guide, is also singularly unsuited for this function; it is far too abstract, far too remote from the concrete social contexts in which individuals find meaning and identity. The family, today as always, remains the institution in which at any rate the very great majority of individuals learn whatever they will ever learn about morality. It is very unlikely that this will change. Once again, this means that the family has a political function of the greatest importance, especially in a democracy.

IBID.

No amount of legislation and court decisions can produce in the individual such basic moral ideas as the inviolability of human rights, the willing assent to legal norms, or the notion that contractual agreements must be respected.

IBID.

[N]either the state nor the judiciary can be moral authorities in and of themselves. When they try to do this, they either are ineffective (the usual case in democracies) or they start out on a path at the end of which lies totalitarianism, in which the political order tries to absorb into itself all values and all institutions in the society (in which case democracy must come to an end).

IBID.

Social order is impossible unless the conduct of individuals is predictable. In human beings, predictability of conduct depends on the development of a stable character and of reliable habits. Everything we know about social psychology indicates that both have their origins in family life. And . . . the bourgeois family has been particularly effective in providing a haven of stability in a rapidly changing society. The tensions of modernization, even under relatively benign circumstances, are trying for the individual; the family is the most important institution in which the child is prepared to withstand these tensions and in which, later on, the adult is given the emotional support to continue withstanding them. While providing this stability, the bourgeois family at the same time cultivates individual independence and initiative—again, personality traits that are particularly important under conditions of rapid social change.

IBID.

For understandable reasons, public policy in the modern welfare state has been aimed toward those who are weak and in need of help. Commonly, the people who fulfill these criteria are rather few . . . and certainly are a minority of the population. This very limited definition of the scope of public policy clashes with the expansionary tendency of the bureaucratic and professional empires spawned by the welfare state. Quite logically, the latter tended to inflate the definitions both of weakness and of need. Ever more families were added to the category of those too weak to cope by themselves, and new needs were invented. Thus, in America, the definition of the family was changed to "families," all of these were supposed to be in "crisis," and at the same time the real needs of certain types of families were magnified and distorted.

IBID.

Public policy with regard to the family should primarily be concerned with the family's capacity to take care of its children, its sick and handicapped, and its aged. The basic principle here should be that, whenever possible, these needs are best taken care of *within* the family—*any* family (barring a very few families to whom one would not entrust those who are weak or in need), regardless of social

or cultural type. This means that the overriding concern of public policy should be to provide support for the family to discharge these caring tasks, rather than to relieve the family of these tasks.

IBID.

[I]f one wants to foster the bourgeois family, the best course to take is to give people freedom of choice. Most of them will choose bourgeois values and bourgeois life-styles—especially people in the "targeted" groups of the poor and disadvantaged.

IBID.

Peter Ludwig Berger (1929–)

A professor at Boston University, where he has directed the Institute for the Study of Economic Culture, Peter Berger has written many books, such as the classic *Invitation to Sociology* (1963) as well as *American Apostasy* (1989), *The Capitalist Revolution* (1986), *Facing Up to Modernity* (1977), and *The War Over the Family* (with Brigitte Berger, 1983).

It is not possible to impose a socialist system without force, since those who are dispossessed in this imposition will not graciously assent to their fate. Hence, as Marx and all the other mainline Marxists argued, there must be a dictatorship. What neither Marx nor most of his epigones understood is that this need for dictatorship increases rather than decreases with the successful establishment of socialism: Central planning of the economy and despotic policies are intrinsically linked phenomena. The degree of power required by "the plan" requires dictatorial powers; . . . there is a natural tendency for a despotic elite to seek control over the economy on which its power rests. Of course, one can imagine different developments—all those included in the vision of a democratic socialism—and no social scientist can confidently assert that such developments are impossible. Yet enough is now known about the empirical workings of "real existing socialism" to make one highly skeptical of the chances for such a future possibility.

THE CAPITALIST REVOLUTION, 1986

Modern capitalism . . . has been a liberating force. The market in and of itself liberates people from the old confines of subsistence economies. It opens up choices, options, that were unheard of in traditional societies. These new choices are not merely economic and technological. Historically and empirically, there is a correlation with social and political choices, and even with choices on the level of consciousness. Thus the modern city, itself a creation of capitalism, has been a liberating force. The old German adage put it succinctly—*"Stadtluft macht frei"* (city air liberates). One may paraphrase: *"Kapitalistische luft macht frei"* (the air of capitalism liberates). *That* is the empirical justification of the ideological proposition that there is an intrinsic connection between economic freedom and all other liberties . . . . However, it does not follow from this that the liberating forces of capitalism are inevitable or irreversible.

IBID.

Walter Fred Berns *(1919–)*

*W*alter Berns has been a Rockefeller Fellow, a Fulbright Fellow, a Guggenheim Fellow, a Phi Beta Kappa lecturer, a winner of the Clark Distinguished Teaching

Award (Cornell University), and a member of the Council of Scholars in the Library of Congress. His books include *The First Amendment and the Future of American Democracy* (1976), *For Capital Punishment: Crime and the Morality of the Death Penalty* (1979), and *Taking the Constitution Seriously* (1987).

A human right properly and originally understood derives from or reflects an aspect of human nature, an aspect that distinguishes human from all other classes of beings and makes it possible for them alone to have rights. Man is not unique in having desires; for example, man and all other animals have planted in them "a strong desire of self-preservation." But only in man's case does this desire for preservation become transformed into a right or, as Locke himself puts it, does it serve as "the foundation of a right," a right to take and use what is "necessary or useful to his being." Insofar as they have desires but not rights, animals are said by Locke to be "inferior" to man; they are directed "by their sense and instinct," whereas man is directed by "his senses and reason." In saying this—and this is all he says directly—Locke suggests that it is man's

rationality that distinguishes him from other animals and allows him to be endowed with rights.

TAKING THE CONSTITUTION SERIOUSLY, 1987

To say that animals do not have rights is not to say we may treat them cruelly. On the contrary, it is human to know what pain is, human to know that we can inflict it and that animals can feel it, and, therefore, human (or humane) to seek to avoid inflicting it on them. When, contrary to the facts, someone issues a declaration to the effect that animals as well as men have rights, his purpose is not to protect animals from other animals but to protect them from other men; no one in his right mind expects the animals themselves to be influenced one way or another by such declarations. These animals can manifest desires, but only man, alone in his rationality, can speak—or has any reason to speak—the language of rights. Only a rational creature can claim a right for himself or recognize a right in another and—and this is the point by so doing, curb, check, restrict, or himself delay the satisfaction of, his own desires. Only a rational creature can understand the need to do this, and how it is in his own interest to do this, and how, in practice, it can best be done. All of which is to say that it is human beings who have rights and, because they have rights, not instincts, are in need of government and capable of instituting it.

IBID.

[T]he Americans of 1776 asserted their rights as men, not as Englishmen; they appealed not to the laws of the realm but to the laws of nature and of nature's God. In this important respect, the Declaration of Independence differs from, say, the celebrated Magna Carta. The barons who on June 15, 1215, met with King John in the meadow at Runneymede demanded and got what they said they were entitled to as English barons: "all the liberties (traditionally enjoyed by) the free men of (John's) kingdom." So, too, does the Declaration differ from the Bill of Rights of 1689. There the British Parliament appealed to and managed to restore "the Protestant Religion and the Lawes and Liberties of (that) Kingdome (which) the late King James the Second (had) endeavor(ed) to subvert and extirpate." As Hannah Arendt correctly pointed out, when, the year before, the Stuarts were expelled and the royal power was placed in the hands of William and Mary—an event known today as the Glorious Revolution—it was not thought of as a revolution at all, "but as a restoration of monarchical power to its former righteousness and glory." But the American appeal was to nature, not to tradition or the customary law . . . .

IBID.

[O]n this foundation [natural law] we built not only a nation of immigrants, but a nation of immigrants from every part of the globe. In the words of the old *Book of Common Prayer*, we became and remain a haven for "all sorts and conditions of men."

This is not to deny that our laws have sometimes been biased or our citizens prejudiced; it is merely to say, what is surely true, that in no other place is a prejudice against foreigners so inappropriate, so foreign, so difficult to justify. Xenophobia is, to use another term for which there is no analogue elsewhere, un-American. Precisely because America is something other than a place and a tradition, because words constitute the principal bond between us, anyone (in principle) may become an American. He has only to be Americanized, and, as I say, all sorts and conditions of men have been able and willing to do that.

IBID.

Locke . . . no longer enjoys an unsullied reputation. Jefferson thought Locke to be one of the three greatest men ever to live, and it used to be customary to refer to him as "America's philosopher"; but that is no longer true—or at least, the designation no longer goes unchallenged. The reason for this change in his status . . . has something to do with property and its ill repute in some contemporary circles. To speak of rights in a Lockean context is to conjure up thoughts of property and, what is thought to be worse, a dynamic rather than a static property: not merely a right to possess and use but a right to acquire. That is what Locke meant by the property right, and fully to secure it is certain to create significant disparities of income and wealth, disparities that are unacceptable to modern egalitarians. Nor is that all that is thought to be wrong with Locke: to secure the right to acquire would seem to promote acquisitiveness, which bears a certain resemblance to covetousness, a mortal sin according to traditional Christian doctrine. To disconnect Jefferson and with him America from John Locke is, for the typical left-wing critic, a moral as well as an intellectual necessity.

IBID.

Allan David Bloom *(1930–1992)*

*A*llan Bloom was co-director of the John M. Olin Center for Inquiry into the Theory and Practice of Democracy at the University of Chicago, where he was also a professor on the Committee of Social Thought. He taught at Yale, Cornell, the University of Toronto, and other universities, and translated and edited Plato's *Republic* and Rousseau's *Emile.* Although he wrote numerous articles, as well as *Shakespeare's Politics* (1964) and *Confronting the Constitution* (1990), he is best known for *The Closing of the American Mind* (1987), a sweeping analysis and critique of contemporary thought.

The black studies programs largely failed because what was serious in them did not interest the students, and the rest was unprofitable hokum. So the university curriculum returned to a debilitated normalcy. But a kind of black domain, not quite institutional, but accepted, a shadow of the university life, was created: permanent quotas in admission, preference in financial assistance, racially motivated hiring of faculty, difficulty in giving blacks failing marks, and an organized system of grievance and feeling aggrieved. And everywhere hypocrisy, contempt-producing lies about what is going on and how the whole scheme is working. This little black empire has gained its legitimacy from the alleged racism surrounding it and from which it defends its subjects. Its visible manifestations are to be found in those separate tables in the dining halls, which reproduce the separate facilities of the Jim Crow South. At Cornell and elsewhere, the black militants had to threaten—and to do—bodily harm to black students with independent inclinations in order to found this system. Now the system is routine . . . .

THE CLOSING OF THE AMERICAN MIND, 1987

The university's acquiescence in the interference with its primary responsibility of providing educational opportunity to those capable of education should be a heavy burden on its collective conscience.

IBID.

Affirmative action now institutionalizes the worst aspects of separatism. The fact is . . . that the university degree of a black student is . . . tainted, and employers look on it with suspicion, or become guilty accomplices in the tolera-

tion of incompetence. The worst part of all this is that the black students, most of whom avidly support this system, hate its consequences. A disposition composed of equal parts of shame and resentment has settled on many black students who are beneficiaries of preferential treatment. They do not like the notion that whites are in the position to do them favors. They believe that everyone doubts their merit, their capacity for equal achievement. Their successes become questionable in their own eyes. Those who are good students fear that they are equated with those who are not, that their hard-won credentials are not credible. They are the victims of a stereotype, but one that has been chosen by black leadership. Those who are not good students, but have the same advantages as those who are, want to protect their position but are haunted by the sense of not deserving it . . . .

IBID.

White students . . . do not really believe in the justice of affirmative action, do not wish to deal with the facts, and turn without mentioning it to their all-white—or, rather, because there are now so many Orientals, non-black—society. Affirmative action (quotas), at least in universities, is the source of what

I fear is a long-term deterioration of the relations between the races in America.

IBID.

[D]emocratic society cannot accept any principle of achievement other than merit.

IBID.

David D. Boaz *(1953–)*

*E*xecutive vice president of the Cato Institute, a Washington, D.C. libertarian think-tank devoted to a belief in minimal government, David Boaz has written many articles and edited a number of works, including *Liberating Schools: Education in the Inner City* (1991) and *Market Liberalism: A Paradigm of the 21st Century* (with Edward H. Crane, 1993).

In the private sector, firms must attract voluntary customers or they fail; and if they fail, investors lose their money, and managers and employees lose their jobs. The possibility of failure, therefore, is a powerful incentive to find out what customers want and to deliver it efficiently. But in the government sector, failures are not punished, they are rewarded. If a government agency is set up to deal with a problem and the problem gets worse, the agency is rewarded with more money and more staff— because, after all, its task is now bigger. An agency that fails year after year, that does not simply fail to solve the problem but actually makes it worse, will be rewarded with an ever-increasing budget.

LIBERATING SCHOOLS, 1991

A key point to keep in mind is that nongovernment schools, which have to offer a better product to stay in business, do a better job of educating children. Defenders of the education establishment have tried to dismiss that success by claiming that the private schools start with a better grade of students—once again, blaming the customers for the enterprise's failure. But that excuse has been exposed time and again. Urban Catholic schools serve a clientele not terribly different from that of the government schools. Marva Collins's school in Chicago received national publicity for its success with poor black children, many of them declared "learning disabled" by the neighborhood government schools. Joan Davis Rateray of the Institute for Independent Education describes . . . the success of many minority-run independent schools. Any remaining doubts should have been eliminated in 1982 when James S. Coleman and his colleagues, after a comprehensive investigation of the results of public versus private schools, concluded that "when family backgrounds that predict achievement are controlled, students in . . . private schools are shown to achieve at a higher level than students in public schools."

IBID.

Daniel J. Boorstin *(1914-)*

Senior historian of the Smithsonian Institution, Daniel Boorstin is an extremely versatile intellectual. Until 1969 he was Preston and Sterling Morton Distinguished Service Professor of American History at the University of Chicago, where he taught for twenty-five years. He earned degrees from Harvard, Oxford, and Yale and practiced law in Massachusetts. He is known for his numerous books, including *The Americans* (a trilogy, 1958–1973), *The Image: A Guide to Pseudo-Events in America* (1964, 1971), *Democracy and Its Discontents* (1971, 1974), and *The Decline of Radicalism* (1969). He also edited the twenty-seven volume *Chicago History of American Civilization* series.

[W]e must abandon the prevalent belief in the superior wisdom of the ignorant. Unless we give up the voguish reverence for youth and for the "culturally deprived," unless we cease to look to the vulgar community as arbiters of our schools, of our art and literature, and of all our culture, we will never have the will to de-provincialize our minds. We must make every effort to reverse the trend in our schools and colleges—to move away from the "relevant" and toward the cosmopolitanizing, the humanizing, and the unfamiliar. Education is learning what you didn't even know you didn't know. The vogue for "Black Studies" itself grew out of the ghetto, and ironically enough, unwittingly became an effort to idealize the ways of the ghetto. The last thing the able young Negro needs is "Black Studies"—which simply reinforces the unfortunate narrowness of his experience and confines him in *his* provincial present. He does need a better, more cosmopolitan educational system, from kindergarten on up, and a freer opportunity to grasp the opportunities in the whole nation.

DEMOCRACY AND ITS DISCONTENTS, 1971, 1974

We must return to the ideal of equality. We must recognize that many of the acts committed in the name of equal opportunity are in fact acts of discrimination. We must reject reactionary programs, though they masquerade under slogans of progress, which would carry us back to Old World prejudices, primitive hatreds, and discriminatory quotas. Our cultural federalism, another name for the fellowship of man in America, must once again emphasize what each can give to us. We must reject the clenched fist for the open hand. We must aim, more than ever before, to become color-blind. We must aim to create conditions of equal opportunity—by improving American schools beginning at the very bottom, and by ruthlessly applying the same standards of achievement to all Americans regardless of race, sex, religion, or national origin—the same standards for admission to institutions of higher learning, for graduation, for the Civil Service, for elected office, and for all other American opportunities. We weaken our nation and show disrespect for all our fellow Americans when we make race or sex or poverty a disqualification—and equally so when we make them a qualification.

IBID.

A more open America is a nation with fewer barriers. It is not a nation of proud, chauvinistic, self-seeking "minorities." We must not allow ourselves to become the Quota States of America.

IBID.

Robert Heron Bork *(1927-)*

*L*awyer, former federal judge, and Reagan Supreme Court nominee, Robert Bork is known for his vast scholarship and his judicial philosophy, which is that of strict constructionism, in which judges are to evaluate laws in relation to the original intent of the Constitution. He taught at Yale Law School, was a resident scholar at the American Enterprise Institute, and wrote *The Anti-Trust Paradox* (1978) and *The Tempting of America* (1990), in which he explains, among other things, his judicial philosophy.

The impact of the academic world is heavily to the left of the general political spectrum. We receive a particular point of view from the media because of the nature of the academic world—through its writing, through its teaching, through its alliance with the media.

When a journalist wants some comments on the current Supreme Court, for example, he calls constitutional law professors. It just happens that he hears very hostile comments about the Burger Court and very friendly comments about the Warren Court.

AMERICAN ENTERPRISE INSTITUTE, 1977

In a constitutional democracy the moral content of law must be given by the morality of the framer or legislator, never by the morality of the judge.

IBID., 1984

Those who made and endorsed our Constitution knew man's nature, and it is to their ideas, rather than to the temptations of utopia, that we must ask that our judges adhere.

THE TEMPTING OF AMERICA, 1990

[W]hen a judge goes beyond [his or her proper function], and reads entirely new values into the Constitution, values the framers and ratifiers did not put there, he deprives the people of their liberty. That liberty, which the Constitution clearly envisions, is the liberty of the people to set their own social agenda through the process of democracy.

STATEMENT AT HEARINGS TO BECOME
A SUPREME COURT JUSTICE, 1987

James Bovard (1956–)

A journalist and policy analyst, James Bovard has written for many magazines, including *Newsweek*, *The New Republic*, and *Reader's Digest*. Among his writings are *The Fair Trade Fraud* (1991) and *Lost Rights: The Destruction of American Liberty* (1994).

The Internal Revenue Service is the authoritarian means to paternalist ends. A government that is anxious to give alms to as many people as possible is even more anxious to commandeer their earnings. Increasingly, the average American's guilt or innocence is left to the eye of the tax auditor, not to the citizen's actual behavior. Federal tax policy is now largely oppression in the name of revenue maximization.

The U.S. Treasury Department defines a tax as "a compulsory payment for which no specific benefit is received in return." No matter how many taxes a person pays, or what politicians promise, the taxpayer is not irrevocably entitled to a single benefit from the government. The level of taxation is thus a stark measure of government's financial power over the individual—a precise gauge of the subjugation of the citizen to the financial demands of the state.

LOST RIGHTS, 1994

Tax rates measure the nation's most important and costly entitlement program—how much of a person's income politicians are entitled to take. According to the Tax Foundation, the average citizen had to work 123 days in 1992 to pay his taxes—from January 1 through May 3 . . . . If the government announced a program of forced labor, and conscripted every taxpayer for over a third of a year without compensation, there would [most] likely be a national revolt. But as long as taxes are seized through payroll tax withholding, most citizens have little opportunity for resistance.

IBID.

Warren T. Brookes (1929–)

*A*n award-winning columnist for Creators Syndicate, Warren Brookes holds a degree in economics from Harvard and is known for his carefully argued economic critiques of liberal thought. He is the author of *The Economy in Mind* (1982).

[T]he whole notion of using the tax system as a method of redistributing wealth rests on a fallacy—namely, that wealth is money, and that all one has to do to transfer wealth is to transfer money.

The trouble with that hypothesis is that money is nothing more than a medium of exchange. Real wealth is the total productive output of the economy in the form of services and goods, which are in turn the product of the energy, resources, and talents of the people who produce them. Thus merely passing money around does little to change a nation's real productive output or wealth, nor does it change the inherent "wealth capacity" of individual citizens. All it does is to reduce the real value of the money itself, through inflation.

THE ECONOMY IN MIND, 1982

The attempt to redistribute wealth by redistributing money through the progressive tax tables only winds up keeping the poor poor, the rich rich, and the middle class struggling even harder to keep up with taxation.

IBID.

Whenever populists use the pejorative term "trickle-down," they are referring to classic supply-side economics. But the plain truth is that in any free society, through invention, creativity, and enterprise, a comparatively small part of the population still contributes the major share of economic growth. In this largest and richest of all industrial democracies, it is still safe to say that 80%–90% of the new jobs and economic growth is contributed by the efforts, imagination, energy, and initiative of less than 5%–10% of all individuals, through whose creativity the great wealth of this country still "trickles down" to the economy.

In the process, of course, this top 5%–10% has become very rich, and not always very nice; but genius seldom seems to equate with meekness and charity. Yet without those well-rewarded individuals who often have risked everything to create the one new enterprise in ten that succeeds, our economy would become stagnant, and trickle-down would quickly be replaced by dole-out, as it has in Poland, Russia, China, Cuba, or even England.

IBID.

[T]rickle-down is really the natural order of things, not merely in economics and business, but in nearly every other facet of life as well. We are all blessed by the genius of relatively few.

Many thousands of books are published each year, but only a few hundred survive the test of time. The world's greatest music is still the work of a comparative handful of great composers, and most of the world's great art is the product of a few hundred brilliant talents. The Bible is the compilation of the ideas and inspiration of a few dozen prophets, yet it enriches the lives of billions.

IBID.

[I]nflation itself has its fundamental roots in the politics of envy—specifically, in the federal government's well-meaning but clumsy efforts to redistribute income from the rich to the poor.

The problem is that today there are not enough rich people around to pay for the more than $500 billion in social spending. Everyone must pay; and since politicians don't like to tax everyone, inflation has become the acceptable but hidden method of transfer.

Each rise in this transfer spending load has increased the tax burden on the entire middle class—and when politicians are afraid to load this tax burden fully on the voters, they resort to increasing use of deficit financing and to printing paper money to accommodate it. Is it really any wonder that the money they print is *green*?

IBID.

In an economy whose wealth is increasingly metaphysical (ideas, inventions, high technology) and whose greatest capital resource is the *individual,* the greatest single threat to economic growth and dynamic development is the growing bureaucratization of our society in both the corporate and the governmental spheres. This was why the best economic news in an otherwise dismal 1981 was that, for the first time in nearly 30 years, government employment had gone down, not up.

It is no coincidence that the productivity of the U.S. economy has declined in almost precise proportion to the rapid buildup in government employment which, between 1950 and 1980, soared by 168%—from 6 million to 16 million. While private employment grew by only 90% during the same period and employment in manufacturing by only 34%, government bureaucratic jobs multiplied six times as fast as blue-collar jobs.

IBID.

Unfortunately, the chief effect of growing regulation by the various state and federal agencies and of tax-subsidized litigation in the courts has been to reduce markedly both the variety and the pace of innovation of virtually all new products now being offered to consumers. Small companies (which have always been the source of most real innovation) can no longer afford the costs and the process of securing product compliance or adequately insured protection from new liability laws and class-action suits.

Meanwhile, the largest conglomerates (whom Naderites profess to hate) are enjoying all of this respite from entrepreneurial competition and are increasingly avoiding the regulatory hassle and playing it safe with proven product winners, instead of taking risks or responding to the marketplace creatively. Instead of genuine breakthroughs, we are seeing more and more in consumer products what we have seen in television shows: safe spinoffs, frequent rip-offs, and modest variations on past success models.

Government regulation also reduces competition in other ways. By setting elaborate and detailed standards and guidelines for products and processes, it automatically decreases either the necessity to produce better products or the incentive for real innovation. Government standards tend to become industry norms, and corporations tend to devote more attention to preserving the status quo than beating the standards . . . .

The effect of such regulation is always to reduce the consumer's ability to force better products and lower prices through the free market, which is the democratic and natural process of supply meeting demand.

IBID.

James McGill Buchanan *(1919–)*

*E*conomist and educator James Buchanan holds a doctorate from the University of Chicago, as well as the Nobel Prize in Economics (1986). He has taught at numerous universities and written numerous books, including *Public Principles of Public Debt* (1958), *The Calculus of Consent* (1962), *The Limits of Liberty* (1975), and *Essays on the Political Economy* (1989).

If we rule out default for the time being, the primary economic consequence of debt-financed spending by government is the guaranteed necessity that we must, as citizens–taxpayers program beneficiaries, give up some part of our incomes in future periods in order to meet interest and amortization charges on debt. A share of our future incomes is obligated to meet the legitimate claims held by creditors of the government. And it makes no difference whatsoever whether these creditors are themselves citizens or foreigners.

ESSAYS ON THE POLITICAL ECONOMY, 1989

The financing of current government spending by debt is equivalent to an "eating up" of our national capital value . . . . By financing current public outlay by debt, we are, in effect, chopping up the apple trees for firewood, thereby reducing the yield of the orchard forever.

IBID.

The person who is faced with a tax bill to finance interest charges . . . will reckon only on the simply observed fact that income that he or she might otherwise use is being taken away in taxes. The result is precisely analogous to the apple orchard example introduced earlier. If the yield of three trees under a person's nominal ownership is committed to debt service, it is fully equivalent to having an orchard with three fewer trees.

IBID.

The descriptive implications of the elementary analysis are clear. The federal government has embarked on a debt-financed spending spree that cannot be permanently sustained. The fact that the government cannot go bankrupt in any sense analogous to a person or business firm does nothing to modify the central proposition. Government's ultimate taxing and money-creation powers can, of course, guarantee that all nominally valued debt claims will be honored, but neither an ever-increasing interest share of tax revenues nor an inflationary monetization of nominal debt claims offers a viable option for permanent reform.

The budgetary deficit must be reduced.

Ibid.

Why is work good, and why is loafing bad? . . . There are gains from the division of labor, from specialization in production accompanied by exchange or trade. Hence the act of entering into the exchange nexus itself generates benefits to everyone else in the nexus, and the work-leisure choice of an individual always involves just such an act.

Think of a simple example. Jones and Smith are frontier farmers. They live side by side, but each one of them is totally self-subsistent. Each grows his own pota-

toes and his own pigs. There is no specialization, no division of labor, and no trade. But each man then realizes that both can gain by entering into a specialization and exchange relationship. Jones begins to specialize in growing potatoes; Smith begins to specialize in growing pigs. Then they swap the potatoes and the pigs. Both are made better off; each can consume both more potatoes and more pigs. Each person has, in choosing to enter this economic arrangement, conferred benefits both on himself and his trading partner.

Ibid.

[W]e must recognize that every time we choose, individually and privately, to work an additional hour, an additional day, an additional week, we are, in so doing, entering the exchange nexus. We are producing goods that are valued by others, and even though we are paid in full for value produced for others, there remains a residue of value to be shared with others. In loafing, there is no spillover share in the excess value produced. The value in loafing is exclusively internal to the person who does the loafing. The argument suggests that there is ethical content in the work-leisure choice of the individual, that the traditional folk wisdom is indeed correct, that we may legitimately and on the basis of a rational choice calculus deem work to be praiseworthy and loafing to be blameworthy. And this conclusion emerges without materialistic or meddlesome preferences for any sort of work or consumption pattern the individual may choose to adopt. So long as work adds something of value in exchange, there is a social spillover benefit that is absent in leisure except as is internal to the person who chooses it.

IBID.

Patrick Joseph Buchanan (1938-)

*P*at Buchanan, who has an M.S. in journalism from Columbia University, has been an editorial writer, a political speechwriter, a special assistant (and executive assistant) to President Richard Nixon, a columnist, and a Republican presidential candidate. He has regularly appeared on cable TV political shows, including *Crossfire*, *The McLaughlin Group*, and *Capital Gang*. Besides his columns, he is known for such books as *The New Majority* (1973), *Conservative Votes, Liberal Victories* (1975), *Right from the*

Beginning (1988, 1990), and *America Asleep* (1991).

When one reflects upon conditions in those societies where government controls four-fifths of the economy, and government devotes itself to the material and moral uplift of the people, it is not difficult to conclude with Dr. [Samuel] Johnson that "a man is never more innocently involved than in the making of money."

CONSERVATIVE VOTES, LIBERAL VICTORIES, 1975

Consider the minimum wage. For many years, conservative economists have argued that the correlation between a high minimum wage and high unemployment among the unskilled is absolute. Others contend that increasing the minimum wage not only prices the least able out of the job market, but threatens others, because of the incentive it provides to automation. Still others view rapid advances in the minimum wage as socially devastating in the inner city, especially to black teenagers who need work experience infinitely more than they need the higher wage few employers will pay a seventeen-year-old.

In brief, the minimum wage is anything but a simple issue. Yet, what comes across the networks is that, "Senator Kennedy and the Democrats called today for a 20-cent increase in the minimum wage; the Republican Administration, however, is opposed, arguing that raising the income of the poorest-paid workers will mean added unemployment."

IBID.

William Frank Buckley, Jr.

(1925–)

*O*ne of the most influential and prolific conservatives of the second half of the twentieth century, William F. Buckley is the editor-in-chief of the *National Review*, author of numerous books, including even some spy thrillers, and a syndicated columnist (for example, "On the Right"). His books include *God and Man at Yale* (1951), *McCarthy and His Enemies* (with Brent Bozell, 1954), *Up from Liberalism* (1959), *Rumbles Left and Right* (1963), *The Unmaking of a Mayor* (1966), *The Jeweler's Eye* (1968), *Inveighing We Will Go* (1972), *Stained Glass* (1978), *A Hymnal* (1978), *Right Reason* (1985), and *Gratitude: Reflections on What We Owe to Our Country* (1990). In addi-

tion, Buckley, whose remarkable debating skills are near-legendary, is known for having hosted since 1966 the extraordinarily literate PBS interview show *Firing Line*.

There is nothing so ironic as the nihilist or relativist (or the believer in the kind of academic freedom that postulates the equality of ideas) who complains of the anti-intellectualism of American conservatives. Such is *our* respect for the human mind that we pay it the supreme honor: we credit it with having arrived at certain great conclusions. We believe that millenniums of intellection have served an objective purpose. Certain problems have been disposed of. Certain questions are closed: and with reference to that fact the conservative orders his life and, to the extent he is called upon by circumstances to do so, the life of the community.

UP FROM LIBERALISM, 1959

It is a part of the conservative intuition that economic freedom is the most precious temporal freedom, for the reason that it alone gives to each one of us, in our comings and goings in our complex society, sovereignty—and over that part of existence in which by far the most choices have in fact to be made, and in which it is possible to make choices, involving oneself, without damage to other people. And for the further reason that without economic freedom, political and other freedoms are likely to be taken from us.

IBID.

The salient economic assumptions of liberalism are socialist.

IBID.

A society has the right to impose negative restraints; but positive acts of compliance it may exact only in extraordinary situations. One may not murder, steal, drive drunkenly, commit libel, undress publicly. But there is not, for each of these prohibitions, a corresponding injunction of an affirmative kind. To require participation in a social enterprise is a fatal habit for a free society to get into.

IBID.

One must bear in mind that the expansion of federal activity is a form of eating for politicians.

NATIONAL REVIEW, SEPT. 8, 1964

When one declares oneself to be a conservative, one is not, unfortunately, thereupon visited by tongues of fire that leave one omniscient. The acceptance of a series of premises is just the beginning.

After that, we need constantly to inform ourselves, to analyze and to think through our premises and their ramifications. We need to ponder, in the light of the evidence, the strengths and the weaknesses, the consistencies and the inconsistencies, the glory and the frailty of our position, week in and week out. Otherwise we will not hold our own in a world where *informed* dedication, not just dedication, is necessary for survival and growth.

IBID., FEB. 8, 1956

One tends to forget that conscription entails the suspension of any number of basic human rights; conscription, for example, allows the government to exact involuntary servitude, and to curtail essential civil liberties . . . . We should applaud any effort to determine whether we could adequately, and at reasonable cost, man the defenses of the nation with volunteers.

IBID., OCT. 27, 1956

The key phrase, for cryptographers who desire to learn the meaning of the Society that is supposed to shape our future, is the following, which you will see repeated time after time: "The Great Society is concerned not with the quantity of our goods but the quality of our lives." . . . [W]hat it does mean is that the Government of the United States, under Lyndon Johnson, proposes to concern itself over the quality of American life. And this is something very new in the political theory of free nations. The quality of life has heretofore depended on the quality of the human beings who gave tone to that life, and they were its priests and its poets, not its bureaucrats.

IBID., SEPT. 7, 1965

Tax *all* the luxuries of the rich and you don't have enough money to buy all the Vatican treasures—it is the middle class and the lower middle classes who are shouldering the great economic load today, for the simple reason that the rich, if you took away everything they had, could relieve the world's poor for a single week.

IBID., APRIL 18, 1967

We [have] become what the philosophers called solipsists—men who recognize reality only in themselves. And when this happens, our own private little worlds, sustained only by our self-love, are easily shattered, and as they shatter we advance the destruction of our entire civilization, and race towards the Apocalypse ever so much faster than thermonuclear bombs will take us there.

IBID., AUGUST 27, 1963

The whole business [of tax reform] is a mess, as is anything which decidedly appeals to different sets of rules. If we desire justice, it should be justice for all. Ideally there would be *no* exemptions, no, not even for colleges or churches or charities; no deductions, no not for business expenses or hospital bills; no subsidies, no not for farmers, or tenants, or small businesses: and lo, if all these deductions, all these business expenses, all these subsidies, were eliminated, the result would be, in effect, a subsidy for all—in the form of uniform, simplified, reduced taxation . . . . It occurs to us that any magazine capable of publishing these noble sentiments should be tax-exempt.

IBID., MAY 6, 1961

It is comforting to tell ourselves that in a free society no fraud can survive for very long after it is publicly discredited; but alas, that is not in fact the case—as witness, for instance, socialism, which is left without serious defenders, but whose forms encroach on us year after year.

RUMBLES LEFT AND RIGHT, 1963

The state is a divine institution. Without it we have anarchy, and the lawlessness of anarchy is counter to the natural law: so we abjure all political theories which view the state as inherently and necessarily evil. But it is the state which has been in history the principal instrument of abuse of the people, and so it is central to the conservatives' program to keep the state from accumulating any but the most necessary powers.

THE CATHOLIC WORLD, MARCH 1961

The not so very long-term objective should be to eliminate the draft in favor of a professional army of volunteers, who would greatly increase the efficiency of the armed services, and relieve the civil population of an experience which, insofar as it is unrelated to true necessity, is debasing, and an unnecessary—and therefore inexcusable—encroachment on individual freedom.

"ON THE RIGHT," APRIL 23, 1964

The new thing in education is the encouragement of privately sponsored, privately administered pedagogical techniques: e.g., "I'll teach your children to read for $75 apiece." An extension of this innovative approach to education is the gradual loosening of the superstition that publicly administered education is the most desirable kind of education for everyone. Parents who want them should receive vouchers, exchangeable at private schools of one's choosing. The social purpose would be to permit pluralism, indi-

viduation, and the adaptation of schools to the special needs of those who have special needs.

IBID., MAY 21, 1968

No one now doubts that what maintains the majority of American students in the public schools in the major cities is economic pressure. Let us admit that if the state were to give each child a voucher, on the order of what is given to veterans under the G.I. Bill of Rights, cashable for sum X at any accredited school, that there would be massive redeployments of children in all the major centers of the United States. And not only the children of the upper middle class. Also poor Negro children, for instance—to private schools especially designed to give special assistance to meet special needs . . . . It is the dawning realization that everybody would be better off under a mixed system in which public schools remained—for those who chose to patronize them. It is even suggested now by pedagogues of great reputation that it might be sound for the public schools to employ private contractors to teach the art of reading to individual students aged four and five and six. Indeed, the day may not be far away when it becomes possible—one is breathless at the prospect—to advocate the voucher system, and take education away from the bureaucrats and the egalitarians and the politicians and return it to the teachers and to the parents.

IBID., JAN. 13, 1968

The government has practically nothing to do with houses, if you consider government-built or subsidized houses as a percentage of the whole. (Between 1950 and 1960, free enterprise built 18,000,000 housing units, while the government, net, destroyed 100,000.) The people of America come within reach of houses as a result of their own exertions, and as a result of the disposition of other people to save. What makes it difficult for people to build their houses is: a) taxes (taken by the government); b) inflation (caused by the government); and c) restrictive labor union policies (protected by the government). The most useful thing the government could do to place decent homes within the reach of its people, is go away.

IBID., JAN. 23, 1968

In effect, the government and the unions and the National Labor Relations Board are suggesting that every business is to some extent a public utility and that therefore the one most crucial decision regarding it, namely, whether it shall

continue to operate or not, is under certain conditions the business of the government rather than that of its owners. The implications of that position shed light on the changing concept of socialism during the past generation. It used to be that socialism meant simply government ownership of the means of production. As far back as twenty years ago a leading theorist of socialism, Mr. G. D. H. Cole, lectured the Fabian Society on the necessity to recognize that outright ownership is merely a technicality. What, he asked, is the purpose of government ownership if, instead, the government can with far greater convenience control corporations by indirect means? What does it matter who owns the title to the business if wages are in effect determined by government (through monopoly rights given to labor unions and through minimum wage laws), if profits are controlled (through taxation), and if production quotas can be set (as during wartime and in periods of emergency)?

IBID., DEC. 17, 1964

Mr. [Lyndon] Johnson has declared "unconditional war" against poverty, but manifestly there are any number of weapons he does not intend to use in order to prosecute that war. He is not, for instance, going to fire any guns, during the forthcoming campaign, on labor union monopolies, which aggravate poverty by extracting artificially high prices from employers, and so cause the price of living to rise. He is not going to drop any shells on his own Department of Agriculture, which pays bonuses to farmers to keep them from growing food, and so aggravates the problem of the poor by raising the cost of bread and butter. He is not going to torpedo the minimum wage laws, which do so much to keep the poor poor, by denying them work at the only price marginal producers are in a position to pay. And above all he is not going to do anything substantial—nothing beyond Mr. Kennedy's proposed reductions—to take government off the back of the people, to leave them freer to work for themselves, to cultivate and distribute the nation's wealth. It is, in short, going to be a sweetheart war. And, by the way, we are not going to win it with Mr. Johnson's choice of weapons.

IBID., JAN. 18, 1964

Government welfare programs are justified only as a means to providing emergency relief for the needy that cannot be, or is not being, provided by nongovernmental sources. As a general rule, the more affluent the society, where the surpluses of private agencies and individuals grow, the less the theoretical need to depend on government welfare. Meanwhile a welfare program ceases to operate in the community interest when it:

—encourages participation in it by persons who have no plausible claim to that community's care;

—encourages participation as a permanent condition, rather than as an expedient to be terminated as quickly as possible through gainful employment or other forms of private support;

—encourages degenerate and socially disintegrating attitudes and practices;

—neglects to provide jobs for participants who are able to work, thus denying them the opportunity, and the discipline, for self-help;

—is administered so as to create unnecessary bureaucratization and waste of public resources.

THE UNMAKING OF A MAYOR, 1966

Edmund Burke *(1729–1797)*

A British statesman and orator, and an excellent and prolific writer, Edmund Burke is commonly viewed as the father of modern conservatism. He is best known for his critique of the French Revolution, *Reflections on the Revolution in France* (1790). (For more on Burke, see the Preface.)

Power gradually extirpates from the mind every humane and gentle virtue.

A VINDICATION OF NATURAL SOCIETY, 1756

The power of perpetuating our property in our families is one of the most valuable and interesting circumstances belonging to it, and that which tends the most to the perpetuation of society itself.

REFLECTIONS ON THE REVOLUTION IN FRANCE, 1790

It is better to cherish virtue and humanity, by leaving much to free will, even with some loss to the object, than to attempt to make men mere machines and instruments of a political benevolence. The world on the whole will gain by a liberty, without which virtue cannot exist.

IBID.

Your literary men and your politicians, and so do the whole clan of the enlightened among us, essentially differ in these points. They have no respect for the wisdom of others, but they pay it off by a very full measure of confidence in their own. With them it is a sufficient motive to destroy an old scheme of things because it is an old one. As to the new, they are in no sort of fear with regard to the duration of a building run up in haste, because duration is no object to those who think little or nothing has been done before their time, and who place all their hopes in discovery. They conceive, very systematically, that all things which give perpetuity are mischievous, and therefore they are at inexpiable war with all establishments. They think that government may vary like modes of dress, and with as little ill effect; that there needs no principle of attachment, except a sense of present convenience, to any constitution of the state. They always speak as if they were of opinion that there is a singular species of compact between them and their magistrates which binds the magistrate, but which has nothing reciprocal in it, but that the majesty of the people has a right to dissolve it without any reason but its will. Their attachment to their country itself is only so far as it agrees with some of their fleeting projects; it begins and ends with that scheme of polity which falls in with their momentary opinion.

IBID.

In a democracy the majority of citizens is capable of exercising the most cruel oppressions upon the minority . . . . Those who are subjected to wrong under multitudes are deprived of all external consolation: they seem deserted by mankind, overpowered by a conspiracy of their whole species.

IBID.

Manners are of more importance than laws. Upon them, in a great measure, the laws depend. The law touches us but here and there, and now and then. Manners are what vex or smooth, corrupt or purify, exalt or debase, barbarize or refine us, by a constant, steady, uniform, insensible operation, like that of the air we breathe in. They give their whole form and color to our lives. According to their quality, they aid morals, they support them, or they totally destroy them.

IBID.

Whatever each man can separately do, without trespassing upon others, he has a right to do for himself . . . .

IBID.

But what is liberty without wisdom, and without virtue? It is the greatest of all possible evils; for it is folly, vice, and madness, without tuition or restraint.

IBID.

Party division, whether on the whole operating for good or evil, are things inseparable from free government.

IBID.

A State without the means of some change is without the means of its conservation.

IBID.

Society is indeed a contract. Subordinate contracts for objects of mere occasional interest may be dissolved at pleasure—but the state ought not to be considered as nothing better than a partnership agreement in a trade of pepper and coffee, calico, or tobacco, or some other such low concern, to be taken up for a little temporary interest, and to be dissolved by the fancy of the parties. It is to be looked on with other reverence, because it is not a partnership in things subservient only to the gross animal existence of a temporary and perishable nature. It is a partnership in all science; a partnership in all art; a partnership in every virtue and in all perfection. As the ends of such a partnership cannot be obtained in many generations, it becomes a partnership not only between those who are living, but between those who are living, those who are dead, and those who are to be born. Each contract of each particular state is but a clause in the great primeval contract of eternal society, linking the lower with the higher natures, connecting the visible and invisible world, according to a fixed compact sanctioned by the inviolable oath which holds all physical and all moral natures, each in their appointed place. This law is not subject to the will of those who by an obligation above them, and infinitely superior, are bound to submit their will to that law. The municipal corporations of that universal kingdom are not morally at liberty at their pleasure, and on their speculations of a contingent improvement, wholly to separate and tear asunder the bands of their subordinate community and to dissolve it into an unsocial, uncivil, unconnected chaos of elementary principles. It is the first and supreme necessity only, a necessity that is not chosen but chooses, a necessity paramount to deliberation, that admits no discussion and demands no evidence, which alone can justify a resort to anarchy. This necessity is no exception to the rule, because this necessity itself is a part, too, of that moral and physical disposition of things to which man must be obedient by consent or force; but if that which is only submission to necessity should be made the object of choice, the law is broken, nature is disobeyed, and the rebellious are outlawed, cast forth, and exiled from this world of reason, and order, and peace,

and virtue, and fruitful penitence, into the antagonist world of madness, discord, vice, confusion, and unavailing sorrow.

IBID.

Government is a contrivance of human wisdom to provide for human wants. Men have a right that these wants should be provided for by this wisdom.

IBID.

When bad men combine, the good must associate; else they will fall, one by one, an unpitied sacrifice in a contemptible struggle.

THOUGHTS ON THE CAUSE OF THE PRESENT DISCONTENTS,
1770

We must all obey the great law of change . . . . All we can do, and that human wisdom can do, is to provide that the change shall proceed by insensible degrees . . . . This gradual course . . . will prevent men . . . from being intoxicated with a large draught of new power, which they always abuse with a licentious insolence.

QUOTED IN RUSSELL KIRK'S *THE CONSERVATIVE MIND,*
1953

Men are qualified for civil liberty in exact proportion to their disposition to put moral chains upon their own appetites; in proportion as their love of justice is above their rapacity; in proportion as their soundness and sobriety of understanding is above their vanity and presumption; in proportion as they are more disposed to listen to the counsels of the wise and good, in preference to the flattery of knaves.

A LETTER TO A MEMBER OF THE NATIONAL ASSEMBLY, 1791

Those who have once been intoxicated with power, and have derived any kind of emolument from it, even though but from one year, can never willingly abandon it.

IBID.

Society cannot exist unless a controlling power upon will and appetite be placed somewhere, and the less of it there is within, the more there must be without.

IBID.

It is ordained in the eternal constitution of things, that men of intemperate minds cannot be free. Their passions forge their fetters.

IBID.

The natural rights of mankind are indeed sacred things, and if any public

measure is proved mischievously to affect them, the objection ought to be fatal to that measure, even if no charter at all could be set up against it. Only a sovereign reason, paramount to all forms of legislation and administration, should dictate.

SPEECH ON CONCILIATION WITH AMERICA, MARCH 22, 1775

All government, indeed every human benefit and enjoyment, every virtue, and every prudent act, is founded on compromise and barter.

IBID.

The people never give up their liberties but under some delusion.

SPEECH, 1784

The only thing necessary for the triumph of evil is for good men to do nothing.

ATTRIBUTED, 1795

The tyranny of a multitude is a multiplied tyranny.

LETTER TO THOMAS MERCER, FEBRUARY 26, 1790

Among a people generally corrupt liberty cannot long exist.

LETTER TO THE SHERIFFS OF BRISTOL, APRIL 3, 1777

Liberty must be limited in order to be possessed.

IBID.

Your representative owes you, not his industry only, but his judgment; and he betrays instead of serving you if he sacrifices it to your opinion.

<small>SPEECH TO THE ELECTORS OF BRISTOL, NOV. 3, 1774</small>

A thing may look specious [*sic*] in theory, and yet be ruinous in practice; a thing may look evil in theory, and yet be in practice excellent.

<small>IMPEACHMENT OF WARREN HASTINGS, FEB. 19, 1788</small>

The greater the power, the more dangerous the abuse.

<small>SPEECH ON THE MIDDLESEX ELECTION, 1771</small>

James Burnham *(1905–1987)*

*F*rom 1932 to 1940 James Burnham was active as a leftist radical. He was once the editor of *The New International*, the chief theoretical journal of the Trotskyists. In 1940, he broke from Marxism and eventually came to write for William F. Buckley's *National Review* for twenty years.

Burnham is especially known for such outstanding works as *The Machiavellians, Defenders of Freedom* (1943), *The Struggle for the World* (1947), *The Coming Defeat of Communism* (1950), *Suicide of the West: An Essay on the Meaning and Destiny of Liberalism* (1964), and *The War We Are In* (1967).

The judgments that liberals render on public issues, domestic and foreign, are as predictable as the salivation of Pavlovian dogs.

<small>*SUICIDE OF THE WEST,* 1964</small>

Modern liberalism, for most liberals, is not a consciously understood set of rational beliefs, but a bundle of unexamined prejudices and conjoined sentiments. The basic ideas and beliefs seem more satisfactory when they are *not* made fully explicit, when they merely lurk rather obscurely in the background, coloring the rhetoric and adding a certain emotive glow.

IBID.

For Western civilization in the present condition of the world, the most important practical consequence of the guilt encysted in the liberal ideology and psyche is this: that the liberal, and the group, nation or civilization infected by liberal doctrine and values, are morally disarmed before those whom the liberal regards as less well off than himself.

IBID.

Government has no right to control individual liberty beyond what is necessary to the safety and well-being of society. Such is the boundary which separates the power of the government and the liberty of the citizen or subject in the political state.

SPEECH, SENATE, JUNE 27, 1848

John C. Calhoun *(1782-1850)*

A champion of states' rights, John C. Calhoun was an American lawyer, a member of the U.S. House of Representatives (1811–1817), a secretary of war (1817–1825), a vice president under John Quincy Adams and Andrew Jackson (1825–1832), a senator (1832–1843, 1845–1850), and a secretary of state (1844–1845). Calhoun's views on human nature and the abuses of political power and his theory of the "concurrent majority" are important to American conservatism.

The very essence of a free government consists in considering offices as public trusts, bestowed for the good of the country, and not for the benefit of an individual or a party.

SPEECH, FEB. 17, 1835

Francis P. Canavan *(1917–)*

A leading American political and religious thinker, Francis Canavan is known especially for *The Political Reason of Edmund Burke* (1960). He is also the author of *Freedom of Expression* (1984) and editor of *The Ethical Dimension of Political Life* (1983).

With the passing of the Warren Court and the dwindling in numbers of the liberal wing, the Court has become more ready to grant states and localities some discretion in judging when freedom of expression is being abused. But the liberal objection remains the same: the public always goes too far, therefore the public must never be allowed to judge . . . [J]uries will surely throw out the pearls with the garbage . . . . This in effect is to hold that common sense and the judgment of ordinary men and women, of the kind who sit on juries, have nothing to do with questions involving the limits of expression.

Underlying this distrust of popular judgment is the centuries-old liberal quest for abstract, utterly impersonal rules of law, that have only to be applied to cases as they arise, without the necessity of any personal judgment at all. Categories such as "obscenity," "defamation," or "advocacy of violent overthrow" must [according to this liberal quest] be rejected because they cannot be precisely defined . . . .

FREEDOM OF EXPRESSION, 1984

Juries, applying general legal definitions and instructed by trial judges, are capable of passing judgment on obscenity and other abuses of freedom of expression. They are often more capable of doing so than civil-liberties lawyers and literary critics who have a vested interest in not recognizing the obvious. When juries err by clear excess, they are subject to correction by appellate courts which will themselves pass prudential judgments on the matter—sound ones, we may hope.

IBID.

[T]here is no escaping the personal judgments of human minds in the application of law to concrete decisions. Personal judgment is unavoidable, in fact, even in the hardest of "hard sciences." Some human minds must judge what constitutes evidence and when the evidence proves a conclusion. There is no set of facts "out there" that talks to men and tells them what is true. All the more so in the area of practical judgment which guides human action, an area that includes the domain of law. Judgment here necessarily requires evaluation of the facts, estimation of the relative weight and force of a multitude of factors and an effort rationally to predict consequences. Practical judgment is not a blind shot in the dark, but neither is it the mathematical demonstration of an ineluctable conclusion.

IBID.

Consider the names of Shakespeare, Molière, Cervantes and Dostoievski. Add Dante and Goethe, if you wish. Not one of them lived in a liberal democracy. Yet critics have compared their writings favorably with the best work of Ernest Hemingway and Norman Mailer. One would be hard put to it, in fact, to come up with the name of a single author of the same stature as these great writers, who lived under a regime of complete freedom of expression or even, for that matter, in a modern liberal democracy.

Neither, of course, did any of the men named above live in Stalin's Russia or under an equally repressive tyranny. Writers need freedom, as do scientists, scholars, teachers and voters. But the question is how much and what kind of freedom? That question can be answered only by addressing oneself to the future question, what do they need freedom for? The purposes of freedom must define its nature and its limits. Inquiry into those purposes will yield a more intelligent theory of freedom of expression than groping for a pearl in the garbage or dreading the loss of a pearl if any garbage at all is thrown out.

IBID.

[W]hile the Constitution must be interpreted and applied by courts of law, it was not written for the convenience of lawyers and courts. It provides basic norms for the government of a nation, which nation is not well served by reducing its constitution to the kind of rules that courts find it easiest to apply. As Chief Justice Burger put it for the Supreme Court, "no amount of 'fatigue' should lead us to adopt a convenient 'institutional' rationale—an absolutist, 'anything goes'

view of the First Amendment—because it will lighten our burdens."

IBID.

George Wescott Carey *(1933–)*

A contributor to several leading political science journals, George Carey has edited such works as *Liberalism Versus Conservatism* (with Willmoore Kendall, 1966) and *A Second Federalist* (with Charles S. Hyneman, 1970), and wrote *In Defense of the Constitution* (1989).

[S]ince at least the advent of the New Deal, . . . the dominant political forces have seen their main task as one of achieving "social democracy" which, when distilled, comes down to greater economic and social equality. The extent of the shift over four decades can hardly be exaggerated. What were formerly regarded as dispensations by government are now looked upon as vested rights. We now have entrenched interests in the bureaucracy whose very livelihood depends upon identifying social "wrongs" and developing long-range plans to ameliorate them. The quest for equality in all spheres of social life seemingly knows no bounds short of repealing the laws of nature.

IN DEFENSE OF THE CONSTITUTION, 1989

Allan C. Carlson *(1949–)*

*P*resident of the Rockford Institute in Illinois and a member of the National Commission on Children, Allan Carlson holds a doctorate in modern history. He has written numerous essays and articles on the family for both popular and scholarly publications, as well as such books as *Family Questions: Reflections on the American Social Crisis* (1988) and *The Swedish Experiment in Family Politics* (1990).

[T]he "comparable worth" doctrine derives whatever federal legal status it has primarily from Title VII of the Civil Rights Act of 1964, which prohibits discrimination in employment on the basis of sex. Yet this critical provision, which is serving as the crucial wedge for the wholesale, government-enforced transformation of sex roles in America, was adopted by Congress without hearings, after less than half a day of confused debate, and somewhat as a joke. Indeed, it was introduced as an amendment to the Civil Rights bill on the floor of the U.S. House of Representatives by Democrat Howard Smith of Virginia, who hoped to scuttle the whole measure by attaching to it an embarrassing, confusing, and silly provision. When he proposed this amendment, it was actually met by a gale of laughter (dutifully recorded in the Congressional Record); Smith had to reassure his colleagues that he was "serious about this thing."

FAMILY QUESTIONS, 1988

The processes by which the "new morality" undermines the "old" are fairly obvious. School-based clinic advocates, for example, are adamant on one point: adolescents have a "right to privacy" which overrides parental control. If the children want contraceptives, parents must not be informed without their offsprings' consent. Indeed, at the national level, this same "right" has served as the legal device through which the federal courts have tossed out the laws in all fifty states that once governed birth control and abortion. At the family or neighborhood level, this same "right" has worked to destroy the traditional means of scrutiny by which parents or other elders governed the fertility of the young. With traditional controls so shattered, only the welfare state—in the guise of state-funded family planning clinics—remains to fulfill the role, albeit through radically different means.

IBID.

The feminist left . . . has . . . an agenda that confronts the core questions that modern family policy must address: "the social construction and control of . . . sexuality and the mix of women's domestic and market labor, especially . . . when young children are present." It is an agenda that also claims to bear historical inevitability: the traditional family, and the wage system which sustained it, is gone forever; a new structure must be created by the state. In its essence, this family agenda involves the socialization of child rearing. It would create child allowances as part of the Social Security system; maternal and child health care as the first stage of a national health insurance scheme; direct governmental subsidization of daycare as a right; and the transformation of corporations into quasi-public agencies for the socialization of children.

In short, it is precisely the "new economic foundation for a higher form of the family and of the relation between sexes" that Karl Marx described in *Capital,* over a century ago.

IBID.

The central lesson of the last one hundred years is that the state can disrupt, but it cannot save families. That task can only be achieved through a revitalized, family-affirming culture. We need a literature that celebrates, rather than denigrates, the familial virtues. We need a popular culture that defends what is wholesome and decent in American life. We need normative social arrangements that reinforce Americans who make a commitment to children and home. We need an educational system that, without apology, presents and upholds marriage, fidelity, and children as the essential framework for the good life. Except at the margins, these are clearly not tasks of government.

IBID.

A familial culture will either emerge out of the popular sentiments of the people, or it will not appear at all. It cannot be imposed by the crude hand of bureaucracy.

Accordingly, a family policy for a free people will largely be one involving the creative disengagement of the state and the reconstruction, to the degree possible, of the natural family economy. From nature, the family can claim prior existence to the state and the exercise of prerogatives that no government can rightfully impair. For families in America, the central task of the next decade is to win back the authority and autonomy which are their due. The alternative can be starkly drawn: the continued socialization of families and childbearing, to their ultimate disappearance, and the ongoing destabilizing of a free and responsible people.

IBID.

Thomas Carlyle (1795-1881)

A Scottish essayist and historian, Thomas Carlyle first gained attention as an interpreter of German romanticism with his *Life of Friedrich Schiller* (1825) and translation of Goethe's *Wilhelm Meister* (1824). Critical of the materialism of his age, Carlyle expressed his views about life in his famous spiritual autobiography, *Sartor Resartus* (1833–1834), and in *French Revolution* (1837). A traditional conservative rather than a libertarian conservative, he believed in a strong government and criticized laissez-faire theory and parliamentary democracy in *On Heroes, Hero-Worship, and the Heroic in History* (1841), *Chartism* (1840), and *Past and Present* (1843).

All great peoples are conservative; slow to believe in novelties; patient of much error in actualities; deeply and forever certain of the greatness that is in law, in custom once solemnly established, and now long recognized as just and final.

PAST AND PRESENT, 1843

All work . . . is noble; work is alone noble . . . . A life of ease is not for any man, nor for any god.

IBID.

Lord Hugh Richard Heathcote Cecil (1869-1956)

A British statesman and the author of *Conservatism* (1912), Lord Hugh Cecil headed, with Winston Churchill, a group of independents in the House of Commons.

Before the Reformation it is impossible to distinguish conservatism in politics, not because there was none, but because there was nothing else.

CONSERVATISM, 1912

Conservatism ought not to be, and at its best is not, the cause of rich people, but it ought to be the cause of the defence of property against unjust treatment. It ought to be so, not only because property is an institution required for the sake of the common good, but also because the owners of it, like other human beings, are entitled to be guarded against undue injury.

IBID.

Virtue is attained in proportion as liberty is attained; virtue does not consist in doing right, but in choosing to do right. This is the great distinction, surely, between the animal and man.

QUOTED IN KENNETH ROSE'S *THE LATER CECILS*, 1975

Whittaker Chambers *(1901–1961)*

*T*he principal witness against Alger Hiss, Whittaker

Chambers is best known for his authorship of *Witness* (1952), in which he related his renunciation of Communism. In 1938, Chambers left the Communist party. He developed strong religious views and joined William F. Buckley's influential circle at the *National Review*. His letters to William F. Buckley, Jr., are collected in *Odyssey of a Friend: Whittaker Chambers' Letters to William F. Buckley, Jr., 1954–1961* (1970).

I saw that the New Deal was only superficially a reform movement. I had to acknowledge the truth of what its more forthright protagonists, sometimes unwarily, sometimes defiantly, averred: the New Deal was a genuine revolution, whose deepest purpose was not simply reform within existing traditions, but a basic change in the social, and, above all, the power relationships within the nation. It was not a revolution by violence. It was a revolution by bookkeeping and lawmaking. In so far as it was successful, the power of politics had replaced the power of business. This is the basic power shift of all the revolutions of our time. This shift *was* the revolution.

WITNESS, 1952

There is one experience which most sincere ex-Communists share, whether or not they go only part way to the end of the question it poses. The daughter of a former German diplomat in Moscow was trying to explain to me why her father, who, as an enlightened modern man, had been extremely pro-Communist, had become an implacable anti-Communist. It was hard for her because, as an enlightened modern girl, she shared the Communist vision without being a Communist. But she loved her father and the irrationality of his defection embarrassed her. "He was immensely pro-Soviet," she said, "and then—you will laugh at me—but you must not laugh at my father—and then—one night—in Moscow—he heard screams. That's all. Simply one night he heard screams."

A child of Reason and the 20th century, she knew that there is a logic of the mind. She did not know that the soul has a logic that may be more compelling than the mind's. She did not know at all that she had swept away the logic of the mind, the logic of history, the logic of politics, the myth of the 20th century, with five annihilating words: one night he heard screams.

IBID.

What Communist has not heard those screams? They come from husbands torn forever from their wives in midnight arrests. They come, muffled, from the execution cellars of the secret police, from the torture chambers of the Lubianka, from all the citadels of terror now stretching from Berlin to Canton. They come from those freight cars loaded with men, women and children, the enemies of the Communist State, locked in, packed in, left on remote sidings to freeze to death at night in the Russian winter. They come from minds driven mad by the horrors of mass starvation ordered and enforced as a policy of the Communist State. They come from the starved skeletons, worked to death, or flogged to death (as an example to others) in the freezing filth of sub-arctic labor camps. They come from children whose parents are suddenly, inexplicably, taken away from them—parents they will never see again.

IBID.

Execution, says the Communist code, is the highest measure of social protection. What man can call himself a Communist who has not accepted the fact that Terror is an instrument of policy, right if the vision is right, justified by history, enjoined by the balance of forces in the social wars of this century?

IBID.

Stephen Chapman (1954–)

*F*ormerly an associate editor for the *New Republic*, Stephen Chapman is a columnist and editorial writer for the *Chicago Tribune* and a syndicated columnist with Creators Syndicate.

Now a quiz to test the academic ability of newspaper readers. Faced with public schools that can't teach students when Columbus landed in America, concerned citizens should: a) provide the schools with more money, b) raise teacher salaries, c) reduce teacher-student ratios, d) ask, in a very loud voice, what in the hell is going on.

If you answered d), you are proof that Americans are not beyond educating. If you answered a), b), or c), you should be aware that in the past decade we have already done all those high-minded things and have very little to show for it.

"FACTS AND FICTIONS OF EDUCATIONAL CHOICE," Nov. 4, 1990

Per-pupil spending has doubled since 1970, after adjusting for inflation, teacher salaries have risen by $13,000 in the past decade, and teachers are better qualified than ever before. We've fiddled with curriculum, instructional methods, graduation requirements and school organization. Nothing has worked. Our children still do worse in international competition than the Jamaican bobsled team . . . .

IBID.

Our schools are supposed to be accountable, but in reality they're accountable only in the way the president is accountable—through slow and clumsy political devices guaranteed to leave many (and often most) people highly dissatisfied. Schools ought to be accountable in the way grocery stores and dry cleaners are accountable— through quick, direct methods that permit a variety of people of different means and desires all to be satisfied at once.

It may sound odd or even callous to think of providing education the way we provide groceries. But if we provided groceries the way we provide education, most of us would starve. If we want nutritious schools, we need to try something different . . . : letting parents send their kids to any school they choose at public expense, and requiring schools to attract students or close down.

IBID.

Mona Charen *(1957–)*

Mona Charen, who holds a law degree from George Washington University, was an editorial associate at the *National Review* and a speechwriter for the Reagan White House as well as for Jack Kemp. Charen's columns are syndicated by Creators Syndicate.

Who is responsible for the run-away spending that has prompted Sen. Rudman to quit in despair? Rudman observes that when he joined the Senate in 1980, Federal payments to individuals, i.e., Social Security, Medicare, Medicaid, Federal retirement and Veterans' benefits amounted to 47 per-

cent of the budget. But those "entitlements" (a perilous word) are growing faster than the rate of inflation. By 1997, Rudman estimates, "entitlements" will chew up 60 percent of federal outlays. Discretionary spending, he warns, will be only 4.3 percent of the budget by then.

. . . Who's to blame? Spineless politicians in Washington who won't bite the bullet and cut the growth of entitlements? Sure. But more than they, *we* are to blame for wanting something for nothing and for electing divided governments and then complaining that nothing gets done. If one party controlled the executive and legislative branches, the philosophy of the party would get a fair trial.

"VOTERS MUST SHARE THE BLAME," MARCH 26, 1992

Linda Chavez *(1947–)*

Linda Chavez has been executive director of the U.S. Commission on Civil Rights and a senior fellow of the Manhattan Institute. She has written numerous articles on Hispanic issues and is the author of *Out of the Barrio* (1991).

The current native-language programs for groups other than Hispanics are few in number. Most Asian parents prefer that their children be taught in English and consider it the parents' responsibility to teach children their native language and culture. The remarkable achievement of many of these children, who figure disproportionately among the recipients of national academic scholarships, testifies to their success in learning English without benefit of bilingual or native-language instruction. The feats of these children, who are immigrants or the children of immigrants, are far from exceptional in historical terms. Rapid social and economic mobility has been the pattern of generations of immigrants; but the key has always been the learning of English in the public schools. Hispanic political leaders chose to break with that tradition in 1968 and have steadfastly held to their position.

OUT OF THE BARRIO, 1991

The number of Hispanic children in bilingual programs grows each year, as does funding for the programs at the local, state, and federal levels. No other ethnic group, including the 250,000 immigrants who come here from Asia each year, is clamoring for the right to have its language and culture maintained in this country at public expense.

Although Hispanics have succeeded in doing so—for the time being—theirs will be a Pyrrhic victory if it is gained at the expense of their ultimate social and economic integration.

IBID.

If Hispanics choose, as many Greek Americans and other select ethnics have, to maintain their native language for use within their families, communities, and churches, they must accept full responsibility for doing so. Hispanics cannot insist, as many of their leaders do, that the larger community must bend to their demand for public recognition of Spanish and that it must pay to preserve Spanish among one segment of the population. Nor should Hispanics expect Americans willingly to abandon more than two hundred years of tradition as a unilingual society. A bilingual future is simply not in the cards.

IBID.

If Hispanic parents want their children to be able to speak Spanish and know about their distinctive culture, they must take the responsibility to teach their children these things. Government simply cannot—and should not—be charged with this responsibility. Government bureaucracies given the authority to create bicultural teaching materials homogenize the myths, customs, and history of the Hispanic peoples of this hemisphere, who, after all, are not a single group but many groups. It is only in the United States that "Hispanics" exist; a Cakchiquel Indian in Guatemala would find it remarkable that anyone could consider his culture to be the same as a Spanish Argentinean's. The best way for Hispanics to learn about their native culture is in their own communities.

IBID.

Important as education is to the progress of Hispanics in this society, Hispanics' lower achievements in this realm must be placed in some perspective. Hispanics are certainly not the first group whose educational gains have proceeded at a slow pace. Italian Americans, for example, did not achieve educational parity with other groups until 1972—nearly six decades after the peak of Italian immigration—but now they experience one of the highest rates of educational mobility of any group. Groups do not all advance at precisely the same rate in this society—sometimes because of discrimination, sometimes because of other factors. As Thomas Sowell and others have pointed out, no multiethnic society in the world exhibits utopian equality of income, education, and occupational status for every one of its ethnic groups. What is impor-

tant is that opportunities be made available to all persons, regardless of race or ethnicity. Ultimately, however, it will be up to individuals to take advantage of those opportunities. Increasing numbers of Hispanics are doing just that. And no government action can replace the motivation and will to succeed that propels genuine individual achievement.

IBID.

San Francisco challenged the right of two Spanish Americans to participate in a department affirmative action program, claiming that the latter's European roots made them unlikely to have suffered discrimination comparable to that of other Hispanics. The group recommended establishing a panel of twelve Hispanics to certify who is and who is not Hispanic. But that is hardly the answer.

Affirmative action politics treats race and ethnicity as if they were synonymous with disadvantage. The son of a Mexican American doctor or lawyer is treated as if he suffered the same disadvantage as the child of a Mexican farm worker; and both are given preference over poor, non-Hispanic whites in admission to most colleges or affirmative action employment programs . . . . It is inherently patronizing to assume that all Hispanics are deprived and grossly unjust to give those who aren't preference on the basis of disadvantages they don't experience. Whether stated or not, the essence of affirmative action is the belief that Hispanics—or any of the other eligible groups—are not capable of measuring up to the standards applied to whites.

IBID.

By 1975 the civil rights movement had changed its goals. It was no longer content to have the same rules apply to whites and blacks, men and women. Rather, it now urged that the rules themselves be changed so that minorities and women could compete under separate standards, provided that the results obtained improved the status of these groups. In other words, as long as more minorities and women were admitted to universities, were hired and promoted, and had their earnings go up relative to those of white males, disparate treatment of minorities and women was not only tolerated but encouraged. In the mid-1960s, the byword was *equal opportunity*; by 1975, it was *equal results*. Ultimately, results could be "equal" only if they were proportional. Everything was seen in terms of the group's right to its share of the pie. A "fair share" came to mean one equal to the group's proportion of the population. This definition applied whether one was talking about the distribution of jobs, the racial composition of schools and neighborhoods, or the voting

rates of minorities. If minorities did not vote in the same proportion as nonminorities, discrimination was presumed to be the cause. Moreover, by 1975 the right to vote was being equated with the right to elect minority candidates. The voting *process* was no longer the focus; the voting *outcome* was.

IBID.

Lord Chesterfield *(1694–1773)*

(Philip Dormer Stanhope, 4th Earl of Chesterfield)

*A*n English statesman and author, Lord Chesterfield was a Whig member of Parliament (1732–1744) and was extremely politically active until he gradually withdrew from politics and society as his hearing worsened. He holds a permanent place in eighteenth-century literature because of his brilliant *Letters to His Son* (posthumous, 1774), written to teach his natural son the manners and standards of worldly people. The letters are shrewd, eloquent, witty, and cynical.

Let us consider, my Lords, that arbitrary Power has seldome [sic] or never been introduced into any Country at once. It must be introduced by slow degrees, and as it were step by step, lest the people should perceive its approach.

"AGAINST LICENSING THE STAGE," A SPEECH WRITTEN FOR DELIVERY TO THE HOUSE OF LORDS, 1737

Gilbert Keith Chesterton

(1874–1936)

*E*nglish journalist and writer, G.K. Chesterton studied art and began his literary career by reviewing art books for *The Bookman*. He later contributed to many English and American journals. After he became Roman Catholic in 1922, Chesterton wrote many works defending his faith. Some of his works are *Heretics* (1905), *The Man Who Was Thursday* (1908), *The Innocence of Father Brown* (1911), *The Wisdom of Father Brown* (1914), *The Uses of Diversity* (1921), *Generally Speaking* (1929), and *The Resurrection of Rome* (1930).

The sin and sorrow of despotism is not that it does not love men, but that it loves them too much and trusts them too little.

THE WISDOM OF FATHER BROWN, 1914

You can never have a revolution in order to establish a democracy. You must have a democracy in order to have a revolution.

TREMENDOUS TRIFLES, 1909

Utopia always seems to me to mean regimentation rather than emancipation; repression rather than expansion. It is generally called a republic and it always is a monarchy . . . because it is really ruled by one man: the author of the book. His ideal world is always the world that he wants; and not the world that the world wants.

GENERALLY SPEAKING, 1929

Marcus Tullius Cicero *(106–43 B.C.)*

A Roman orator, statesman, and philosopher, Cicero, as a young man, studied law, oratory, and Greek literature and philosophy. He associated the idea of a free society with a constitutional republic, in which persuasion rather than violence is the instrument of political power. He believed, however, that even in a constitutional republic, freedom can be lost without effective, conscientious leadership.

Ignorance of good and evil is the most upsetting fact of human life.

DE FINIBUS, BEGUN 45 B.C., PUBLISHED POSTHUMOUSLY

The good of the people is the highest law.

DE LEGIBUS, BEGUN 52 B.C., PUBLISHED POSTHUMOUSLY

Law is the highest Reason implanted in Nature, which commands what ought to be done, and forbids the opposite.

IBID.

The more laws, the less justice.

DE OFFICIIS, 44 B.C.

Stephen Grover Cleveland

(1837–1908)

*T*wenty-second and twenty-fourth president of the United States,

Grover Cleveland was known for his strong belief in unregulated economic markets, as when he favored reducing tariffs. He opposed currency inflation and blocked undeserved Civil War pensions.

Though the people support the government, the government should not support the people.

VETO, TEXAS SEED BILL, FEBRUARY 16, 1887

Robert Keith Corbin *(1928–)*

*R*obert Corbin is a former president of the National Rifle Association.

Unless you live on a mountaintop, you can't escape it: Politicians and bureaucrats at every level nationwide are demanding hundreds of new gun prohibitions in possibly the highest flood tide of anti-gun hysteria ever. As always, instead of focusing on the criminal and the system that abets him, they attack firearms, touting their latest gun laws as "first steps" in reducing crime. But we've taken 20,000 anti-gun "first steps" already. All they've led us to is the highest violent crime rates in history; yet still politicians demand more. It's time to break that cycle and focus attention, outrage and proven solutions on the genuine crime problems.

AMERICAN RIFLEMAN, MAY 1993

[W]hen it comes to the lawless, politicians do nothing but huff and puff about crime, and pass yet more laws that only disarm the law-abiding and pry into our lives. So while the law*makers* and law*breakers* take more from us and grow stronger each day, we law-*obeyers* are disarmed and deserted. Which for thousands of Americans means tears, terror, bloodshed and an early death. And it could, one day, mean the end of our republic.

Wake up, America! Little by little, your freedom and safety are being robbed, along with your last and best means to get them back. Don't be fooled: The gun debate isn't just about waiting periods, semi-automatic bans, licensing, registration, handgun bans or the Second Amendment. It's about liberty, and the fundamental beliefs that make democracy possible.

IBID., JUNE 1993

Stanley Crouch *(1945–)*

*B*lack cultural critic Stanley Crouch is a writer for the *Village Voice* and the author of *Notes from a Hanging Judge: Essays and Reviews, 1979–1989* (1990). His writings especially emphasize the importance of personal responsibility.

We [cannot] ignore the way in which too many irresponsible intellectuals— black and white—have submitted to the youth culture and the adolescent rebellion of pop music, bootlegging liberal arts rhetoric to defend Afrofascist rap groups like Public Enemy, on the one hand, while paternalistically defining the "gangster rap" of doggerel chanters such as Ice Cube as expressive of the "real" black community.

QUOTED IN *SECOND THOUGHTS ABOUT RACE IN AMERICA*, 1991

Richard Marvin DeVos *(1926–)*

*I*n 1959, Rich DeVos co-founded, with Jay Van Andel, AMWAY

Corporation, one of the world's largest privately held companies, having more than two million independent distributors around the world. DeVos served as AMWAY president until 1994. A speaker and author, he recorded *Selling America*, an award-winning tape, and wrote *Believe* (1975) and *Compassionate Capitalism* (1993).

One way or the other, we all participate in this great free-enterprise system. We can benefit from its advantages or we can miss our chance forever, but we must never forget that the spirit and promise of free enterprise flow through our veins just as they flowed through the veins of the Rockefellers, du Ponts, and Carnegies. The entrepreneurial spirit was born in us right along with our need to eat and drink, to love and be loved, to learn, to grow, and to achieve.

COMPASSIONATE CAPITALISM, 1993

Guided by the principles of Adam Smith, capitalism has produced the greatest prosperity the world has ever known. There have been failures. Karl Marx was just one of the critics of capitalism who made that perfectly clear. We all know the stories of greedy capitalists, child-labor exploiters, and robber barons. Nevertheless, these are the exceptions

and not the rules. Capitalism remains the only economic system that gives us hope that we can pull the world and all her people back from the brink of bankruptcy and forward into an age of prosperity and peace.

IBID.

Entrepreneurship is a way of seeing—seeing a need and filling it. It does not matter whether that need is for soap (a business entrepreneur) or compassionate service (a social entrepreneur); the same kind of vision is involved. In fact, entrepreneurship and compassion go hand in hand . . . .

IBID.

Martin Diamond *(1919–1977)*

*M*artin Diamond, who earned a doctorate in political science in 1956, taught at the University of Chicago, the Illinois Institute of Technology, Claremont Men's College, Claremont Graduate School, and Northern Illinois University. A fellow at many think tanks, such as the Rockefeller Foundation, Diamond was asked to give advice to many prominent persons, including members of the United States Senate and House of Representatives. His essays are posthumously collected in *As Far As Republican Principles Will Permit* (edited by William A. Schambra, 1992).

The principle of equality, more and more people have come to believe, means that each person is equally entitled to live a fully human life. Not, mind you, to try to do so, to have equal opportunity with others, to be equally free of the rule of others; not equally free to pursue happiness, but to have it, to live a fully human life. That is the new claim of democracy. But this runs head on into that inequality which I have claimed to be the deepest principle of human existence. Very few are complete human beings; most of us are very far from it indeed . . . . Is there not something misleadingly utopian in a determination that all shall be equally fully human?

. . . That utopian expectation increasingly has become the standard against which men measure their happiness; and the result is despair and malaise. By that misleading expectation, democracy is made to promise everybody that he will have all the pleasures of body, spirit, and mind that belong to the complete human being. And life—mockingly, eternally—teaches that this is simply not possible. It teaches that the complete human life is achieved only by some and by a hard, tortuous ascent. Properly understood, democracy promises only that there will be no artificial barriers to everyone's opportunity; that no man must be kept from fulfilling his capacity because of his origin. That is the first aspiration of democracy. But now we try to go beyond that. We say we are going to make everyone not only equally free, but equally, fully human. And since it simply cannot be done, we invest delusive shortcuts and deceive ourselves that we are accomplishing our objective.

AS FAR AS REPUBLICAN PRINCIPLES WILL ADMIT, 1992

Albert Venn Dicey *(1835–1922)*

A jurist, A. V. Dicey wrote *The Law of the Constitution* (1885), a standard work, as well as other works, including *Lectures on the Relation between Law and Public Opinion in England During the Nineteenth Century* (1905).

[One of the grounds for a preference for collectivism] is the sentiment or conviction which is entertained by every collectivist, that an individual probably does not know his own interest, and certainly does not know the interest of the class to which he belongs, as well as does the trade union, or ultimately the State of which he is a member . . . .

LECTURES ON THE RELATION BETWEEN LAW AND PUBLIC OPINION IN ENGLAND DURING THE NINETEENTH CENTURY, 1905

Of the members of every community the greater number cannot obtain the comforts or the enjoyments which fall to the lot of their richer and more fortunate neighbours. Against this evil of property the State ought, it is felt by collectivists, to protect the wage-earning class, and in order to give this protection must go a good way towards securing for every citizen something like the same advantages, in the form of education, or of physical well-being, as the rich can obtain by their own efforts. This extension of the idea and practice of protection by the State has not, it is true, in England led as yet to anything like that enforced equality popularly known as communism, but, during the latter part of the nineteenth century, it has produced more legislation tending towards

that equalisation of advantages among all classes which, in practice, means the conferring of benefits upon the wage-earners at the expense of the whole body of the tax-payers.

IBID.

James Clayton Dobson, Jr. *(1936–)*

*C*hild psychologist and author, James Dobson received his Ph.D. from the University of Southern California in 1967 and was an assistant professor—and later associate clinical professor of pediatrics—at the U.S.C. School of Medicine from 1966 to 1983. He has served on both President Carter's task force for White House conferences on the family and President Reagan's National Advisory Council, Office of Juvenile Justice and Delinquency Prevention. Dobson is the founding president of Focus on the Family and the author of numerous books.

My mission in writing is to help preserve the health and vitality of the

American family, which is undergoing a serious threat to its survival. It is my view that our society can be no more stable than the foundation of individual family units upon which it rests. Our government, our institutions, our schools . . . indeed, our way of life are dependent on healthy marriages and loyalty to the vulnerable little children around our feet. Thus, my professional life is devoted to the integrity of the family and the God who designed it.

QUOTED IN *CONTEMPORARY AUTHORS*, 1972, 1978

Robert J. Dole *(1923–)*

A Republican senator from Kansas, Bob Dole is one of Washington's most powerful people. First elected to Congress in 1960, he is also one of the most senior senators. *The Almanac of American Politics*, published by the *National Journal*, has called Dole "an old-fashioned kind of Republican: old-fashioned in what he believes in, old-fashioned in how he operates, old-fashioned in . . . grit and determination . . . ."

When political action committees give money, they expect something in return other than good government.

QUOTED IN PHILIP STERN'S *THE BEST CONGRESS MONEY CAN BUY*, 1988

If you're hanging around with nothing to do and the zoo is closed, come over to the Senate. You'll get the same kind of feeling and you won't have to pay.

ADDRESS TO CONFERENCE OF NEW YORK OFFICIALS, *NEW YORK TIMES*, MAY 9, 1985

As long as there are 3 to 4 people on the [Senate] floor, the country is in good hands. It's only when you have 50 to 60 in the Senate that you want to be concerned.

IBID.

John Dos Passos *(1896–1970)*

A n American author, John Dos Passos wrote many works, including *Adventures of a Young Man* (1939), *The Ground We Stand On* (1941), and *Occasions and Protests* (1964). Although Dos Passos was a Marxist during his early career, he became an active anti-Communist in the late thirties and even condemned the New Deal as excessively collectivist.

Actually the world is becoming a museum of socialist failures.

OCCASIONS AND PROTESTS, 1964

Socialism in Great Britain accomplished little more than to freeze the capitalist economy at its point of least efficiency.

IBID.

Marxism has not only failed to promote human freedom. It has failed to produce food.

IBID.

While we can't get away from the fact that most everybody in the world today believes in his heart that life is more worth living for the average man in North America than anywhere else, we still don't feel secure. Indeed we feel we lack that minimum of security necessary to keep a human institution a going concern. Too many Americans have let in among their basic and secret beliefs the sour postulate that American democracy is rotten. In spite of the ritual phrases and the campaign slogans out of our national folklore, like the frogs in Aesop's fable, many of us are croaking that we

are sick of King Log and that we want to be ruled by King Stork. "When fascism comes to America," said Huey Long, one of the smartest aspirants for the position of King Stork that ever stuck his head out of our frogpond, "it will come as antifascism." It won't matter what name we call King Stork by, if we let him in he'll eat us up just the same. Under the verbal pieties of democratic phraseology the state of mind of a good deal of the country is summed up by a man I heard cap a long irate political argument by shouting: "This man Roosevelt's got too much power: what we need's a dictator."

THE GROUND WE STAND ON, 1941

I myself believe that we are going to stick to our old King Log, that our peculiar institutions have a future, and that this country is getting to be a better place for men to live in instead of a worse . . . .

IBID.

Dinesh D'Souza (1961-)

*D*inesh D'Souza has been a White House domestic policy analyst, an editor of *Policy Review* (from the Heritage Foundation), and a research fellow at the American Enterprise

Institute. He is a skillful debater who has jousted with a number of liberals and is known especially for his provocative critique of liberal education's views and policies in *Illiberal Education* (1991). He is also the author of *The End of Racism* (1995).

The American system is based on the conviction that equality is not inconsistent with excellence; indeed, the philosophical conjunction of the two principles supports the vaunted notion of "equality of opportunity." By applying the same standard to everyone, natural talent and hard work are permitted and expected to distinguish individuals on the plane of achievement. Proportional representation for ethnic groups directly violates the democratic principle of equal opportunity for individuals, and the underlying concept of group justice is hostile both to individual equality and to excellence.

ILLIBERAL EDUCATION, 1991

The question is not whether universities should seek diversity, but what kind of diversity. It seems that the primary form of diversity which universities should try to foster is diversity of mind. Such diversity would enrich academic discourse, widen its parameters, multiply its objects of inquiry, and increase the probability of obscure and unlikely terrain being investigated. Abroad one typically encounters such diversity of opinion even on basic questions such as how society should be organized . . . .

By contrast, most American students seem to display striking agreement on all the basic questions of life. Indeed, they appear to regard a true difference of opinion, based upon convictions that are firm and intensely held, as dangerously dogmatic and an offense against the social etiquette of tolerance. Far from challenging these unconventional prejudices, college leaders tend to encourage their uncritical continuation.

IBID.

William Durant *(1885–1981)* and Ariel Durant *(1898–1981)*

*O*f all their important works, *The Story of Civilization* is Will and (his wife) Ariel Durant's best-known work. Written from 1935 to 1975, the book spreads from prehistory to the eighteenth century. They also wrote *Caesar and Christ* (1944) and *The Lessons of History* (1968).

The experience of the past leaves little doubt that every economic system must sooner or later rely upon some form of the profit motive to stir individuals and groups to productivity. Substitutes like slavery, police supervision, or ideological enthusiasm prove too unproductive, too expensive, or too transient.

THE LESSONS OF HISTORY, 1968

Nothing is clearer in history than the adoption by successful rebels of the methods they were accustomed to condemn in the forces they deposed.

IBID.

Utopias of equality are biologically doomed, and the best that the amiable philosopher can hope for is an approximate equality of legal justice and educational opportunity. A society in which all potential abilities are allowed to develop and function will have a survival advantage in the competition of groups.

IBID.

A great civilization is not conquered from without until it has destroyed itself within. The essential cause of Rome's decline lay in her people, her morals, her class struggle, her failing trade, her bureaucratic despotism, her stifling taxes, her consuming wars.

CAESAR AND CHRIST, 1944

Max Eastman *(1883-1969)*

*A*merican poet, critic, and social thinker, Max Eastman was originally a radical of the left who, from 1922 to 1924, associated with Leon Trotsky in the Soviet Union. In 1933, Eastman began to lose faith in the Soviet system, and in 1941 he repudiated even socialism. Eastman became an important voice for William F. Buckley's *National Review.* His arguments against socialism are presented in *Stalin's Russia and the Crisis in Socialism* (1939), *Marxism: Is it a Science?* (1940), and *Reflections on the Failure of Socialism* (1955).

I still think the worst enemy of human hope is not brute facts, but men of brains who will not face them. For that reason I had no high expectations of the liberal [American] intelligentsia when it came to acknowledging that the "revolution of our times," as so far conceived and conducted, is, has been, and will be, a failure. I never dreamed, however, that they [the American intelligentsia] could sink to the depths of maudlin self-deception and perfectly abject treason to truth, freedom, justice, and mercy that many of them have reached in regard to the Russian debacle. That has indeed profoundly, and more than any other shock, whether emotional or intellectual, disabused me of the dream of liberty under a socialist state. If these supposedly elevated and detached minds [of the American intelligentsia], free of any dread, of any pressure, of any compulsion to choose except between truth and their own mental comfort, can not recognize absolute horror, the absolute degradation of man, the end of science, art, law, human aspiration, and civilized morals, when these arrive in a far country, what will they be worth when the pressure is put upon them at home? They will be worth nothing except to those dark powers which will most certainly undertake to convert state-owned property into an instrument of exploitation beside which the reign of private capital will seem to have been, in truth, a golden age of freedom and equality for all.

REFLECTIONS ON THE FAILURE OF SOCIALISM, 1955

Thomas Stearns Eliot *(1888–1965)*

*B*orn in America, T. S. Eliot became a British subject. A motif running through his poetry and literary criticism is an esteem for tradition, without which, he believed, neither social life nor culture could be understood. A social conservative, Eliot believed that individual freedom and traditional order are inextricably linked. In *The Idea of a Christian Society* (1939) and *Notes Towards the Definition of Culture* (1949), he attempted to explain the social philosophy underlying his poems and literary criticism.

Envy is everywhere. / Who is without envy? And most people / Are unaware or unashamed of being envious.

THE ELDER STATESMAN, 1958

The difference between being an elder statesman/And posing successfully as an elder statesman/Is practically negligible.

IBID.

The historical sense involves a perception, not only of the pastness of the past, but of its presence.

"TRADITION AND THE INDIVIDUAL TALENT," *THE SACRED WOOD*, 1920

It is not enough to understand what we ought to be, unless we know what we are;

and we do not understand what we are,
unless we know what we ought to be.
"RELIGION AND LITERATURE," 1935

We know too much, are convinced of
too little. Our literature is a substitute
for religion, and so is our religion.
"A DIALOGUE ON DRAMATIC POETRY," 1928

Ebenezer Elliott (1781–1849)

*A*n English poet who composed
the romantic poetry in *The
Vernal Walk* (1801), *Night* (1818), and
The Village Patriarch (1829), Ebenezer
Elliott was called "the Corn-Law
Rhymer" because he attributed all
national misfortunes to the "bread
tax," which he denounced in *Corn-Law
Rhymes* (1831), and *The Splendid
Village* (1833–1835).

What is a Communist? One who has
yearnings
    For equal division of unequal earnings.
    Idler or bungler, or both, he is willing,
    To fork out his copper and pocket
your shilling.

CORN-LAW RHYMES, 1831

Rowland Evans, Jr. (1921–) and Robert David Sanders Novak (1931–)

*R*owland Evans, Jr. and Robert
Novak are best known for their
joint syndicated column, which they
have been writing since 1963, and for
which they have become famous as simply "Evans and Novak." In addition,
they have co-written *Lyndon B.
Johnson: The Exercise of Power*
(1967), *Nixon in the White House: The
Foundation of Power* (1971), and *The
Reagan Revolution* (1981). Before his
association with Novak, Evans was
associated with the AP Washington
Bureau and the New York *Herald
Tribune.* Novak began his writing
career as a newspaper reporter and
eventually became a commentator on
the Cable News Network (CNN) as well
as a syndicated columnist. In 1965,
Novak wrote *The Agony of the GOP,*
and in 1990, he received the ACE
award from the Cable Broadcasting
Industry.

The bashing of . . . two very different Bush lieutenants reflects the way big-time politics works in Washington today. The assault on each, rooted more in personalities than issues, originated with the new media. Yet the ordeals of John Sununu and Dan Quayle are really linked to ideology. They are both committed conservatives in an administration dominated by pragmatists . . . .

Just why Quayle is targeted by the news media after two years of an essentially error-free record in the vice-presidency is a matter of considerable discussion in Republican circles. His problem is viewed as resentment against the sudden, unexpected elevation to power of somebody who inherited wealth and social position but lacked gravitas . . . .

In the case of both men, ideology is really at stake. Quayle has been considerably more circumspect than Sununu, but they have been together in the forefront of today's cutting-edge social issue: racial quotas. Quayle . . . has quietly pursued a conservative agenda, most recently against excessive environmental regulation . . . .

. . . [T]he president [George Bush] knows that what is at stake is not an arrogant chief of staff or an incompetent vice president but whether he will try to wobble away from his own policies.

"MEDIA PROMOTE THE BASHING OF BUSH'S MEN,"
MAY 8, 1991

Jerry L. Falwell *(1933–)*

*J*erry Falwell is the founding minister of the Thomas Road Baptist Church (1956), founder of Liberty University (1971), and founder of the Moral Majority, later Liberty Federation (1979–1989). He is also the host of the *Old Time Gospel Hour* television show, author of several books, including *Listen, America!* (1980), *Finding Inner Peace and Strength* (1982), and *New American Family* (1992), and the recipient of numerous awards and other distinctions, including that of *Conservative Digest*'s Number One Most Admired Conservative Man Not in Congress.

Today America is turning her back on her biblical heritage and thus precipitating her downfall. Because I believe we are in a fateful decade, I wrote *Listen, America!* to awaken apathetic Americans to the fact that our beloved nation can only be saved if moral Americans will act quickly.

QUOTED IN *CONTEMPORARY AUTHORS*, 1981

It is my conviction that the family is God's basic unit in society. God's most important unit in society. No wonder then . . . we are in a holy war for the survival of the family. Before a nation collapses the families of that nation must go down first.

DECEMBER 2, 1979

and greed. Such an elitism is a recognition of . . . human inequality . . . .

. . . Elitism isn't a dirty word, just a recognition of reality.

MAY 18, 1992

Don Feder *(1946–)*

*D*on Feder's columns, syndicated by Creators Syndicate, often focus on the importance of personal responsibility and document the numerous failures of bureaucrats and social engineers. His principal focus is on domestic issues and on the different ways in which conservatives and liberals approach them. A collection of his works is gathered in *A Jewish Conservative Looks at Pagan America* (1993).

Philosophical elitism is born of pessimism about the human condition, the realization that man is flawed, and rare is the individual who can rise above his nature. Man must be educated and trained to overcome inherent weakness, the natural tendencies to indolence, envy

Edwin John Feulner, Jr. *(1941–)*

*P*resident of the Heritage Foundation since 1977, Edwin Feulner has also been a member of the staff of the U.S. secretary of defense under Melvin Laird (1969–1970), an administrative assistant to U.S. Congressman Philip M. Crane (1970–1974), a public affairs fellow at Stanford University's Hoover Institute (1965–1967), and publisher of *Policy Review*. Feulner, who holds a doctorate from the University of Edinburgh, is the author of *Trading with the Communists* (with Samuel F. Clabaugh, 1968), *Congress and the New International Order* (1976), *Looking Back* (with Herb B. Berkowitz, 1981) and *Conservatives Stalk the White House* (1982, 1983).

In the NIEO [new international economic order] rhetoric, the call for "self-determination" is actually a disguised claim, not for control over one's own resources and wealth, but for control and possession of the wealth of other nations and their citizens.

CONGRESS AND THE NEW INTERNATIONAL ORDER, 1976

The wealth which the LDC's [less developed countries] wish to redistribute does not exist internally, or where it does exist the leadership elite refuses to redistribute it. The leaders of those nations have decided to redistribute someone else's wealth.

IBID.

The U.S. has not been sufficiently direct in refusing to accept the sense of guilt NIEO would impose on the developed world—guilt for being more developed, for "exploiting" the LDC's, and for failing to develop the LDC's to an equal status. The key to the success of NIEO is the success of its advocates in persuading the developed nations that they are the cause of the underdevelopment of LDC's.

IBID.

[T]he demand that developed nations and the industries of those nations do everything possible to provide the underdeveloped nations with wealth, economic growth, and power is blatantly incompatible with self-reliance.

IBID.

Suzanne Fields *(1936–)*

*C*olumnist, author, and social observer Suzanne Fields earned a doctorate in English literature from Catholic University. She is a columnist for the *Washington Times* (since 1984) and the Los Angeles Times Syndicate (since 1988). She is the author of *Like Father, Like Daughter* (1983).

Welfare doesn't work. We all know that. It provides the wrong incentives. It undercuts the family and encourages long-term dependence.

Long ago the dispensers of welfare made a pact with the devil and his disciples—i.e., us—that a woman on welfare shouldn't be married to a man who is employed, nor should she work, either. She would be better off not marrying at all. In the government scale (with a bureaucratic thumb on it), an illegitimate child is worth more than a legitimate one.

Welfare not only sends the wrong message, it fails to raise the poor from poverty to prosperity, or even self-sufficiency. The statistics of generational cycles and debacles are grim: a child who grows up in a welfare family is three times more likely than other children to become a welfare client when he grows up.

Combined benefits for a single mother with two children are worth between $8,500 to $15,000 a year depending on the state. A Heritage Foundation memo addressed to President Clinton shows that illegitimacy increases when welfare benefits increase. A study by the University of Washington finds that an increase of $200 per month in state welfare benefits to a family causes an increase of 150 percent in teen-age illegitimacy rates.

These families lack a lot more than money.

Single welfare mothers rarely learn the relationship between hard work and hard-earned money, disciplined behavior and personal rewards, delayed gratification and long-term goals. Their children can't understand these connections, either. You don't need an expert to tell you that when welfare supports bad habits, it reinforces them.

"WELFARE NEEDS REFORM, NOT ANOTHER TEACH-IN," FEB. 8, 1993

Antony Flew (1923-)

*B*orn in London and educated at Kingswood School, Bath, and at St. John's College, Oxford, Antony Flew has taught philosophy in England as well as North America, Australia, and Malawi. He has written numerous books, including *An Introduction to Western Philosophy* (1971), *Crime or Disease?* (1973), *Sociology, Equality and Education* (1976), and *The Politics of Procrustes: Contradictions of Enforced Equality* (1981).

The wholesale, utopian, social engineer determined to impose his long-term policies no matter what the immediate discontents, is by his cloth precluded from learning from his mistakes. Nor can he take account of the insight that there will always be unintended consequences, whether good, bad, or mixed.

THE POLITICS OF PROCRUSTES, 1981

Benjamin Franklin (1706–1790)

*A*merican statesman, scientist, philosopher, and author, Benjamin Franklin is known especially for his aphorisms, inventions, and government service. His aphorisms were published in *Poor Richard's Almanack*

(1732–1757), under the pseudonym of Richard Saunders. His inventions include an improved heating stove (about 1744). He began public life in 1754 as Pennsylvania's delegate to the Albany Congress. In 1775, Franklin was a member of the Second Continental Congress and of the committee to draft the Declaration of Independence—and a signer of the Declaration. He was appointed commissioner, with John Jay and John Adams, in 1781 to negotiate peace with Great Britain; and on February 12, 1790, Franklin signed a memorial to Congress asking for the abolition of slavery.

In Rivers and bad Governments, the lightest Things swim at top.

POOR RICHARD'S ALMANACK, 1754

In general I would only observe that commerce, consisting in a mutual exchange of the necessities and conveniences of life, the more free and unrestrained it is, the more it flourishes; and the happier are all the nations concerned in it. Most of the restraints put upon it in different countries seem to have been the projects of particulars for their private interest, under pretense of public good.

THE WRITINGS OF BENJAMIN FRANKLIN (1905–1907), 1783

I have seen so much embarrassment and so little advantage in all the restraining and compulsive systems, that I feel myself strongly inclined to believe that a state which leaves all her ports open to all the world upon equal terms will, by that means, have foreign commodities cheaper, sell its own productions dearer, and be on the whole the most prosperous.

IBID.

Industry need not wish, as *Poor Richard* says, *and he that lives upon hope will die fasting. There are no gains without pains; then help hands, for I have no lands,* or if I have, they are smartly taxed. And, as *Poor Richard* likewise observes, *He that hath a trade hath an estate; and he that hath a calling, hath an office of profit and honor;* but then the *trade* must be worked at, and the *calling* well followed. . . . If we are industrious, we shall never starve; for, as *Poor Richard* says, *At the working man's house hunger looks in, but dares not enter.* Nor will the bailiff or the constable enter, for *Industry pays debts, while despair increaseth them,* says *Poor Richard.* What though you have found no treasure, nor has any rich relation left you a legacy, *Diligence is the mother of good luck,* as *Poor Richard* says, *and God gives all things to industry. Then plow deep, while sluggards sleep, and you shall have corn to sell and to keep,* says Poor Dick. Work while it is called today, for you know not how much you may be hindered tomorrow, which makes *Poor Richard* say, *One today is worth two tomorrows,* and farther, *have you somewhat to do tomorrow, do it today.* If you were a servant, would you not be ashamed that a good master should catch you idle? Are you then your own master, *be ashamed to catch yourself idle.*

IBID., 1757

The ordaining of laws in favor of *one* part of the nation, to the prejudice and oppression of *another,* is certainly the most erroneous and mistaken policy.

IBID., 1774

To relieve the misfortunes of our fellow creatures is concurring with the Deity; it is godlike. But if we provide encouragement for laziness, and supports for folly, may we not be found fighting against the order of God and nature, which perhaps has appointed want and misery as the proper punishments for, and cautions against, as well as necessary consequences of, idleness and extravagance? Whenever we attempt to amend the scheme of Providence, and to interfere with the government of the world,

we had need be very circumspect, lest we do more harm than good.

IBID., 1753

I wish they were benefited by this generous provision in any degree equal to the good intention with which it was made, and is continued; but I fear the giving [to] mankind a dependence on anything for support, in age or sickness, besides industry and frugality during youth and health, tends to flatter our natural indolence, to encourage idleness and prodigality, and thereby to promote and increase poverty, the very evil it was intended to cure; thus multiplying beggars instead of diminishing them.

IBID., 1768

In my youth I traveled much, and I observed in different countries that the more public provisions were made for the poor, the less they provided for themselves, and of course became poorer. And, on the contrary, the less was done for them, the more they did for themselves, and became richer. There is no country in the world where so many provisions are established for them [as in England]; so many hospitals to receive them when they are sick or lame, founded and maintained by voluntary charities; so many almshouses for the aged of both sexes, together with a solemn general law made by the rich to subject their estates to a heavy tax for the support of the poor. Under all these obligations, are our poor modest, humble, and thankful? And do they use their best endeavors to maintain themselves, and lighten our shoulders of this burden? On the contrary, I affirm that there is no country in the world in which the poor are more idle, dissolute, drunken, and insolent. The day you passed that act, you took away from before their eyes the greatest of all inducements to industry, frugality, and sobriety, by giving them a dependence on somewhat else than a careful accumulation during youth and health, for support in age or sickness.

In short, you offered a premium for the encouragement of idleness, and you should not now wonder that it has had its effect in the increase of poverty. Repeal that law, and you will soon see a change in their manners. *Saint Monday* and *Saint Tuesday* will soon cease to be holidays. *Six days shalt thou labor*, though one of the old commandments long treated as out of date, will again be looked upon as a respectable precept; industry will increase, and with it plenty among the lower people; their circumstances will mend; and more will be done for their happiness by inuring them to provide for themselves

than could be done by dividing all your estates among them.

IBID., 1772

I have long been of [the] . . . opinion that your [England's] legal provision for the poor is a very great evil, operating as it does to the encouragement of idleness. We have followed your example, and begin now to see our error, and, I hope, shall reform it.

IBID., 1789

Printers do continually discourage the printing of great numbers of bad things, and stifle them in the birth. I myself have constantly refused to print anything that might countenance vice, or promote immorality; though by complying in such cases with the corrupt taste of the majority I might have got much money. I have also always refused to print such things as might do real injury to any person, how much soever I have been solicited, and tempted with offers of great pay; and how much soever I have by refusing got the ill will of those who would have employed me.

IBID., 1731

A law might be made to raise . . . wages; but if our manufactures are too dear, they will not vend abroad, and all that part of employment will fail, unless by fighting and conquering we compel other nations to buy our goods, whether they will or no, which some have been mad enough at times to propose.

IBID., 1768

They that can give up essential liberty to obtain a little temporary safety deserve neither liberty nor safety.

"MOTTO OF THE HISTORICAL REVIEW OF PENNSYLVANIA," 1759

Where liberty dwells, there is my country.

LETTER TO B. VAUGHN, MARCH 14, 1783

Milton Friedman *(1912–)*

A Nobel laureate in economics, Milton Friedman is a leading monetary theorist and a defender of laissez-faire capitalism, whose ideas about a free-market economy have exercised great influence on conservatives as well as libertarians. He is the author of such works as *Capitalism and Freedom* (1962), *A Monetary History of the United States, 1867–1960*

(1963), *Free to Choose* (with Rose Friedman, 1980), and *Tyranny of the Status Quo* (with Rose Friedman, 1984).

One popular explanation for crime is poverty and inequality. People are driven to steal, to rob, to murder because they have no other means to avoid hunger and deprivation. Or they are driven to crime because of the spectacle of rich versus poor, a spectacle that feeds a sense of injustice and unfairness, not to speak of the less admirable motive of envy. However plausible this explanation is of why some people turn to crime, it cannot explain the *rise* in crime over recent decades in the United States.

TYRANNY OF THE STATUS QUO, 1984

[E]very program enacted to benefit a specific interest, even if the program is a price knowingly paid for gaining political support and campaign funds, is described as promoting the general welfare. Worse, if at all possible, the cost is buried in a total in order to disguise a sop to a special interest. Consider one particularly transparent case. "Conservation of agricultural resources" seems an appropriate object for governmental concerns—until you realize that it is a euphemism for a program to subsidize farmers to keep land out of cultivation in order to keep up the price of farm products and the income of farmers.

IBID.

Television, the breakdown of the family, other cultural changes in recent decades—all have been indicted in examining the poor performance of our public schools. They have undoubtedly contributed to the deterioration in schooling, but they are not the major causes. In our opinion, centralization and bureaucratization of public schooling are the fundamental reasons for the deterioration. As financing of public schools has moved further and further away from local control, the educational bureaucracy has tended to replace parents in deciding what and how our children should learn. The most expedient, and perhaps the only, way to return control to parents is an arrangement whereby parents can choose the schools their children attend—and if you are not satisfied—can move their children from one school to another.

IBID.

Deficits allow our representatives to vote for spending without having to vote taxes to pay for it, and that creates irresponsibility.

IBID.

Viewed as a means to the end of political freedom, economic arrangements are important because of their effect on the concentration or dispersal of power. The kind of economic organization that provides economic freedom directly, namely, competitive capitalism, also promotes political freedom because it separates economic power from political power and in this way enables the one to offset the other.

CAPITALISM AND FREEDOM, 1962

Unions have . . . not only harmed the public at large and workers as a whole by distorting the use of labor; they have also made the incomes of the working class more unequal by reducing the opportunities available to the most disadvantaged workers.

IBID.

Fundamentally there are only two ways of coordinating the economic activities of millions. One is central direction involving the use of coercion—the technique of the army and of the modern totalitarian state. The other is voluntary cooperation of individuals—the technique of the market place . . . . Exchange can bring about coordination without coercion.

IBID.

There's only one place where inflation is made: that's in Washington.

QUOTED IN *THE MACMILLAN BOOK OF BUSINESS AND ECONOMIC QUOTATIONS* (1984), 1977

If an exchange between two parties is voluntary, it will not take place unless both believe they will benefit from it. Most economic fallacies derive from the neglect of this simple insight, from the tendency to assume that there is a fixed pie, that one party can gain only at the expense of another.

IBID., 1981

"Environment" and "safety" are fine objectives, but they have become sacred cows about which it is almost heresy to ask whether the return justifies the cost.

QUOTED IN *MILTON FRIEDMAN'S MONETARY FRAMEWORK,* EDITED BY ROBERT J. GORDON, 1974

The objectives [behind the explosion in welfare and other entitlement programs] have all been noble; the results disappointing. Social Security expenditures have skyrocketed, and the system is in deep financial trouble. Public housing and urban renewal programs have subtracted from rather than added to the housing available to the poor. Public assistance rolls mount despite growing employment. By general agreement, the welfare program is a "mess" saturated with fraud and corruption. As government has paid a larger share of the nation's medical bills, both patients and physicians complain of skyrocketing costs and of the increasing impersonality of medicine. In education, student performance has dropped as federal intervention has expanded.

The repeated failure of well-intentioned programs is not an accident. It is not simply the result of mistakes of execution. The failure is deeply rooted in the use of bad means to achieve good objectives.

FREE TO CHOOSE, 1980

David Lloyd George (1863–1945)

A British statesman known for his brilliance in debating, Lloyd George held many governmental posts, including that of M.P., president of the Board of Trade (1905–1908), chancellor of the exchequer, minister of munitions, secretary of state for war, and prime minister (1916–1922). He arranged a conference (1921) with Irish leaders, leading eventually to the founding of the Irish Free State. Lloyd George wrote *War Memoirs* (6 vols., 1933–1936) and *The Truth about the Peace Treaty* (2 vols., 1938).

A young man who isn't a Socialist hasn't got a heart; an old man who is a Socialist hasn't got a head.

QUOTED IN *THE BUSINESSMAN'S ENCYCLOPEDIA*

What protection teaches us, is to do to ourselves in time of peace what enemies seek to do to us in time of war.

PROTECTION OR FREE TRADE, 1886

To put political power in the hands of men embittered and degraded by poverty is to tie firebrands to foxes and turn them loose amid the standing corn.

PROGRESS AND POVERTY, 1879

Henry George *(1839–1897)*

*A*lthough Henry George was an American economist who believed that the idea of socialism was "grand and noble," his *Progress and Poverty* (1879) has nonetheless influenced tax legislation in many countries and his *Protection or Free Trade* (1886) is a significant defense of free trade. George believed that the great contrast between poverty and wealth stemmed from only a few persons' profiting from the rental of land and the unearned increase in land values. He proposed a single property tax, applying entirely to land, to pay for government.

George Franklin Gilder *(1939–)*

*G*eorge Gilder has been a fellow of the Kennedy School of Government at Harvard and a speechwriter for Ronald Reagan. He has written for numerous publications and is the author of such books as *Wealth and Poverty* (1981), *Visible Man* (1978), *Naked Nomads* (1974), *Sexual Suicide* (1973), and *The Spirit of Enterprise* (1984).

Capitalists are motivated not chiefly by the desire to consume wealth or indulge their appetites, but by the freedom and power to consummate their entrepreneurial ideas. Whether piling up coconuts or designing new computers, they are movers and shakers, doers and givers, obsessed with positive visions of change and opportunity. They are men with an urge to understand and act, to master something and transform it, to work out a puzzle and profit from it, to figure out a part of nature and society and turn it to the common good. They are inventors and explorers, boosters and problem solvers; they take infinite pains and they strike fast.

WEALTH AND POVERTY, 1981

Are they [capitalists] greedier than doctors or writers or professors of sociology or assistant secretaries of energy or commissars of wheat? Yes, their goals seem more mercenary. But this is only because money is their very means of production. Just as the sociologist requires books and free time and the bureaucrat needs arbitrary power, the capitalist needs capital . . . . Capitalists need capital to fulfill their role in launching and financing enterprise. Are they self-interested? Presumably. But the crucial fact about them is their deep interest and engagement in the world beyond themselves, impelled by their imagination, optimism and faith.

IBID.

The man has the gradually sinking feeling that his role as provider, the definitive male activity from the primal days of the hunt through the industrial revolution and on into modern life, has been largely seized from him; he has been cuckolded by the compassionate state.

IBID.

A successful economy depends on the proliferation of the rich, on creating a large class of risk-taking men who are willing to shun the easy channels of a comfortable life in order to create new enterprise, win huge profits, and invest them again.

IBID.

Entrepreneurs understand the inexorable reality of risk and change. They begin by saving, forgoing consumption, not to create an ersatz security but to gain the wherewithal for a life of productive risks and opportunities. Their chief desire is not money to waste on consumption but the freedom and power to consummate their entrepreneurial ideas.

THE SPIRIT OF ENTERPRISE, 1984

Whether sorting potatoes or writing software, they [entrepreneurs] are movers and shakers, doers and givers, brimming with visions of creation and opportunity.

They are optimists, who see in every patch of sand a potential garden, in every man a potential worker, in every problem a possible profit. Their self-interest succumbs to their deeper interest and engagement in the world beyond themselves, impelled by their curiosity, imagination, and faith.

IBID.

Entrepreneurs seek money chiefly for positive reasons: to perform their central role in economic growth. Just as a sociologist needs free time and access to libraries and research aides, and a scientist needs a laboratory and assistants, and a doctor needs power to prescribe medicine and perform surgery—just as intellectuals need freedom to write and publish—capitalists need economic freedom and access to capital to perform their role in launching and financing enterprise.

IBID.

Entrepreneurs must be allowed to retain the wealth they create because only they, collectively, can possibly know how to invest it productively among the millions of existing businesses and the innumerable visions of new enterprise in the world economy.

IBID.

By the very process of acquiring profits, they [entrepreneurs] learned how to use them. By the very process of building businesses, they gained the discipline to avoid waste and the knowledge to see value. By the process of creating and responding to markets, they orient their lives toward the service of others. Entrepreneurs who hoard their wealth or seek governmental protection from rivals or revel in vain consumption or retreat to selfish isolation betray the very essence of their role and responsibility in the world. To that degree, they are no longer entrepreneurs or capitalists but relics of the feudal and static societies of the precapitalist era.

IBID.

Entrepreneurs provide a continuing challenge both to men who refuse a practical engagement in the world, on the grounds that it is too dangerous or corrupt, and to men who demand power over others in the name of ideology or expertise without first giving or risking their wealth. Capitalism offers nothing but frustrations and rebuffs to those who wish—because of claimed superiority of intelligence, birth, credentials, or ideals— to get without giving, to take without risking, to profit without sacrifice, to be exalted without humbling themselves to understand others and meet their needs.

IBID.

Newton Leroy Gingrich (1943–)

S peaker of the House Newt Gingrich received his Ph.D. in European history from Tulane University in 1968 and went on to serve in Congress as representative of his 6th Georgia District (1979–), becoming the house minority whip in 1989 and then Speaker of the House in 1995. Gingrich co-founded the Conservative Opportunity Society, the congressional military caucus, and the space caucus, and wrote *Window of Opportunity* (with Marianne Gingrich, 1984) and *To Renew America* (1995).

As a historian, I argue that American civilization cannot survive with twelve-year-olds having babies, fifteen-year-olds shooting one another, seventeen-year-olds dying of AIDS, and eighteen-year-olds graduating with diplomas they cannot read.

COMMENTARY, AUG. 1994

American history offers us great models of [vigorous conservative] leadership. Just read the biography of Benjamin Franklin. He is an inventor of self-government: the creator of our public library, post office, and volunteer fire department. The list of his social inventions includes many that are volunteer or local, some that are national. Look at every great wave of American activism, and think about what it changed. The Republican Party from 1854 to 1928 authored the Homestead Act, which offered a free farm to every man who would settle on it and improve it. The transcontinental railroad: it was built with subsidies, but we did not need a Department of Railroads. Because we wanted productivity on the American farm we established the Land Grant colleges, the agricultural laboratories, and field agents. Opening up the West: government paid for Lewis and Clark's expedition. Building the Panama Canal all of us wanted to keep? We invented a nation, built a canal, manned the canal, cured yellow fever, and had a Navy to protect it.

All I am suggesting is that we have had a remarkably vigorous conservatism that said, "I want to protect individual freedom. I want stability. I want a lean bureaucracy. I will reshape the market to encourage certain behaviors. But within that framework, I want maximum individual liberty." Read the preamble of the Constitution: " . . . establish justice, insure domestic tranquillity, provide for the common defense, promote the general welfare, and secure the blessings of liberty to ourselves and our posterity . . ."

The challenge to you is very simple. Ronald Reagan and Barry Goldwater carried us to this evening. It is our turn.

THE HERITAGE FOUNDATION, APRIL 21, 1988

[W]e must replace the false compassion of our bureaucratic welfare state with a truly caring humanitarian approach based on common sense. If you measure results rather than intentions, products rather than processes, the facts are painfully obvious. Our inner city school systems are collapsing, leaving an entire generation of Americans without the tools they need to care for themselves and their families. Our health care system is too expensive, too bureaucratic and too inaccessible for many Americans. Our welfare system actually sickens the poor, teaches destructive habits and values, encourages the collapse of families, and traps people in poverty. We have too much red tape and too little technology, too much bureaucracy and too little entrepreneurship in our effort to protect the environment.

IBID., AUGUST 22, 1990

The answers will be found in thousands of local experiments and thousands of local efforts. The federal government must free up the system to undertake those efforts. Bureaucratic rules cannot take the place of common sense; red tape cannot replace initiative and individual effort. Unfeeling bureaucracies are no substitute for the basic American values of helping your neighbor and contributing to your community. Instead of raising taxes to pay for more bureaucracy, we must replace the bureaucratic welfare state with a system that elevates those basic American values.

IBID.

[F]or two generations the government has been more important than the family in setting our national tax policy. Back in 1947 we had almost no taxes on an average worker with a wife and two children. The deduction per child as a share of average income was the equivalent of over $6,000 in today's money. The Social Security tax was so small—$30 a year—that it was not even noticed. Today taxes are so high they force many mothers to work. Today's taxes are anti-child, anti-family and anti-work. Furthermore, our tax system is anti-savings, anti-investment and anti-jobs.

IBID.

Nathan Glazer *(1923–)*

*N*athan Glazer, a sociologist, has been coeditor of *The Public Interest* and has written a number of books, including *American Judaism* (1957, 1972), *Beyond the Melting Pot* (with Daniel P. Moynihan, 1963), *Affirmative Discrimination* (1976), *Ethnic Dilemmas, 1964–1982*, (1983), and *The Limits of Social Policy* (1988).

The reality that many people try to resist is that equality of opportunity and of treatment, insofar as we can measure it, will not automatically lead to an equal outcome for all groups—at least not rapidly. It appears that the simple liberty to compete, regardless of our effort to equalize the starting points, will lead some students to move far ahead and will prevent an equal outcome. We will find the same patterns in economic life: a measured equality of starting point seems to have only a modest influence on eventual outcome, as measured by income and occupation.

ETHNIC DILEMMAS, 1964–1982, 1983

The liberty to compete educationally and economically will lead to inequality, even starting from an equal position, and even, indeed, taking into account the fact that some groups start with initial handicaps of private and public discrimination. It is well known that minorities in many countries are disproportionately successful educationally or economically even though such minorities face discrimination. These minorities include Jews, Lebanese, Chinese, Indians, Armenians, Ibos, and many other groups, though no one makes the claim that persons from these groups are uniformly successful in all circumstances. This is not to say that the discrimination such groups have faced, and do face, is irrelevant to success educationally and economically: even the groups that are disproportionately successful, one assumes, would have achieved more in the absence of discrimination.

IBID.

If . . . liberty leads to inequality, even when an initial equality exists, even indeed when certain achieving groups are handicapped severely (of course it is more common for handicapped groups to fall behind, but . . . this is by no means always the case, nor are the exceptions inconsequential), a dilemma is created for a democracy that judges its success by the degree to which each group approximates the average in key indicators of success and well-being. If, further, lawyers insist that any difference that exists is attributable to an unfair and now illegal discrimination by public authorities and private individuals and institutions, and no cause of group difference other than discrimination, past or present, is admitted, legal reasoning will simply lose touch with reality. For one overwhelming fact undermines interpretations of difference as owing to discrimination: Some minorities that have met discrimination have not only achieved equality but more than equality in many significant measured areas.

IBID.

To live with the two fraternities—the fraternity of the racial and ethnic groups and the fraternity of the larger American society—means to acknowledge, and to accept, differences that are not the result of unfair discrimination but are themselves the result of a concrete group life. Every contemporary society tries to reduce differences and inequalities, and ours should too. But what is problematic is the attempt to treat every difference as the result of discrimination and as a candidate for governmental action to reduce

it. In a multiethnic society, such a policy can only encourage one group after another to raise claims to special treatment for its protection.

IBID.

The demand for special treatment will lead to animus against other groups that already have it, by those who think they should have it and don't. One sees the opportunity for the growth of antagonisms with a potentiality for evil that all such ethnic and group antagonisms possess. And the fact that among the victims might be that old elite that practiced discrimination in the past and that might therefore in some sense "deserve" its fate would scarcely reassure us: as in Lebanon today, the former discriminators and the discriminated against would go down together.

IBID.

[T]he rising emphasis on group differences which government is called upon to correct might mean the destruction of any hope for the larger fraternity of all Americans, in which people are tied to one another in what they feel to be a common good society, and in which the tie is close enough to allow tolerance for their range of differences.

IBID.

William Godwin *(1756–1836)*

*E*nglish philosopher and novelist William Godwin wrote novels and essays, as well as *History of the Commonwealth* (1824–1828) and *An Enquiry Concerning Political Justice* (1793), in which he emphasized the importance of personal liberty.

Government can have no more than two legitimate purposes—the suppression of injustice within the community, and the common defense against external invasion.

AN ENQUIRY CONCERNING POLITICAL JUSTICE, 1793

Johann Wolfgang von Goethe *(1749–1832)*

*G*erman poet Goethe has been called "The German Shakespeare" and in fact helped establish the Shakespearean form of drama on the German stage. A prolific poet and author, he exercised a dominant influence on German literature. For example, *The Sorrows of Young Werther* (1774), an epistolary novel of morbid sensibility, influenced the sentimental school and his *Faust* (1832) influenced the modern spirit in literature.

Legislators and revolutionaries who promise liberty and equality at the same time are either utopian dreamers or charlatans.

QUOTED IN *MAXIMS AND REFLECTIONS*, NO. 953

What is the best government? That which teaches us to govern ourselves.

IBID.

Freedom! A fine word when rightly understood. What freedom would you have? What is the freedom of the most free? To act rightly!

EGMONT, 1788

Barry Goldwater *(1909–)*

*B*arry Goldwater was the 1964 Republican presidential candidate. The author of *Conscience of a Conservative* (1960), he has been a strong proponent of little governmental intervention in the economy, of states' rights, and of individual responsibility. An extremely influential thinker, Goldwater is widely regarded as the father of twentieth-century American conservatism as a political movement.

If the Conservative is less anxious than his Liberal brethren to increase Social Security "benefits," it is because he is more anxious than his Liberal brethren that people be free throughout their lives to spend their earnings when and as they see fit.

CONSCIENCE OF A CONSERVATIVE, 1960

The conscience of the Conservative is pricked by *anyone* who would debase the dignity of the individual human being. Today, therefore, he is at odds with dictators who rule by terror, and equally with those gentler collectivists who ask our permission to play God with the human race.

IBID.

The only way to persuade farmers to enter other fields of endeavor is to stop paying inefficient farmers for produce that cannot be sold at free market prices.

IBID.

How can he [one] be free if the fruits of his labor are not his to dispose of, but are treated, instead, as part of a common pool of public wealth? Property and freedom are inseparable: to the extent government takes the one in the form of taxes, it intrudes on the other.

IBID.

The graduated tax is a *confiscatory* tax. Its effect, and to a large extent its aim, is to bring down all men to a common level.

IBID.

The effect of Welfarism on freedom will be felt later on—after its beneficiaries have become its victims, after dependence on government has turned into bondage and it is too late to unlock the jail.

IBID.

Welfare programs cannot help but promote the idea that the government *owes* the benefits it confers on the individual, and that the individual is entitled, by right, to receive them.

IBID.

Let us, then, not blunt the noble impulses of mankind by reducing charity to a mechanical operation of the federal government . . . . Let welfare be a private concern.

IBID.

William Franklin (Billy) Graham *(1918–)*

*E*vangelist Billy Graham received his Th.B. from the Florida Bible Seminar in Tampa (1940) and was ordained to the ministry in the Southern Baptist Convention. He is the founder of World Wide Pictures (1949), and the Billy Graham Evangelistic Association, and has supervised world-wide evangelistic campaigns. He has hosted the weekly *Hour of Decision* radio program since 1950. A recipient of numerous awards, such as the Bernard Baruch award (1955), the Horatio Alger award (1965), and the International Brotherhood award of the National Conference of Christians and Jews (1971), Graham is the author of over a dozen books.

We [Americans] have taught during the past few decades that morals are relative, and now we are reaping the harvest. The tendency of the educational system, the courts, and the mass communication media is often to ignore the victim of a crime and to coddle the criminal. In some cases, we even make the criminal a hero.

WORLD AFLAME, 1965

Theirs [Communists' philosophy] is an "end justifies the means" philosophy. Wrong though they are, they have a goal, a purpose, and a sense of destiny. It is clear that we can never cope with Communism simply by fearing it and hating it. We must recapture our own national sense of purpose, our devotion to a great cause, and a vital faith, if we are to vie successfully with a foe who is making plans to bury us.

IBID.

We speak of Communism being a great challenge to Christianity, and ideologically it is; but no system can be seriously threatened by an enemy "without" until it has been weakened by some enemy "within." While I am diametrically opposed to Communism *per se,* I am more concerned about the lack of zeal for Christianity than I am about the zeal and purposes of the Communists.

IBID.

It is . . . true, as Will Durant said: "No great nation has ever been overcome until it has destroyed itself." Republics, kingdoms, and empires all live their uncertain lives and die. In America we are now on the verge of seeing a democracy gone wild. Freedom has become license. Moral law is in danger of being abandoned even by the courts. To what degree can we expect immunity from the inevitable law of regress that sets in when nations defy the laws of God?

IBID.

Communism can never succeed unless Christianity fails.

IBID.

Communism does not have the ultimate answer or the final hope. With whatever vigor and effort Communism may attack the problems of the world's disinherited masses, it has no answer for man's real problem—the problem of the human spirit in search of God. This is one of the reasons why Communism will ultimately fail.

IBID.

Satan's masterpiece in our times is the philosophy of communism. Its godless, materialistic interpretation of life has had untold effects upon the moral life of the nation.

QUOTED IN *THE QUOTABLE BILLY GRAHAM*, 1966

The "great society" concept is not new. Plato formulated his "Republic"; Sir Thomas More his "Utopia"; Karl Marx his "classless society"; and many others have made attempts to create a picture of the ideal social order. But while the motivation may have been genuinely humanitarian, past efforts have failed miserably. The dreams have cracked up on the rocks of reality.

IBID.

William Philip Gramm (1942-)

A United States Republican senator from Texas, Phil Gramm is also an economist who holds a doctorate in economics and has taught at Texas A & M University. Through his own tenacity—as well as discipline from his parents, neither of whom graduated from high school—Gramm earned a doctorate despite having failed third, seventh, and ninth grades. Gramm is a fiscal conservative, with a profound respect for hard-working taxpayers.

In 1981, on the day the Reagan-Bush Economic Program passed in the House,

I was walking down the steps of the Capitol and a reporter came running up to me and said,

"Congressman Gramm, in your 1,350 page budget how did you decide what programs ought to grow and what programs ought to be cut?"

I said,

"I used the Dicky Flatt test . . . .

"I looked at every program in the federal government. And then I tried to think of a real, honest-to-God working person in my Congressional District. And I often thought of a printer from Mexia [Texas] named Dicky Flatt. And I thought about Dicky Flatt because he works for a living. He is in business with his wife; his momma; and his brother and brother's wife. They have a print shop. They sell stationery and school and office supplies. They work till 7 or 8 o'clock every week night; and they're open on Saturday. And whether you see Dicky Flatt at the PTA or the Boy Scouts or at his church, try as he may he never quite gets that blue ink off the end of his fingers . . . .

"I looked at each program and I thought about Dicky Flatt and I asked a simple question: will the benefits to be derived by spending money on this program be worth taking the money away from Dicky Flatt to pay for it?"

Let me tell you something, there are not a hell of a lot of programs that will stand up to that test. The Dicky Flatt test is the Republican test and when Congress starts using that test we are going to lick this deficit problem once and for all.

SPEECH AT THE REPUBLICAN NATIONAL CONVENTION, HOUSTON, TEXAS, AUGUST 18, 1992

Edward Grimsley *(1927–)*

*E*dward Grimsley is a prominent syndicated columnist for Creators Syndicate.

Gone are the days when it was commendable for people to practice the precepts of Ben Franklin ("Early to bed and early to rise makes a man healthy, wealthy and wise," "A penny saved is a penny earned" and so forth) and inspire Horatio Alger rags-to-riches stories. No longer is it universally considered to be an admirable feat for people to climb the ladder of success in this glorious land of opportunity. Today the individual who rises from poverty to become president of Amalgamated Motors and earn a few million dollars a year at the job is likely to be vilified as a parasite.

Nor is it safe for a politician to capitalize on the fact that he rose from a log cabin to a mansion. Today that would make him the target of an investigation by a special federal prosecutor.

To be wealthy, then, is to be politically incorrect.

"DEMOCRATS ARE A THREAT TO THE MIDDLE CLASS,"
FEB. 21, 1992

John Hamilton Hallowell *(1913–)*

*J*ohn Hallowell earned a doctorate in political science from Princeton and then taught at a number of leading universities, including U.C.L.A., Duke University, and the University of Chicago. Much of his writing emphasizes the importance of traditional conservative values, including a sense of the transcendent. He has written such books as *The Decline of Liberalism as an Ideology* (1943), *Main Currents in Modern Political Thought* (1950), and *The Moral Foundation of Democracy* (1954).

The sickness of the modern world is the sickness of moral confusion, intellectual anarchy, and spiritual despair. The revolution of nihilism, born of this confusion and despair, is peculiar not alone to any one country or people but in varying degrees is taking place everywhere. With almost frantic zeal we search for the political or economic panacea that will save us and the world from disaster, not seeing, apparently, that the disaster is already upon us and that for the cure we must examine the state of our own souls . . . . In his despondency he is tempted to strike out against the enemy he cannot identify, whose name he does not know, in desperate action. In his anxiety to escape from utter futility and meaningless existence he is tempted to give up his most priceless heritage—his freedom—to any man who even promises deliverance from insecurity. He is tempted to put his faith in the most absurd doctrine, to submit his will to the most brutal dictator, if only in such a way he can find that for which he longs with all the passion of his being—a meaningful existence, a life worth living, a life worth dying to preserve.

MAIN CURRENTS IN MODERN POLITICAL THOUGHT, 1950

The beliefs . . . in the absolute moral worth of the individual, in the spiritual

89

equality of individuals, and in the essential rationality of man were a heritage from the Middle Ages and have their roots deep in Christian and Greek thought. We can repudiate these ideas only by repudiating our humanity. It is the belief in the absolute moral worth of the individual that prevents the individual from being submerged, if not obliterated, in a conception of the race, the class, the nation, or some other collectivity that regards the individual as a means rather than as an end in himself.

THE MORAL FOUNDATION OF DEMOCRACY, 1954

Real consent is a spontaneous expression of approval. It is a positive force arising out of inner conviction. It is not synonymous with passive acquiescence or voluntary submission. It is found as the basis of government in greater proportion to constraint only in nations where there is a community of values and interests, that is, where there is positive affirmation of certain fundamental values and interests common to nearly all individuals and groups within the nation. It is, indeed, the existence of this community of values and interests that makes democratic, parliamentary government possible. A minority will agree to temporary rule by the majority only because certain common interests in maintaining the political

system transcend partisan interests. The breakdown of democracy comes when this community of values disintegrates, when common agreement on fundamentals no longer exists, when partisans no longer endeavor to work through the state but to become the state.

THE DECLINE OF LIBERALISM AS AN IDEOLOGY, 1943

Alexander Hamilton *(1755–1804)*

*T*he first secretary of the treasury (1789–1795), Alexander Hamilton was also secretary and aide-de-camp to George Washington and a member of the Continental Congress (1782, 1783, 1787, 1788). He supported the new constitution by contributions (with James Madison and John Jay) to the *Federalist Papers* (1787–1788). As secretary of the treasury, Hamilton planned and executed policies that strengthened central government, established a national fiscal system, stimulated trade and enterprise, and developed national resources.

Why has government been instituted at all? Because the passions of men will not conform to the dictates of reason and justice without constraint.

THE FEDERALIST, #15, 1788

We are now forming a republican government. Real liberty is neither found in despotism or [sic] the extremes of democracy, but in moderate government.

DEBATES OF THE FEDERAL CONVENTION, JUNE 26, 1787

There can be no truer principle than this—that every individual of the community at large has an equal right to the protection of government.

ADDRESS, CONSTITUTIONAL CONVENTION, JUNE 29, 1787

John Marshall Harlan *(1833–1911)*

*K*entucky-born John Marshall Harlan served in the Union army in the Civil War and became attorney general of Kentucky and associate justice of the U.S. Supreme Court (1877–1911). Harlan was the sole dissenter in the *Plessy v. Ferguson* case (1896), which ruled racially separate but equal accommodations constitutional, and which was overturned by *Brown v. Board of Education of Topeka* (1954).

It is not within the functions of government . . . to compel any person in the course of his business and against his will, to accept or retain the personal services of another, or to compel any person, against his will, to perform personal services for another.

ADAIR V. U.S. (THE YELLOW DOG CONTRACT CASE), 1908

Jeffrey Peter Hart *(1930–)*

*J*effrey Hart has been an English professor as well as an editor of *National Review* and a syndicated columnist. His works include *The American Dissent: A Decade of Modern Conservatism* (1966), *When the Going was Good: American Life in the Fifties* (1982), *Acts of Recovery* (1989), and *From This Moment On: America in 1940* (1987).

What is the explanation for the liberal character of academic culture? You will note that a college faculty is by no means a random sample of the general population. It is, rather, a self-selected and rather special sample. In my opinion, the original act of career choice is probably fundamental here. The choice of an academic career is, at the same time, a negative decision—as much a choice not to be a lawyer, a general, or a businessman as to be a Shakespearean, a scholar or an expert in structural linguistics. I do not think the academy makes people liberals, but that individuals who are already on uneasy terms with ordinary society tend to choose the academy.

Naturally, the choice is dressed up as something much more flattering to the ego. The academic individual is a "critic of society" and an "independent thinker." Within their own environment, however, we do not seem to encounter much criticism or independence—merely a lot of people who tend . . . to "sound the same."

ACTS OF RECOVERY, 1989

One answer to the liberal content of academic opinion, applicable over the last century or more, takes a "history of ideas" form. It argues that the traditional attitudes and ideas of Western culture form, so to speak, the thesis, while liberalism constitutes the antithesis, the negative image. Thus, from the liberal perspective, most traditional virtues become negative qualities. If the

traditional thesis is Christian, the liberal antithesis must be secularist. If ordinary human nature admires victory, the liberal cherishes victims, real and contrived. If the ordinary fellow roots for the Marines and the cowboys, the liberal roots for the Vietcong or the Indians. The sense of alienation from customary attitude is total. You can sense this alienation in the language itself, and language always carries cultural values in it. The English word "abortion" possesses powerful negative overtones—you simply cannot say, "I had a marvelous abortion the other day." In his negative culture, the liberal converts abortion into a positive cause. Figures who are pariahs in the ordinary culture—the pornographer, the Communist, or whatever—become in the negative liberal culture the objects of special solicitude.

IBID.

In my own experience, liberalism is relentlessly moralistic, even puritanical. I groan inwardly at a general meeting of the Dartmouth faculty, listening to them moralize away about virtually everything. Liberals are perpetually engaged in a kind of moral Easter-egg hunt, seeking out supposed victims. These victims, hereafter known as

Victims, must be rescued from supposed oppressors, whom we will now call Oppressors. In this melodrama the result is always predictable and therefore boring.

IBID.

The human emotion of pity is valid, of course, but it cannot be allowed to preempt all other emotions and values. The liberal converts pity into a kind of nervous tic, the habitual response to everything. The liberal seems constantly to be rejecting the spectrum of powerful and valid human emotions that have nothing to do with pity. There really do exist values in the world other than concern for Victims, real or phony. Such potent worldly values include vitality, form, style, beauty in all its modes, heroism, pleasure, freedom, wealth, creativity, and joy. The liberal seems constantly to be repressing or ignoring all of those in favor of routinized and quickly boring pity. I recall, a couple of years ago, a moralistic attack from the liberals upon the notion of choosing a Carnival Queen. They charged that the girl was being singled out on the basis of "mere beauty." That language— "mere beauty"—just about

tells it all. Mere beauty happens to be intensely important to me.

IBID.

In the search for a new symbol to replace the bushwhacked Dartmouth Indian, it has occurred to me that we might consider The Liberal. Various astonishing skits could be devised for this figure, all of them self-abasing and moralistic. We might even commission a Cigar-Store Liberal, life-sized, carved out of wood. This Cigar-Store Liberal—unisex, of course—might be posed rejecting a bunch of grapes, or forcing a kid onto a bus, or surrendering, or kissing the foot of some Third World windbag.

IBID.

The vast slide is under way. Communism has been the dominant fact of the 20th century, fascism a mere blip by comparison. Perhaps 100 million people have been killed, 30 million by the Soviets, about the same number by Mao, several million by Pol Pot, several million by the Hanoi communists, about a million now in Central America and Cuba—all in the name of ushering in a socialist Utopia. Well, so much for that. During his first term as president, Ronald Reagan said two things that aroused fury on the left. He said that the Soviet Union is an "evil empire" and that communism is a vast historical mistake. He was correct on both accounts.

"COMMUNISM: IT'S ALL OVER," JUNE 8, 1989

Paul Harvey *(1918–)*

*N*ews commentator, author, and columnist, Paul Harvey delights listeners with his speaking voice and delivery ("And now you know the *rest* of the story"). His professionalism as well as his homespun wisdom and unswerving commitment to traditional values have won him numerous honors and awards, including eleven Freedoms Foundation awards (1952–1976), the American of the Year award from Lions International (1975), the Outstanding Broadcast Journalism award (1980), and the Golden Radio award of the National Radio Broadcasters Association (1982).

You are familiar with *Who's Who Among American High School Students.* Each year our nation's outstanding high school students are studied to see what makes them outstanding.

This year *Who's Who* conducted a study of their parents in an effort to discover what made these young people standout students . . . .

Two thousand parents were surveyed, and most had inspired their children with the imperatives of good education, work and respect for authority.

In a word, today's star students come from "old-fashioned" homes. Old-fashioned only in that they reflect hard work, self-reliance, respect for family and community—in a phrase: "family values."

"FAMILY VALUES AREN'T OUT OF DATE," OCTOBER 1, 1992

The Census Bureau, based on a single statistic, has declared that 30 million Americans fall below the poverty threshold of $13,942 for a family of four.

But the Bureau's statisticians ignore the fact that 40 percent of those people own their own homes . . . .

That their average home is a three-bedroom house with a garage, porch and patio . . . .

More than half of the poor live in homes or apartments with twice as much living space as the average Japanese, four times more than the average Russian.

"WE ARE 'NAMES,' NOT 'NUMBERS,'" SEPT. 11, 1992

USDA studies have affirmed that the average consumption of protein, vitamins and minerals in the United States is virtually [the] same for both poor and middle-class children.

And in most cases it is well above recommended norms.

Far from being chemically hungry and malnourished, "poor" children in the United States are in fact super-nourished, growing up to be an inch taller and 10 pounds heavier than the average American soldier in World War II.

IBID.

I am fed up with politicians trashing our country when it is the best country on this planet.

Recession is worse in every other industrial nation than it is in ours. And yet with the willing complicity of much of the media, our country is mean-mouthed day in and day out until a lie begins to sound like the truth.

IBID.

Friedrich August von Hayek

(1899–1992)

*A*ustrian-born economist Friedrich Hayek, who became a British subject in 1938, was a leading defender of free-market economics and the whig tradition of political thought. Hayek wrote such works as *The Road to Serfdom* (1944) and *The Constitution of Liberty* (1960), and he shared the 1974 Nobel Prize in economics with Gunnar Myrdal.

The more the state "plans" the more difficult planning becomes for the individual.

THE ROAD TO SERFDOM, 1944

In a directed economy, where the authority watches over the ends pursued, it is certain that it would use its powers to assist some ends and to prevent the realization of others. Not our own view, but somebody else's, of what we ought to like or dislike would determine what we should get.

IBID.

We have progressively abandoned that freedom in economic affairs without which personal and political freedom has never existed in the past.

IBID.

It is now often said that democracy will not tolerate "capitalism." If "capitalism" means here a competitive system based on free disposal over private property, it is far more important to realize that only within this system is democracy possible. When it becomes dominated by a collectivist creed, democracy will inevitably destroy itself.

IBID.

There is no justification for the belief that, so long as power is conferred by democratic procedure, it cannot be arbitrary; the contrast suggested by this statement is altogether false: it is not the source but the limitation of power which prevents it from being arbitrary.

IBID.

It is of the essence of the demand for equality before the law that people should be treated alike in spite of the fact that they are different.

THE CONSTITUTION OF LIBERTY, 1960

The greatest danger to liberty today comes from the men who are most needed and most powerful in modern government, namely, the efficient expert administrators exclusively concerned with what they regard as the public good.

IBID.

Liberty not only means that the individual has both the opportunity and the burden of choice; it also means that he must bear the consequences of his actions and will receive praise or blame for them. Liberty and responsibility are inseparable. A free society will not function or maintain itself unless its members regard it as right that each individual occupy the position that results from his action and accept it as due to his own action.

IBID.

[The] belief in individual responsibility, which has always been strong when people firmly believed in individual freedom, has markedly declined, together with the esteem for freedom. . . . Responsibility . . . often evokes the outright hostility of men who have been taught that it is nothing but circumstances over which they have no control that has determined their position in life or even their actions. This denial of responsibility is, however, commonly due to a fear of responsibility, a fear that necessarily becomes a fear of freedom.

IBID.

[The fundamental issue] is whether it is desirable that people should enjoy advantages in proportion to the benefits which their fellows derive from their activities or whether the distribution of these advantages should be based on other men's views of their merits.

IBID.

[T]he impersonal process of the market . . . can be neither just nor unjust, because the results are not intended or foreseen . . . .

"'SOCIAL' OR DISTRIBUTIVE JUSTICE," IN
THE ESSENCE OF HAYEK, 1984

[W]e consent to . . . uniform rules for an [economic] procedure which has greatly improved the chances of all to have their wants satisfied, but at the price of all individuals and groups incurring the risk of unmerited failure . . . .
. . . [The] game of competition in a market . . . means that some must suffer unmerited disappointment.

IBID.

Henry Hazlitt *(1894–1993)*

*A*uthor, journalist, editor, reviewer, and economist, Henry Hazlitt, who lived for nearly 100 years—and wrote for nearly as many years—popularized economic thinking, criticized the economic theory of John Maynard Keynes, and contributed to moral philosophy. Hazlitt's numerous books include *The Way to Will Power* (1922), *The Anatomy of Criticism* (1933), *Economics in One Lesson* (1946), *Will Dollars Save the World?* (1947), *The Failure of the "New Economics": An Analysis of the Keynesian Fallacies* (1959), *What You Should Know About Inflation* (1960), *The Foundations of Morality* (1964), *Man vs. the Welfare State* (1969), and *The Conquest of Poverty* (1973).

[T]he "private sector" of the economy is, in fact, the *voluntary* sector; and . . . the "public sector" is, in fact, the *coercive* sector. The voluntary sector is made up of the goods and services for which people voluntarily spend the money they have earned. The coercive sector is made up of the goods and services that are provided, regardless of the wishes of the individual, out of the taxes that are seized from him.

QUOTED IN *THE WISDOM OF HENRY HAZLITT*, 1993

[As the coercive] sector grows at the expense of the voluntary sector, we come to the essence of the welfare state. In this state nobody pays for the education of his own children but everybody pays for the education of everybody else's children. Nobody pays his own medical bills, but everybody pays everybody else's medical bills. Nobody helps his own old parents, but everybody else's old parents. Nobody provides for the contingency of his own unemployment, his own sickness, his own old age, but everybody provides for the unemployment, sickness, or old age of everybody else. The welfare state . . . is the great fiction by which everybody tries to live at the expense of everybody else.

IBID.

[The welfare state] is bound to be a failure. This is sure to be the outcome whenever effort is separated from reward. When people who earn more than the average have their "surplus," or the greater part of it, seized from them in taxes, and when people who earn less than the average have the deficiency, or the greater part of it, turned over to them in hand-outs and doles, the production of all must sharply decline; for the energetic and able lose their incentive to produce more than the average, and the slothful and unskilled lose their incentive to improve their condition.

IBID.

Patrick Henry *(1736–1799)*

*P*atrick Henry was an American Revolutionary leader who practiced law in Virginia and served in the Virginia legislature. When he introduced resolutions opposing the Stamp Act, he ended his speech with, "Ceasar had his Brutus; Charles the First, his Cromwell; and George the Third—may profit by their example." With Thomas Jefferson and Richard Henry Lee, he initiated the intercolonial committee of correspondence. Henry was a member of the First Continental Congress (1774), and at Virginia's second revolutionary convention in March 1775, he spoke his most famous words: "Give me liberty, or give me death." He was instrumental in causing the adoption of the first ten amendments to the U.S. Constitution.

[R]eligion, or the duty which we owe to our creator, and the manner of discharging it, can be directed only by reason and conviction, not by force or violence; and therefore all men are equally entitled to the free exercise of religion, according to the dictates of conscience; and this is the mutual duty of all to practice Christian forbearance, love, and charity towards each other.

VIRGINIA BILL OF RIGHTS, ARTICLE 16, JUNE 12, 1776

Is life so dear or peace so sweet as to be purchased at the price of chains and slavery? Forbid it, Almighty God! I know not what course others may take, but as for me, give me liberty, or give me death.

SPEECH, VIRGINIA CONVENTION, MARCH 23, 1775

Gertrude Himmelfarb (1922–)

*P*rofessor emeritus of history at the Graduate School of the City University of New York, Gertrude Himmelfarb is a fellow of the British Academy, the Royal Historical Society, the American Philosophical Society, and the American Academy of Arts and Sciences. A prolific author, she is particularly learned in the history of ideas. Her books include *Lord Acton: A Study in Conscience and Politics* (1952), *Darwin and the Darwinian Revolution* (1959), *On Liberty and Liberalism: The Case of John Stuart Mill* (1974), *The Idea of Poverty: England in the Early Industrial Age* (1984), and *On Looking into the Abyss* (1994).

With the rise of communism and Nazism, many liberals, normally inclined to a moderate, pluralistic, pragmatic view of liberty, were persuaded that the only security against an absolutistic regime was an absolute principle of liberty. Anything less appeared incommensurate with the enormity of the evil. Totalitarianism, they believed, could be effectively opposed only by an ideology as total and uncompromising as the enemy with whom they were contending. Against absolute despotism the only adequate response seemed to be absolute liberty.

This was—and still is—the psychological basis of the "slippery slope" argument. Any deviation from absolute liberty is seen as a capitulation to tyranny . . . . This is the argument used by liberals in support of government subsidies for such "art" as the photograph of a crucifix submerged in urine, the painting of Christ as a drug addict with a needle in his arm, or a sexual performance compared with which the old striptease is positively puritanical. Yet the same liberals who advocate the largest freedom for artists (including the freedom to be subsidized) also tend to support, in the name of the same freedom, the strictest separation of church and state—with the curious result that the photograph of a crucifix immersed in urine can be exhibited in a public school, but a crucifix not immersed in urine cannot be exhibited.

ON LOOKING INTO THE ABYSS, 1994

[A more serious problem is] the tendency of absolute liberty to subvert the very liberty it seeks to preserve. By making particular liberties dependent on an absolute principle of liberty, by invalidating all those other principles—history, custom, law, interest, opinion, religion—which have traditionally served to support particular liberties, the absolute principle discredits these particular liberties together with the principles upon which they are based. So far from making liberty absolutely secure, the absolutistic doctrine may have the unwitting effect of depriving specific liberties, including the most basic ones, of the security they enjoy under more traditional, modest auspices. And when that absolute principle proves inadequate to the exigencies of social life, it is abandoned absolutely, replaced not by a more moderate form of liberty but by an immoderate form of government control.

IBID.

Liberals have always known that absolute power tends to corrupt absolutely . . . . [W]e are now discovering that absolute liberty also tends to corrupt absolutely. A liberty that is divorced from tradition and convention, from morality and religion, that makes the individual the sole repository and arbiter of all values and puts him in an adversarial relationship to society and the state—such a liberty is a grave peril to liberalism itself. For when that liberty is found wanting, when it violates the moral sense of the community or is incompatible with the legitimate demands of society, there is no moderating principle to take its place, no resting place between the wild gyrations of libertarianism and paternalism.

IBID.

Thomas Hobbes *(1588–1679)*

*C*ontroversial in his day, the English philosopher Thomas Hobbes has had a continuing influence on Western political thought. Hobbes held that self-preservation is the principal motive that causes people to give up some of their freedom to seek the protection of a powerful sovereign. For Hobbes, a sovereign's rule, though supreme, is derived from the people. His concept of the social contract influenced others, especially Locke, Spinoza, and Rousseau, who formed their own social contract theories.

Intemperance is naturally punished with diseases; rashness, with mischance; injustice, with violence of enemies; pride, with ruin; cowardice, with oppression; and rebellion, with slaughter.

LEVIATHAN, 1651

For the laws of nature (as justice, equity, modesty, mercy, and, in sum, *doing to others as we would be done to*) of themselves, without the terror of some power, to cause them to be observed, are contrary to our natural passions, that carry us to partiality, pride, revenge and the like.

IBID.

[In a state of nature, that is, life without any law or government:] No arts; no letters; no society; and which is worst of all, continual fear and danger of violent death; and the life of man, solitary, poor, nasty, brutish, and short.

IBID.

Eric Hoffer *(1902–1983)*

A San Francisco longshoreman-turned-author, Eric Hoffer achieved immediate fame for his book *True Believer* (1951), in which he described the underlying logic of mass movements, such as Nazism and Communism, and the characteristics of their followers. He also wrote *The Passionate State of Mind* (1955) and *The Ordeal of Change* (1963).

We clamor for equality chiefly in matters in which we ourselves cannot hope to obtain excellence.

THE PASSIONATE STATE OF MIND, 1955

No matter how noble the objectives of a government, if it blurs decency and kindness, cheapens human life, and breeds ill will and suspicion—it is an evil government.

IBID.

We cannot win the weak by sharing our wealth with them. They feel our generosity as oppression.

THE ORDEAL OF CHANGE, 1963

There can be no freedom without
freedom to fail.

IBID.

I doubt if the oppressed ever fight for
freedom. They fight for pride and
power—the power to oppress others.
The oppressed want above all to imitate
their oppressors; they want to retaliate.

THE TRUE BELIEVER, 1951

It is to escape the responsibility for
failure that the weak so eagerly throw
themselves into grandiose undertakings.

IBID.

Samuel Phillips Huntington

(1927-)

A political science educator,
Samuel P. Huntington has been
the director of the John M. Olin
Institute for Strategic Studies at
Harvard. Some of his books include
The Soldier and the State (1957), *The
Common Defense* (1961), *Political
Order in Changing Societies* (1968),
American Politics (1981), and *The
Third Wave: Democratization in the
Late Twentieth Century* (1991).

The basic ideas of the American
Creed—equality, liberty, individualism,
constitutionalism, democracy—clearly do
not constitute a systematic ideology, and
they do not necessarily have any logical
consistency. At some point, liberty and
equality may clash, individualism may
run counter to constitutionalism, and
democracy or majority rule may infringe
on both. Precisely because it is not an
intellectualized ideology, the American
Creed can live with such inconsistencies.

AMERICAN POLITICS, 1981

Logically inconsistent as they seem to
philosophers, . . . all the varying elements
in the American Creed unite in imposing
limits on power and on the institutions of
government. The essence of constitutionalism is the restraint of governmental
power through fundamental law. The
essence of liberalism is freedom from governmental control—the vindication of
liberty against power . . . . The essence of
individualism is the right of each person
to act in accordance with his own conscience and to control his own destiny
free of external restraint, except insofar as
such restraint is necessary to ensure comparable rights to others. The essence of
egalitarianism is rejection of the idea that
one person has the right to exercise power
over another. The essence of democracy is
popular control over government directly

or through representatives, and the responsiveness of government officials to public opinion. In sum, the distinctive aspect of the American Creed is its antigovernment character. Opposition to power, and suspicion of government as the most dangerous embodiment of power, are the central themes of American political thought.

IBID.

The political climate of the late 1970s was distinguished by the increasing ascendancy of conservative, antigovernment attitudes among the public at large and of conservative, antigovernment ideas among the intellectual elite. This shift to the right was first marked in the 1976 election results, as Carter defeated his liberal opponents for the Democratic nomination and Ronald Reagan almost unseated an incumbent Republican President. It was marked again in 1978 by the defeat of liberal candidates for state and local office and the victory of conservative, antitaxation referenda in several states. It continued in 1980 with the primary victories of Carter and Reagan, the defeat of Carter in the November election, and the unseating of a number of liberal Democratic senators. Americans were not only distrustful of governmental authority, they were also hostile to governmental activity.

IBID.

In 1959, . . . when asked to identify which was "the biggest threat to the country in the future," only 14 percent of the public picked "big government," compared to 41 percent who picked "big labor" and 15 percent who chose "big business." In 1978, in contrast, 47 percent of the public picked big government for this honor, compared to 19 percent each for big business and big labor. Similarly, in 1964 only 43 percent of the American public thought the government in Washington was "too big"; by 1976 over 58 percent of the public believed this, and in both 1972 and 1976, 50 percent or more of those identifying themselves as liberals, moderates, and conservatives held this view.

IBID.

Reed John Irvine (1922–)

*M*edia critic and corporate executive Reed Irvine has done postgraduate work at the University of Colorado and the University of Washington and earned a Master of Literature degree from Oxford University. He was on the board of governors of the Federal

Reserve System (1951–1963) and served as an advisor on international finance (1963–1977). Irvine has been chair of Accuracy in Media (AIM)—a media watchdog organization—editor of the *AIM Report*, and chair of Accuracy in Academia, as well as a syndicated columnist and radio commentator. He is the author of *Media Mischief and Misdeeds* (1984) and *Profiles of Deception* (with Cliff Kincaid, 1990), a collection of some of his columns and radio commentary.

The Public Broadcasting Service (PBS) finished airing a four-hour series condemning the use of covert action by U.S. intelligence agencies in mid-February. For four hours, Bill Kurtis, the former co-host of the CBS *Morning News* program, reviewed what he portrayed as the futility and folly of American efforts to try to achieve our foreign policy objectives by using covert action, sometimes labeled "dirty tricks," against our enemies. To make his case, Kurtis went back 35 years to review covert CIA operations in Iran and Guatemala in 1953. These have long been considered good examples of successful covert actions, but Kurtis presented them as both wicked and as failures . . . .

. . . Our successes may not have ushered in a millennium of paradise in the countries we tried to help, but our failures have in every case resulted in unending hell for those who fell under the yoke of communism. Communism in the Third World has meant bloodbaths, boat people, masses of political prisoners, millions of refugees, loss of freedom, impoverishment, and war. The PBS series never discussed that . . . .

"'DIRTY TRICKS' BY PBS," MARCH 11, 1989

[I]n the period 1982–83 . . . [and] 1986–87, . . . bad news about the economy was frequently the only news [that was reported on network evening news programs]. And the bad economic news was often attributed to the policies of the Reagan Administration. By contrast, the Administration was seldom given credit for good economic news. It was presented as if it just happened. The major media may have felt vindicated when the stock market crashed in October 1987. The market dropped a record 24 percent. What they didn't point out was that, during the preceding 5 years, the market had staged a 250 percent increase.

"BAD NEWS IS THE ONLY NEWS," NOV. 18, 1988

Harry Victor Jaffa *(1918–)*

*H*arry Jaffa is the author of books on the Lincoln-Douglas debates as well as such works as *Equality and Liberty* (1965), *How to Think About the American Revolution* (1978), *American Conservatism and the American Founding* (1984), and *Original Intent and the Framers of the Constitution* (1993).

Liberalism and Radicalism both reject the wisdom of the past, as enshrined in the institutions of the past, or in the morality of the past. They deny legitimacy to laws, governments, or ways of life which accept the ancient evils of mankind, such as poverty, inequality, and war, as necessary—and therefore as permanent—attributes of the human condition. Political excellence can no longer be measured by the degree to which it ameliorates such evils. The only acceptable goal is their abolition. Liberalism and Radicalism look forward to a state of things in which the means of life, and of the good life, are available to all. They must be available in such a way that the full development of each

individual—which is how the good life is defined—is not merely compatible with, but is necessary to, the full development of all. Competition between individuals, classes, races, and nations must come to an end. Competition itself is seen as the root of the evils mankind must escape. The good society must be characterized only by cooperation and harmony.

How to Think About the American Revolution, 1978

The Old Liberalism saw life as a race, in which justice demanded for everyone only a fair or equal chance in the competition. But the New Liberalism sees the race itself as wrong. In every race there can be but one winner, and there must be many losers. Thus the Old Liberalism preserved the inequality of the Few over and against the Many. It demanded the removal of artificial or merely conventional inequalities. But it recognized and demanded the fullest scope for natural inequalities. But the New Liberalism denies natural no less than conventional inequalities.

Ibid.

In the Heaven of the New Liberalism, as in that of the Old Theology, all will be rewarded equally. The achievement of the good society is itself the only victory.

But this victory is not to be one of man over man, but of mankind over the scourges of mankind. No one in it will taste the bitterness of defeat. No one need say, "I am a loser, but I have no right to complain. I had a fair chance." The joys of victory will belong to all. Unlike the treasures of the past, the goods of the future will be possessed by all. They will not be diminished or divided by being common. On the contrary, they will for that very reason increase and intensify. No one will be a miser—or a Conservative.

IBID.

Thomas Jefferson *(1743–1826)*

*T*he principal author of the Declaration of Independence and third president of the United States (1801–1809), Thomas Jefferson was a strong advocate of religious freedom, and his emphasis on limited constitutional government, states' rights, and individual liberty has enormously influenced conservative political theory. (For more on Jefferson, see the Preface.)

Sometimes it is said that man cannot be trusted with the government of himself. Can he, then, be trusted with the government of others? Or have we found angels in the form of kings to govern him?

FIRST INAUGURAL ADDRESS, MARCH 4, 1801

Still one thing more, fellow citizens—a wise and frugal government, which shall restrain men from injuring one another, which shall leave them otherwise free to regulate their own pursuits of industry and improvement, and shall not take from the mouth of labor the bread it has earned. This is the sum of good government, and this is necessary to close the circle of our felicities.

IBID.

All, too, will bear in mind this sacred principle, that though the will of the majority is in all cases to prevail, that will, to be rightful, must be reasonable; that the minority possess their equal rights, which equal laws must protect, and to violate which would be oppression.

IBID.

I would rather be exposed to the inconveniences attending too much liberty than those attending too small a degree of it.

LETTER TO ARCHIBALD STUART, DEC. 23, 1791

Offices are as acceptable here as else-where, and whenever a man has cast a longing eye on them, a rottenness begins in his conduct.

LETTER TO TENCH COXE, MAY 21, 1799

The republican is the only form of government which is not eternally at open or secret war with the rights of mankind.

LETTER TO WILLIAM HUNTER, MARCH 11, 1790

The legitimate powers of government extend to such acts only as are injurious to others.

"NOTES ON THE STATE OF VIRGINIA," 1781–1785

Every government degenerates when trusted to the rulers of the people alone. The people themselves are its only safe depositories.

IBID.

All men shall be free to profess, and by argument to maintain, their opinion in matters of religion; and . . . the same in no wise diminish, enlarge, or affect their civil capacities.

"VIRGINIA STATUTE FOR RELIGIOUS FREEDOM," 1779

The natural progress of things is for liberty to yield and government to gain ground.

LETTER TO E. CARRINGTON, MAY 27, 1788

Were we directed from Washington when to sow, and when to reap, we should soon want bread.

AUTOBIOGRAPHY, 1821

Paul Johnson (1928–)

*B*ritish historian, journalist, and broadcaster Paul Johnson was educated at Stonyhurst and Magdalen College, Oxford. He has edited many journals, especially the *New Statesman*, and was professor of communications at the American Enterprise Institute in Washington, D.C. Some of his works include *The Offshore Islanders* (1972), *Elizabeth I: A Study in Power and Intellect* (1974), *Pope John XXIII* (1975), *A History of Christianity* (1976), *Enemies of Society* (1977), *Intellectuals* (1988), and *Modern Times* (1991).

The disillusion with socialism and other forms of collectivism, which became the dominant spirit of the 1980s, was only one aspect of a much wider loss of faith in the state as an agency of benevolence. The state was, up to the

1980s, the greater gainer of the twentieth century; and the central failure. Before 1914 it was rare for the public sector to embrace more than 10 percent of the economy; by the end of the 1970s, and even beyond, the state took up to 45 percent or more of the GNP in liberal countries, let alone totalitarian ones. But whereas, at the time of the Versailles Treaty in 1919, most intelligent people believed that an enlarged state could increase the sum total of human happiness, by the 1990s this view was held by no one outside a small, diminishing and dispirited band of zealots, most of them academics. The experiment had been tried in innumerable ways; and it had failed in nearly all of them. The state had proved itself an insatiable spender, an unrivalled waster. It had also proved itself the greatest killer of all time. By the 1990s, state action had been responsible for the violent or unnatural deaths of some 125 million people during the century, more perhaps than it had succeeded in destroying during the whole of human history up to 1900. Its inhuman malevolence had more than kept pace with its growing size and expanding means.

MODERN TIMES, 1991

Samuel Johnson *(1709–1784)*

*E*nglish author, poet, and lexicographer, Samuel Johnson is perhaps most famous for his pioneering *Dictionary of the English Language* (1755), which established the practice of clarifying definitions by quotations from leading authors. He wrote many other works, including *The Rambler*, a book of essays (1750–1752), the satirical *Rasselas*, a fictional assault on metaphysical optimism (1759), and *Lives of the English Poets* (1779–1781). His political views were very much like those of Edmund Burke: conservative, traditional, and distrustful of radical social upheavals. Johnson was immortalized by his biographer James Boswell, who wrote *Life of Samuel Johnson* (1791).

It is better that some should be unhappy than that none should be happy, which would be the case in a general state of equality.

QUOTED IN *LIFE OF SAMUEL JOHNSON*, APRIL 7, 1776

Your levellers wish to level down as far as themselves; but they cannot bear levelling up to themselves.

IBID., 1791

Most of the misery which the defamation of blameless actions or the obstruction of honest endeavors brings upon the world is inflicted by men that propose no advantage to themselves but the satisfaction of poisoning the banquet which they cannot taste, and blasting the harvest which they have no right to reap.

THE RAMBLER, 1751

Jack French Kemp (1935–)

A former U.S. congressman from New York (1971–1989) and secretary of Housing and Urban Development (1989–1992), Jack Kemp was also a special assistant to the governor of California and a special assistant to the chair of the Republican national convention. He has been a strong advocate of free enterprise, as when he has supported programs enabling industrious people in public housing to become self-sustaining and to buy their homes. His appreciation of the entrepreneurial spirit and his manifest enthusiasm and optimism have appealed to millions of people. Kemp is the author of *An American Renaissance: A Strategy for the 1980's* (1979).

We are the most free and most educated, creative, talented, energetic, and healthy people on earth—and we are now operating at less than half our potential, perhaps less than a third our potential! There's no telling what we can accomplish if only the government would get out of the way and let us load the wagon. The American Dream is not a sniveling, envious hope that everyone be leveled with everyone else. It is the freedom and encouragement to climb as high up the ladder of opportunity as possible, and obtain a just reward based upon our efforts and abilities.

AN AMERICAN RENAISSANCE: A STRATEGY FOR THE 1980's, 1979

Lyndon Johnson's Great Society was built on an invigorating, exciting, but nonetheless erroneous, idea that government sharing can end poverty and urban squalor by taxing away resources from the "haves" and giving them to the "have nots." As is usual, the resources were taxed away from middle-class Americans and, except in the rare instance, never got to the lower-income classes. Giant federal bureaucracies were established to run programs and dispense funds that would lead to this Great Society, and by the time the federal tax dollars got through the bureaucratic "in" and "out" baskets there were left only nickels and dimes. The war on poverty became a war on the middle class—and on the poor.

IBID.

Where tax dollars were actually spent [in Lyndon Johnson's Great Society], there almost always occurred an increase in bitterness and frustration in the segment of society that was supposed to benefit. All over the nation poor blacks, Hispanics, and whites, were trained by government bureaucrats for jobs that didn't exist in the private sector. Urban renewal meant that low-income housing, designated "substandard" by government bureaucrats, was torn down to make way for gleaming new—and taxable—offices, factories, and shopping malls. In 1979, a dozen years later, the nation is pockmarked with the razed acreage of defunct projects. Those evicted generally had to fend for themselves, and because they usually could only move to housing they could not afford the government had to begin new programs to transfer income to citizens it had displaced. And since only a tiny number of such projects resulted in the expected taxable properties, the unlucky people whose properties surround the pockmarked urban-renewal areas now have to pay off bonds floated to ravage their towns and cities.

IBID.

The most frequent barriers to opportunity today are not "whites only" factories or businesses to which "no Irish need apply." They are factories and businesses that never were because it wasn't worth it for anyone to build them! They are the inner-city wrecks that stand empty now because their occupants couldn't afford to retool. They are the jobs that will never be because your would-be employer can't afford to pay your wages and then pay the government more in payroll taxes, unemployment insurance, Social Security charges, and the like *because* he hired you.

IBID.

There must be taxes to pay for those things that require collective effort. Some regulations are essential for public health and safety. But it is the job of those in public life to find and eliminate barriers that serve no social good.

IBID.

Those who have convinced themselves that higher taxes are a cure for inflation naturally view our tax-rate reduction proposals as inflationary. Yet reduced tax rates are inflationary only if they result in larger budget deficits and those larger deficits are financed by creating more money. A constructive reduction of steep marginal tax rates can increase the tax base by increasing the volume of work, saving, and investment, and by reducing the incentive to evade taxes. A growth-oriented tax policy also reduces the clamor for federal spending to support incomes of the unemployed or otherwise needy.

IBID.

Willmoore Kendall *(1909–1967)*

*W*idely praised for his impressive teaching gifts when he taught political science, Willmoore Kendall was chair of the department of economics and politics at the University of Dallas. A Trotskyist in the early thirties, he came to be increasingly anti-Communist. In 1955, Kendall became an editor of William F. Buckley's *National Review*. He wrote articles for almost every major political science journal in the United States. His books include *John Locke and the Doctrine of Majority Rule* (1941), *The Conservative Affirmation* (1963), and *The Basic Symbols of the American Tradition* (with George W. Carey,

1970). Kendall also edited *Liberalism Versus Conservatism* (with George W. Carey, 1966).

All the current hullaballoo about civil liberties, about desegregation, about redistricting on a one-man-one-vote basis, is, I am saying, the result of one thing, namely, the Supreme Court decision, a few years ago, to revise its own traditional interpretation of the Fourteenth Amendment. From now on, it said in effect, the Fourteenth Amendment is going to require not equal protection under existing laws, but the revision of existing laws so that they will give equal protection. And the effect of that change of mind and heart on the part of the Supreme Court was, quite simply, this: It put the Supreme Court into the business of upsetting the deal—the deal between the federal government and the states—written into the Philadelphia Constitution and the Tenth Amendment.

IN *WILLMOORE KENDALL CONTRA MUNDUM*, 1971

The Conservative . . . *still* regards the suffrage, the relations between Church and State, the drawing of lines for legislative districts, education—he *still* regards these things as the business exclusively of the states, as not, therefore, the business of the federal government, and not, therefore, the business of the Supreme Court. He still regards the equal protection and due process clauses of the Fourteenth Amendment as guarantees merely of impartial enforcement of existing laws.

IBID.

James Jackson Kilpatrick, Jr.

(1920–)

A prolific columnist and author, James J. Kilpatrick began his long writing career as a newspaper reporter, then became an editorial writer, and later a syndicated columnist (currently syndicated by Universal Press Syndicate). He has been a television commentator, won numerous awards (including the Medal of Honor for Distinguished Service in Journalism from the University of Missouri), and written several books, including *The Sovereign States* (1957), *The Smut Peddlers* (1960), and *The Writer's Art* (1984).

The one great, precious factor that distinguishes a free society from a totalitarian society is the absence of unwarranted governmental restraint upon the free man. Within the broadest possible limits the free man may work as he pleases, come and go as he pleases, think, read, write, vote, and worship as he pleases. His liberties, of course, are not absolute . . . but . . . extend to the point at which Citizen A causes some serious loss, risk, or inconvenience to Citizen B.

THE SMUT PEDDLERS, 1960

I had supposed it to be a fundamental principle of conservatism to challenge *every* doubtful intrusion of the state upon the freedom of the individual. The more serious the intrusion, the more it must be resisted. Only the most compelling interests of society can justify a major invasion by the government of a person's rights to be left alone . . . . If these are not fundamental principles of conservatism, I have wasted thirty years in the contemplation of that philosophy.

NATIONAL REVIEW, 1967

In a trillion-dollar budget, the NEA [National Endowment for the Arts] grants are nickels and dimes. The outlays are small; the principle is large. How can Congress justify grants to individual towns for construction of sewerage?

Surely the building of local sewers is a local responsibility. Let us inquire into the constitutional authority for the endless time-wasting seminars and conferences sponsored by the Department of Education. The federal budget teems with appropriations that rest upon a flimsy basis or no basis at all.

It is this failure to recognize constitutional restraints that leads directly to the fiscal mess we are in. Congress operates on the airy assumption that its powers are unlimited. Anything goes. In the closing hours of this session, Congress voted for a study of jazz, for a study of Acadian culture in the state of Maine, for the protection of fish in the Corejos River of Colorado and for the establishment of a Japanese-American museum. Bills were flying to enactment faster than reporters could keep up with them. And in the midst of this blizzard of activity, members were still arguing over ways to prevent the NEA from subsidizing dirty pictures. Sometimes one despairs.

The dirty pictures matter and the dirty "rap" sessions matter, for they contribute to the steady erosion of old values of modesty, taste and sheer decency, but they don't matter greatly . . . .

What matters, and matters deeply, is the casual irresponsibility of Congress in spending our money on programs not sanctioned by our Constitution. If today's topic is obscenity, look no further than Capitol Hill. Now, that's obscene.

"CONGRESS HAS NO BUSINESS IN ARTS BUSINESS,"
OCT. 23, 1990

The reformers [of higher education] desire to replace traditional courses in part with untraditional courses—with courses that would place heavy emphasis upon the cultures of Africa. They would send many dead white male poets into exile, and replace them with writers of obscure reputation or no reputation at all . . . .

Nothing is wrong, and a great deal is right, about "diversity" and "multicultural" teaching. As the planet shrinks, all of us will have to deal in some fashion with alien cultures. True diversity has great appeal to those who love individual freedom. But first things first. When Milton is exiled because Milton is a sexist, students of English literature are being shortchanged.

"RADICALS POISON THE GROVES OF ACADEME,"
APRIL 10, 1991

Russell Amos Kirk (1918–1994)

*O*ne of the most influential conservatives of the twentieth century, Russell Kirk earned a Doctor of Literature at St. Andrews University in Scotland and received numerous awards, including the Ingersoll prize for scholarly writing (1984), the Presidential Citizen's Medal (1989), and the Salvatori prize for historical writing (1991). A distinguished fellow of the Heritage Foundation, Kirk wrote and edited numerous books, including *The Conservative Mind* (1953), *A Program for Conservatives* (1954), *Academic Freedom* (1955), *Confessions of a Bohemian Tory* (1963), *Edmund Burke* (1967), *Decadence and Renewal in Higher Learning* (1978), *Portable Conservative Reader* (1982), *The Conservative Constitution* (1990), *The Politics of Prudence* (1993), and *America's British Culture* (1993).

Conservatism is not a fixed and immutable body of dogma, and conservatives inherit from Burke a talent for re-expressing their convictions to fit the time. As a working premise, nevertheless, one can observe here that the essence of social conservatism is preservation of the ancient moral traditions of humanity. Conservatives respect the wisdom of their ancestors (this phrase was Strafford's, and Hooker's, before Burke

illuminated it); they are dubious of wholesale alteration. They think society is a spiritual reality, possessing an eternal life but a delicate constitution: it cannot be scrapped and recast as if it were a machine. "What is conservatism?" Abraham Lincoln inquired once. "Is it not adherence to the old and tried, against the new and untried?" It is that, but it is more. Professor Hearnshaw, in his *Conservatism in England*, lists a dozen principles of conservatives, but possibly these may be comprehended in a briefer catalogue. I think that there are six canons of conservative thought—

(1) Belief in a transcendent order, or body of natural law, which rules society as well as conscience. Political problems, at bottom, are religious and moral problems. A narrow rationality, what Coleridge called the Understanding, cannot of itself satisfy human needs. "Every Tory is a realist," says Keith Feiling: "he knows that there are great forces in heaven and earth that man's philosophy cannot plumb or fathom." True politics is the art of apprehending and applying the Justice which ought to prevail in a community of souls.

(2) Affection for the proliferating variety and mystery of human existence, as opposed to the narrowing uniformity, egalitarianism, and utilitarian aims of most radical systems; conservatives resist

what Robert Graves calls "Logicalism" in society. This prejudice has been called "the conservatism of enjoyment"—a sense that life is worth living, according to Walter Bagehot "the proper source of an animated Conservatism."

(3) Conviction that civilized society requires orders and classes, as against the notion of a "classless society." With reason, conservatives often have been called "the party of order." If natural distinctions are effaced among men, oligarchs fill the vacuum. Ultimate equality in the judgment of God, and equality before courts of law, are recognized by conservatives; but equality of condition, they think, means equality in servitude and boredom.

(4) Persuasion that freedom and property are closely linked: separate property from private possession, and Leviathan becomes master of all. Economic levelling, they maintain, is not economic progress.

(5) Faith in prescription and distrust of "sophisters, calculators, and economists" who would reconstruct society upon abstract designs. Tradition, sound prejudice, and old prescription are checks both upon man's anarchic impulse and upon the innovator's lust for power.

(6) Recognition that change may not be salutary reform: hasty innovation may be a devouring conflagration, rather than

a torch of progress. Society must alter, for prudent change is the means of social preservation; but a statesman must take Providence into his calculations, and a statesman's chief virtue, according to Plato and Burke, is prudence.

Various deviations from this system of ideas have occurred, and there are numerous appendages to it; but in general conservatives have adhered to these articles of belief with a consistency rare in political history.

THE CONSERVATIVE MIND, 1953

Conservatism's most conspicuous difficulty in our time is that conservative leaders confront a people who have come to look upon society, vaguely, as a homogeneous mass of identical individuals whose happiness may be obtained by direction from above, through legislation or some scheme of public instruction. Conservatives endeavor to teach humanity once more that the germ of public affections (in Burke's words) is "to learn to love the little platoon we belong to in society." A task for conservative leaders is to reconcile individualism—which sustained nineteenth century life even while it starved the soul of the nineteenth century—with the sense of community that ran strong in Burke and Adams. If conservatives cannot redeem the modern masses from the sterile modern mass-mind, then a miserable collectivism impoverishing body and soul impends over Britain and America—the collectivism that has submerged eastern Europe and much of Asia and Africa, the collectivism (as Orwell wrote) of "the stream-lined men who think in slogans and talk in bullets."

IBID.

Subjecting the failure of twentieth-century American liberalism to close analysis would be breaking a butterfly upon the wheel.

IBID.

The humanitarian's indiscriminate utilitarian method engenders hostility toward that hierarchy of values which erects distinctions between saint and sinner, scholar and barbarian.

IBID.

[M]isguided "liberal" measures have worked mischief that may not be undone for decades or generations, especially in the United States. Miscalled "urban renewal" (actually the creation, often, of urban deserts and jungles), undertaken out of mixed humanitarian and profiteering motives, has uprooted in most American cities whole classes and local communities, under dubious cover of federal statute; inordinate building of

highways has had the same consequence. Urban rioting, the swift increase of major crimes, and the boredom that encourages addiction to narcotics are products of such foolish programs. In the phrase of Hannah Arendt, "the rootless are always violent." So it is that the conservative talks of the need for roots in community, not of more measures of "mass welfare."

IBID.

The conservative is not afraid of the abused word "discipline." Without discipline, men and women must spend their lives either in mischief or in idleness.

IBID.

Jeane (Duane) Jordan Kirkpatrick *(1926–)*

A former U.S. ambassador to the United Nations and a syndicated columnist, Jeane Kirkpatrick is the recipient of the Presidential Medal of Freedom (1985) and the author of such books as *Political Woman* (1974), *Dictatorships and Double Standards* (1982), *The Reagan Phenomenon* (1983), and *The Withering Away of the Totalitarian State* (1990).

[Democrats] can't get elected unless things get worse—and things won't get worse unless they get elected.

TIME, JUNE 17, 1985

A government is not legitimate merely because it exists.

IBID.

Tradition, to be sure, does not filter out bestial conceptions any more than it eliminates brutal practices . . . . But traditional ideas [unlike rationalist theories and ideals] have at least the merit of being integrally related to actual societies and social practices.

DICTATORSHIPS AND DOUBLE STANDARDS, 1982

The fact is that government cannot produce equality, and any serious effort to do so can destroy liberty and other social goods.

IBID.

[B]ecause regulation uses the coercive power of government to alter outcomes, it diminishes individual liberty: people are persuaded by the threat of sanctions to act differently than they would otherwise prefer.

IBID.

In any election, the character of the candidates is much more important than their positions on specific issues. Issues change with circumstance. Character persists. It is expressed in the lives, choices and public records of candidates . . . .

Character determines the quality of leadership a candidate can bring to the presidency. His outlook on politics and government and his philosophy on public affairs will determine the direction in which he intends to lead.

"WHY CHARACTER IS MORE IMPORTANT THAN ISSUES,"
OCT. 25, 1992

Arthur Koestler *(1905 1983)*

A Hungarian-born English author, Arthur Koestler was a Communist in the 1930s who left the party over Stalin's purge trials. His best-known novel, *Darkness at Noon* (1941), describes the purge of a Bolshevik "deviationist."

If we survey history and compare the lofty aims, in the name of which revolutions were started, and the sorry end to which they came, we see again and again how a polluted civilization pollutes its own revolutionary offspring.

ESSAY IN *THE GOD THAT FAILED,*
RICHARD CROSSMAN, ED. 1949

The reformer is equally apt to forget that hatred, even of the objectively hateful, does not produce the charity and justice on which a utopian society must be based.

IBID.

The [Communist] party denied the free will of the individual—and at the same time it exacted its willing self-sacrifice. It denied his capacity to choose between two alternatives—and at the same time it demanded that he should always choose the right one. It denied his power to choose between good and evil—and at the same time it spoke accusingly of guilt and treachery.

DARKNESS AT NOON, 1941

Irving Kristol *(1920–)*

A former Trotskyist who later cofounded *Encounter*, an anti-Communist journal, Irving Kristol is editor of the journal *The Public Interest* and an influential columnist whose most notable book is *Two Cheers for Capitalism* (1978). Like other neoconservatives, Kristol is a former liberal who has come to criticize Great Society liberalism.

The distribution of income under capitalism is an expression of the general belief that it is better for society to be shaped by the interplay of people's free opinions and free preferences than by the enforcement of any one set of values by government.

But there have always been many people in this world who do not believe that liberty is the most important political value. These people are sincere dogmatists. They believe they know *the* truth about a good society; they believe they possess *the* true definition of distributive justice; and they inevitably wish to see society shaped in the image of these true beliefs. Sometimes they have prized religious truth more than liberty (e.g., the Marxist philosophy); and sometimes they have prized equality more than liberty. It is this last point of view that is especially popular in some circles—mainly academic circles—in the United States today.

TWO CHEERS FOR CAPITALISM, 1978

Professor Ronald Dworkin, one of our most distinguished liberal legal philosophers, has written that "*a more equal society is a better society even if its citizens prefer inequality.*" (Italics mine.) From which it follows that "social justice" may require a people, whose preferences are corrupt (in that they prefer liberty to equality), to be coerced into equality. It is precisely because they define "social justice" and "fairness" in terms of equality that so many liberal thinkers find it so difficult genuinely to detest left-wing (i.e., egalitarian) authoritarian or totalitarian regimes. And, similarly, it is precisely because they are true believers in justice-as-equality that they dislike a free society, with all its inevitable inequalities.

IBID.

As one who does like a free society, I have to concede to . . . [the "liberals"] the right to hold and freely express . . . [their] opinions. But I do find it ironical that their conception of "social justice" should be generally designated as the "liberal" one. Whatever its other merits, an authentic attachment to liberty is not one of them.

IBID.

[I]n contrast to previous societies organized around an axis of aristocratic or religious values it [capitalism] relegates them to the area of personal concern whether of the isolated individual or of voluntary associations of individuals . . . . What previous cultures would have called "the domestic virtues" are what capitalism most prizes in its citizens: prudence, diligence, trustworthiness, and an ambition largely channeled toward "bet-

tering one's condition." As for the rest, well, that is one's private affair, to be freely coped with as best one can.

Now, the first thing to be said about this extraordinary (in historical terms) conception of a social order is that it works. It works in a quite simple, material sense: people who, individually or collectively, subscribe to the social philosophy of a capitalist order, and to those bourgeois virtues associated with it, do indeed better their condition. The history of the past two centuries affirms this truth unequivocally. It is also the case—as some critics quickly point out—that this prosperity is not equally shared. But over the longer term everyone does benefit, visibly and substantially.

IBID.

Our revolutionary message—which is a message not of the Revolution itself but of the American political tradition from the *Mayflower* to the Declaration of Independence to the Constitution—is that a self-disciplined people *can* create a political community in which an ordered liberty will promote both economic prosperity and political participation. To the teeming masses of other nations, the American political tradition says: To enjoy the fruits of self-government, you must first cease being "masses" and become a "people," attached to a common way of life, sharing common values, and existing in a condition of mutual trust and sympathy as between individuals and even social classes . . . . What the American political tradition says is that the major function of government is, in Professor [Michael] Oakeshott's phrase, to "tend to the arrangements," and that free people do not make a covenant or social contract with their government, or with the leaders of any "movement," but among themselves.

REFLECTIONS OF A NEOCONSERVATIVE, 1983

In the end, what informs the American political tradition is a proposition and a premise. The proposition is that the best national government is, to use a phrase the founding fathers were fond of, "mild government." The premise is that you can only achieve mild government if you have a solid bedrock of local self-government, so that the responsibilities of national government are limited in scope. And a corollary of this premise is that such a bedrock of local self-government can only be achieved by a people who—through the shaping influence of religion, education, and their own daily experience—are capable of governing themselves in those small and petty matters which are the stuff of local politics.

IBID.

[O]ur political leaders, when they come to praise civil rights in one world forum or another, do not argue in favor of limited government—perhaps because they no longer really believe in it. They always talk as if their mission is to persuade authoritarian or totalitarian governments to make a gift of civil rights to their people. Not only is this a silly and fruitless exercise; it also suggests that our leaders have quite forgotten the relation of civil rights to limited government, and seem to believe that the people's civil rights are distributed by a paternalistic government as part of a general welfare program.

IBID.

It is an observable fact that not all people who are statistically poor are everywhere equally miserable or have an equal sense of being "badly off." The past and the future always shape our sense of the present. So much, therefore, depends on the hopes one may have for one's children, the faith one may have in the ultimate benignity and "fairness" of Providence, on the assurance and solace one may derive from traditions. Poverty does not always dehumanize, and relative affluence can have its costs in human terms—costs that are actually, if often dimly felt.

IBID.

[O]n the street where I lived until recently there was a Chinese family, recent immigrants, who ran a basement laundry. The parents and their five children shared the two tiny rooms at the back of the tiny store, and I shudder to think what this family did to our official poverty statistics. Still, those parents expressed great confidence that their children would "get ahead"—and, in fact, all five ended up as college graduates. Ought not one to incorporate that *prospect* in any estimate of the family's economic well-being? In contrast, on the same street there were several welfare families, whose incomes, in cash and kind and services, may well have been larger than that of our Chinese family, but who were in various stages of a dependency-induced corruption, with little family stability and with the children involved in drugs and delinquency. Would an increase in their welfare receipts really have improved their economic well-being? If it had merely accelerated their demoralization, how would that relate to economic well-being?

IBID.

William Kristol *(1952-)*

*W*riter and political consultant William Kristol, the son of Irving Kristol and Gertrude Himmelfarb, holds a doctorate from Harvard. He was an assistant professor of political science at the University of Pennsylvania and an assistant professor of public policy at Harvard. Kristol was special assistant chief of staff at the Department of Education (1985–1989). Later, he was Vice President Dan Quayle's domestic policy advisor and then his chief of staff.

[I]f, once upon a time, conservatives felt a Burkean responsibility to uphold sound social habits and traditional customs against liberal debunking, now it is liberalism that constitutes the old order, dictating "correct" habits and permissible customs, while conservatives can become the exponents of light and air, of free and open debate, of demystification and even of political and intellectual liberation. The bankruptcy of liberalism invites the possibility of a new, governing conservatism.

"A CONSERVATIVE LOOKS AT LIBERALISM,"
COMMENTARY, SEPT. 1993

Wayne R. LaPierre, Jr. (1949–)

*W*ayne LaPierre is the executive vice president of the
National Rifle Association (founded
1871) and an outspoken defender of the
Second Amendment right to bear arms.

If you hunt with a gun that chambers
a new round every time you pull the
trigger—as millions of us do—then
you'd better watch out. Lawmakers in
Congress claim that you're the owner of
an "assault weapon," and that just own-
ing such a gun somehow places you in
the same category as this nation's most
violent criminals.

. . . [Lawmakers] ask you to believe
your semi-automatics are the new-found
weapons of choice of violent criminals and
drug-dealers. They expect you to believe
they'll stop after one or 10 or 100 of these
arbitrarily chosen semi-automatics have
been banned. And they ask you to forget
that their "new" semi-auto technology
actually dates back to the turn of the century, and has been used in hunting
firearms since the days of Teddy Roosevelt.

. . . By the U.S. Department of
Defense definition, real assault weapons
are capable of fully automatic fire and

have been strictly controlled by federal
law for almost 60 years.

AMERICAN RIFLEMAN, JULY 1993

The problem isn't legal firearm avail-
ability. It's a criminal justice system that
has utterly crashed. A system that frees
the average convicted murderer before he
serves even *one third* of his sentence. A
system that nurtures violence such that
in Washington, D.C., one in nine people
is under criminal court supervision. A
system so completely in ruins that New
York City averages more murders each
year than 23 states *combined.*

IBID., MARCH 1993

The anti-gun movement promised
not to leave a stone unturned in 1994.
That's why their list of Second
Amendment larceny remains as long as it
is ambitious.

IBID., FEBRUARY 1994

To hear supporters tell it, the Brady
Act is a law-and-order miracle, anti-gun
legislation that fights crime better than
Batman.

Yet the truth is, Brady's a bad bust—a
law left wide open to abuse, a waste of
time and money, a sham that throws a
monkey wrench into the machinery of
handgun purchases by law-abiding citizens, and does little or nothing to keep

guns away from those who use them to commit crimes.

IBID., JUNE 1994

William Edward Hartpole Lecky *(1838–1903)*

*I*rish historian and essayist W. E. H. Lecky won success with his work *History of Rationalism in Europe* (1865) and its companion, *History of European Morals from Augustus to Charlemagne* (1869). He also wrote *Democracy and Liberty* (1896), but he is famous for his magnum opus, *The History of England in the Eighteenth Century* (8 vols., 1878–1890).

It is obvious that a graduated tax is a direct penalty imposed on saving and industry, a direct premium offered to idleness and extravagance. It discourages the very habits and qualities which it is most in the interest of the State to foster, and it is certain to operate forcibly where fortunes approach the limits at which a higher scale of taxation begins. It is a strong inducement at that period, either to cease to work or to cease to save. It is at the same time perfectly arbitrary. When the principle of taxing all fortunes on the same rate of computation is abandoned, no definite rule or principle remains. At what point the higher scale is to begin, or to what degree it is to be raised, depends wholly on the policy of Governments and the balance of parties. The ascending scale may at first be very moderate, but it may at any time, when fresh taxes are required, be made more severe, till it reaches or approaches the point of confiscation.

DEMOCRACY AND LIBERTY, 1896

[With a graduated tax, no] fixed line or amount of graduation can be maintained upon principle, or with any chance of finality. The whole matter will depend upon the interests and wishes of the electors; upon party politicians seeking for a cry and competing for the votes of very poor and very ignorant men. Under such a system all large properties may easily be made unsafe, and an insecurity may arise which will be fatal to all great financial undertakings. The most serious restraint on parliamentary extravagance will, at the same time, be taken away, and majorities will be invested with the easiest and most powerful instrument of oppression. Highly graduated taxation realises most completely the supreme danger of democracy, creating a state of things in which one class imposes on another burdens which it is not asked to share, and impels the State into vast schemes of extravagance, under the belief that the whole cost will be thrown upon others.

IBID.

John Leo *(1935–)*

*A*n outspoken critic of contemporary liberalism, John Leo writes a column entitled "On Society," which regularly appears in *U.S. News and World Report*.

The minority liberalism of the New Deal narrowed and hardened into a sectarian movement that Prof. William Galston of the University of Maryland calls "liberal fundamentalism." It was presided over by a top-bottom coalition of elite professionals and the poor, with less and less room for the middle class and the working class and their values. Along the way, a great many Democrats came to see the party as indifferent, if not hostile, to their moral sentiments

and not much interested in their economic struggles either . . . .

. . . [G]alston, in a paper, co-authored with Elaine Kamarck, warned that for many Americans, "Democrats are part of the problem: Democrats have become the party of individual rights but not individual responsibility, of self-expression but not self-discipline, of sociological explanation but not moral accountability." That helped keep the national party out of touch with voters for a generation.

U.S. NEWS AND WORLD REPORT, DEC. 7, 1992

Pope Leo XIII *(1810–1903)*

(Gioacchino Vincenzo Pecci)

*G*ioacchino Vincenzo Pecci was pope of the Roman Catholic Church from 1878–1903. An eminent scholar whose classical education enabled him to write excellent Latin poetry and prose, he wrote a number of important encyclicals on various matters, including marriage, freemasonry, Biblical study, education, and socialism.

The main tenet of Socialism, namely, the community of goods, must be rejected without qualification, for it would injure those it pretends to benefit, it would be contrary to the natural rights of man, and it would introduce confusion and disorder into the commonwealth.

RERUM NOVARUM, MAY 15, 1891

Max Lerner *(1902–1992)*

A social scientist and professor as well as an author and a political columnist, Max Lerner edited *The Encyclopedia of Social Sciences.* He was on the faculty of a number of colleges and universities, including Sarah Lawrence. He wrote over a dozen books, including *Ideas are Weapons* (1939), *The Unfinished Country* (1959), *Tocqueville and American Civilization* (1969), and *America as a Civilization* (1987).

The great force that has thus far broken the shock of the periodic assaults on freedom from within American life has been the civil liberties tradition—the historical commitment of Americans to the public protection of the freedom of the individual person. Its roots go deep into the history of American thought and attitudes.

We may start with the Puritan (and generally Protestant) emphasis on the importance of the individual conscience. Beyond that there was the teaching, from the religious tradition, of the intensity of sacrifice for individual conscience and for the ideal of justice and equality. Broadening out still further, there was the emphasis on the individual personality and its sanctity, resting on the tradition of natural rights, the religious belief that each person has a soul, and the premise of potential individual creativeness. Add to this the property complex which has put a premium on the value of individual effort and its relation to reward, and the success complex which has linked freedom with the sense of competitive worth and the impulse for self-improvement.

AMERICA AS A CIVILIZATION, 1987

[There are] two basic American attitudes toward freedom as an ingredient in the social process. One is the pragmatic attitude expressed in Holmes's phrase about the competition of ideas, which is a more astringent way of putting Milton's " . . . who ever knew Truth put to the worse, in a free and open encounter?" It says in effect that the idea which survives may not be necessarily the truth, but what better way does a society have for choosing the ideas it will live by? The second is the belief that the individual personality is more productive if it functions in freedom than if it must obey someone else's authoritarian behest.

IBID.

It [the preservation of civil liberty] is not the possession of any single group in American life, nor can it be left to the sole guardianship of any group—not even of the Supreme Court. The labor groups care about freedom of collective bargaining and freedom from strike-breaking violence, yet they may themselves be scornful of the civil rights of Negro workers whom some unions still exclude. The business managers are concerned about their freedom from government controls, yet American history is filled with the denials of freedom by employers to workers who sought to organize. Liberals claim the civil-liberties tradition as their own, yet some of the staunchest defenders of civil liberties have been conservatives, from John Adams through men like Charles E. Hughes and Henry L. Stimson. Some who have called themselves "liberals" have been known to run from the defense of freedom as soon as the firing became hot; while, in a different grain of "liberalism," there have been some so bemused by the "world revolution" of Communism that they did not face with realism the nature of the Communist threat to freedom.

IBID.

Clive Staples Lewis *(1898–1963)*

A prolific British novelist and critic, C. S. Lewis is known for his defense of Christianity and traditional moral values. He wrote such works as *Mere Christianity* (1943) and *The Abolition of Man* (1944), though he is also well known for his works of fantasy and is best known for *The Screwtape Letters* (1942), a diabolical view of humanity.

That invaluable man Rousseau first revealed it. In his perfect democracy, you remember, only the state religion is permitted, slavery is restored, and the individual is told that he has really willed (though he didn't know it) whatever the Government tells him to do.

THE SCREWTAPE LETTERS, 1942

The basic principle of the new education is to be that dunces and idlers must not be made to feel inferior to intelligent and industrious pupils. That would be "undemocratic." Entrance examinations must be framed so that all, or nearly all, citizens can go to universities, whether they have any power (or wish) to profit by higher education or not. The bright pupil thus remains democratically fettered to his own age group throughout his school career, and a boy who would be capable of tackling Aeschylus or Dante sits listening to his coeval's attempts to spell out A CAT SAT ON A MAT. And what we must realize is that "democracy" in the diabolical sense (*I'm as good as you . . .*) is the finest instrument we could possibly have for extirpating political democracies from the face of the earth.

IBID.

supervisor (1957–1962), a lawyer with a private practice (1962–1966), an assistant district attorney (1966–1969), a candidate for the U.S. Congress (1968), a special assistant in the Bureau of Narcotics and Firearms Control (1969–1970), an advisor on the White House Domestic Council and member of the White House "plumbers" (1971), and a general counsel for the Committee to Re-Elect the President (CREEP, 1971–1972). Because of his involvement in the Watergate break-in, he was imprisoned for more than four and one-half years and released in 1977. He is the author of the best-selling *Will: The Autobiography of G. Gordon Liddy* (1980) and the novels *Out of Control* (1979) and *The Monkey Handlers* (1991).

George Gordon Battle Liddy *(1930–)*

*H*ost of a phenomenally popular syndicated radio talk show (*The G. Gordon Liddy Show*), G. Gordon Liddy has been an FBI field agent and

What's the point of it [gun control legislation], other than to inconvenience the honest citizen who follows the rules? . . . I can assure you that the guys I met in the nine prisons I served my sentence in did not get their guns at the gun store.

QUOTED IN *PEOPLE*, JAN. 10, 1994

The right of the private citizenry to keep and bear arms predates the United States Constitution. The Second

Amendment *merely* declares that the Congress does not have the authority to infringe upon that right. The right of the private citizen to keep and bear arms is based on the right to hunt to feed one's family; the right to protect one's self, family and property against outlaws; to protect one's community against foreign and domestic enemies; and as a guarantee against tyranny.

THE LIDDY LETTER, MAY 1994

The Second Amendment specifically mentions one of the benefits of an armed citizenry, the ability of community members to come together in a time of crisis and protect one another. "A well regulated Militia, being necessary to the security of a free state . . ." The liberals hated watching on their television sets the live coverage of the Militia in the Korea-town section of Los Angeles, during the riots [of April 1992], successfully defending their families and property against the domestic enemy intent on destroying their homes and putting bricks through the heads of their family members and neighbors . . . .

IBID.

The liberals want to take away your ability to take care of yourself because in their view, we have "evolved" into a "better world" where we call the nanny state when we have problems. [They] . . .

want you to call 9-1-1 when your home is being invaded by marauders. Look at what happened to the people in L.A. who called 9-1-1. The line was busy and they got bricks thrown at their heads and crowbars in their ribs . . . . Thousands lost their homes to roving bands of thieves. "Well, that's what insurance is for" say the academics and the liberals . . . . Insurance my ass! I'll tell you who had insurance. The Korean-Americans had insurance. And they didn't get it from State Farm . . . they got it from the United States Constitution, the Bill of Rights, with a little help from Smith & Wesson, Browning, Remington, and the good folks at Colt in Connecticut. Those Korean-American heroes were successful, in part, because they had detachable magazines with capacities in excess of five rounds. The liberals don't like that. It is not statist. It does not conform to their vision of a Nanny state.

IBID.

Just as a rose by any other name would smell as sweet, Hillary's Socialized Healthcare Plan, renamed the Gephardt-Mitchell Congressional Healthcare Bill, stinks just as foul.

The renaming of Clinton's plan for socialized medicine is another example of the arrogance of the Clinton White House. They know the American people have soundly rejected the monstrosity which emerged from Hillary's . . . secret meetings with socialized medicine lobbyists. But she does not care what the American people want. For domestic ideals, she has only lip service. Hillary went to Wellesley and Yale Law School. She is smarter than the commoners. She believes that if all Americans were as smart as she, they too would believe in government control of our Healthcare . . . .

IBID., AUGUST 1994

[T]he Clintons cannot get enough votes in Congress to pass their [healthcare] plan . . . . What is the solution? Should the Congress give the American people what they want—Healthcare Reform which provides for portable insurance [that] workers can keep when they switch jobs and reform allowing Americans with pre-existing conditions to buy insurance? *"No!"* screams Hillary [Clinton]. "You will get my plan, but we will call it somebody else's plan so it will pass in Congress."

IBID.

The "Congressional" [healthcare] plan will still have government-selected commissioners deciding what service your doctor can prescribe to you. It will still force men, including the elderly and Pro-Life Americans like Catholic priests

and nuns, to buy abortion insurance. . . . [T]he Congressional plan will tax businesses to pay for the new government entitlement, causing a dramatic rise in prices of goods and services and millions of lost jobs. The Congressional plan will do everything Hillary's plan will do because they are the same plan . . . .

IBID.

Rush Hudson Limbaugh *(1951–)*

*O*ne of America's most famous and successful citizens, Rush Limbaugh is host of the radio talk show called *The Rush Limbaugh Show* on the EIB ("Excellence In Broadcasting") Network (since 1988) and of the syndicated television show of the same name (since 1992). He is the author of *The Way It Ought To Be* (1992) and *See, I Told You* (1993), both huge best sellers.

Do you know what the single biggest item in the federal budget is? It's not Defense. It's Health and Human Services, Housing and Urban Development. It's social spending. We spend almost $800 billion a year on human resources and welfare programs and things are worse now in the inner cities than they were 25 years ago. Homelessness, crime, illegitimacy, broken families, drugs, the collapse of schools, all worse . . . despite all this "investment." . . .

. . . But still this drumbeat, this notion that we're not spending enough on our people, continues. General David Dinkins, Mayor of New York, recently blamed urban decline on (guess what?) "12 years of neglect of the cities."

THE LIMBAUGH LETTER, JUNE 1993

Why have so many of the things that hold society together crumbled? We have allowed the values that permit people to seize opportunities—self-discipline, hard work, responsibility—to be ridiculed. Instead, we have handed people excuse after excuse: they have been victims, they have been oppressed, they have been disadvantaged.

IBID.

It is a dangerous notion to believe the federal government can fix all this . . . . [I]t's axiomatic in the human condition that people are the only ones who can help themselves. You save yourself. You save your family. Your family, working together, saves you. You don't have a prayer of contentment or prosperity if you depend on a monolithic government for it.

IBID.

There is a decline in the ability of people to say, "That's wrong. That shouldn't happen." Let me confront the idea that we accept an illegitimacy rate that is five times what it was thirty years ago . . . . People say, "Well, kids are going to have sex. You can't stop them." . . .

Then how is it that in 1979, 1969, 1959 teenage pregnancy wasn't as prevalent as it is now? If more kids could be prevented from having sex in the past, why do we accept the way it is now as the standard?

But anyone who raises such questions is castigated: "You're a hatemonger. You're a bigot. You're a sexist." . . . "You're just trying to impose your morality on people." No, I'm trying to maintain the standards of a decent, great society, or as close to it as you can get.

IBID., MARCH 1993

Government doesn't fix the economy. You do. If you think otherwise, ask yourself this question: If government spending and "investment" created prosperity, why haven't the past 2 years of massive deficit-enlarging spending been a boom, rather than the recession we all know so well? It is people, engaging in that wonderful activity known as commerce—not government policy—which fuels and drives our economic engine.

IBID., APRIL 1993

There is nothing so compelling, so potent, as a rugged individual pursuing excellence. It is the force that has moved history. An individual with passion, conviction, drive, has always confounded and frightened those obsessed with making regulations for "fairness"—that is, mediocrity. And the reason is simple: Such rugged individuals cannot, ultimately, be controlled or crushed.

All you must do to understand this is recall one image: a lone Chinese citizen standing defiant in the path of a government tank. There is no better metaphor for the contest between the state and the individual. Anyone who witnessed that scene knew, immediately and instinctively, who possessed the greater power. It is irrational on its face, but you know it is true. The tank could have killed the man instantly. But yet the man was stronger. Clearly there was a spiritual element to the equation. And this is why socialism has never worked, and can never work. The human heart, and the human soul, is individual; singular; unique.

IBID.

Socialism has never, ever worked. Usually the failures are measured in economic terms relative to capitalistic societies—but the largest cost has been borne in the trampling of the human spirit. It is an ideology of bondage.

. . . Socialism means collective or government ownership, with central bureaucracies controlling economic planning—instead of the brilliance that results from free people making millions of daily decisions in a free market. The socialist distrust and hatred of private ownership is not just a fatal flaw. It is also a serious misunderstanding of that yearning for freedom with which all human beings are endowed.

IBID.

Something happens when an individual owns his home or business. He or she will always invest more sweat, longer hours and greater creativity to develop and care for something he owns than he will for any government-inspired project supposedly engineered for the greater social good . . . . The desire to improve oneself and one's family's lot, to make life better for one's children, to strive for a higher standard of living, is universal and God-given. It is honorable. *It is not greed.*

IBID.

Abraham Lincoln *(1809–1865)*

*T*he sixteenth president of the United States, Abraham Lincoln was a member of the U.S. House of Representatives (1847–1849) and was nominated for the Republican presidential ticket in 1860. He opposed slavery even before he became president, as when he debated Democratic opponent Stephen Douglas in a series of debates conducted for the Illinois senatorial race. Known for issuing the Emancipation Proclamation, which declared the freedom of all slaves in the rebelling states, and for the Gettysburg Address, Lincoln thought that the institution of slavery contradicted America's founding principles.

What constitutes the bulwark of our own liberty and independence? It is not our crowning battlements, our bristling sea coasts, the guns of our war steamers, or the strength of our gallant and disciplined army . . . . Our reliance is in the *love of liberty* which God has implanted in us . . . . Destroy this spirit, and you have planted the seeds of despotism at your own doors. Familiarize yourselves with the chains of bondage and you prepare your own limbs to wear them. Accustomed to trample on the rights of others, you have lost the genius of your own independence and become the fit subjects of the first cunning tyrant who rises among you.

SPEECH, EDWARDSVILLE, ILLINOIS, SEPT. 11, 1858

This is a world of compensations; and he who would *be* no slave must consent to *have* no slave. Those who deny freedom to others deserve it not for themselves, and, under a just God, cannot long retain it.

LETTER TO HENRY L. PIERCE AND OTHERS, APRIL 6, 1859

And by virtue of the power and for the purposes aforesaid, I do order and declare that all persons held as slaves within said designated states and parts of states are, and henceforward shall be, free; and that the executive government of the United States, including the military and naval authorities thereof, will recognize and maintain the freedom of said persons.

EMANCIPATION PROCLAMATION, JANUARY 1, 1863

This *declared* indifference, but as I must think, covert *real* zeal for the spread of slavery, I can not but hate. I hate it because of the monstrous injustice of slavery itself. I hate it because it deprives our republican example of its just influence in the world—enables the enemies of free institutions, with plausibility, to taunt us as hypocrites—causes the real friends of liberty to doubt our sincerity and especially because it forces so many really good men amongst ourselves into an open war with the very fundamental principles of civil liberty—criticizing the Declaration of Independence, and insisting that there is no right principle of action but *self-interest.*

REPLY TO STEPHEN DOUGLAS, PEORIA, ILLINOIS, OCT. 18, 1854

Let us have the faith that right makes might; and in that faith let us to the end dare to do our duty as we understand it.

ADDRESS AT COOPER INSTITUTE, FEB. 27, 1860

I believe that each individual is naturally entitled to do as he pleases with himself and the fruit of his labor, so far as it in no wise interferes with any other man's rights; that each community, as a state, has a right to do exactly as it pleases with all the concerns within that State that interfere with no other State . . . .

SPEECH, CHICAGO, JULY 10, 1858

Always be in mind that your own resolution to succeed is more important than any other one thing.

LETTER TO I. REAVES, NOV. 5, 1855

Success does not so much depend on external help as on self-reliance.

ADDRESS ON NEGRO COLONIZATION, AUG. 14, 1862

I take it that it is best for all to leave each man free to acquire property as fast as he can. Some will get wealthy. I don't believe in a law to prevent a man from getting rich; it would do more harm than good.

SPEECH, NEW HAVEN, CONNECTICUT, MARCH 6, 1860

John Locke *(1632–1704)*

*E*nglish philosopher John Locke is known especially for his theory of knowledge and his political philosophy (which deeply influenced America's founders). His views on religious liberty were expressed in *An Essay Concerning Toleration* (1667), and his views on political liberty and obligation were expressed in *Two Treatises on Civil Government* (1690). An influential social contract theorist, Locke argued that the overarching purpose of the state is to protect an individual's natural rights to life, liberty, and property. He held that a state that systematically violates the natural rights of its citizens is tyrannical and should be overthrown. Much of the social, economic, and ethical theory of the eighteenth century was rooted in Locke's social contract theory. Many of the principles embodied in the U.S. Constitution, including the concept of governmental checks and balances, found their inspiration in the philosophy of Locke.

Man being born, as has been proved, with a title to perfect freedom, and an uncontrolled enjoyment of all the rights and privileges of the law of nature equally with any other man or number of men in the world, hath by nature a power not only to preserve his property—that is, his life, liberty, and estate—against the injuries and attempts of other men, but to judge of and punish the breaches of that law in others as he is persuaded the offense deserves, even with death itself, in crimes where the heinousness of the fact in his opinion requires it.

Two Treatises on Civil Government, 1690

The great and *chief end* therefore of Mens [sic] uniting into Commonwealths, and putting themselves under

Government, *is the Preservation of their Property.*

Ibid.

Freedom of man under a government is to have a standing rule to live by, common to every one of that society, and made by the legislative power vested in it.

Ibid.

The great question which, in all ages, has disturbed mankind, and brought on them the greatest part of their mischiefs, which has ruined cities, depopulated countries, and disordered the peace of the world, has been, not whether there be power in the world, nor whence it came, but who should have it.

Ibid.

The natural liberty of man is to be free from any superior power on earth, and not to be under the will or legislative authority of man, but to have only the law of nature for his rule. The liberty of man in society is to be under no other legislative power but that established by consent in the commonwealth; nor under the domain of any will or restraint of any law but what the legislative [sic] shall enact according to the trust put in it.

Ibid.

Glenn Cartman Loury *(1948–)*

A political economist, Glenn
Loury rose from the ghettos of
South Chicago to earn a doctorate from
M.I.T. and tenured posts at Harvard
University and Boston University. He
has delivered a number of influential
lectures and written many influential
articles, emphasizing personal respon-
sibility and the importance of the fam-
ily, church, and private community
organizations. Some of his articles
include "The Need for Moral
Leadership in the Black Community"
(*New Perspectives*, Summer 1984),
"Beyond Civil Rights" (*New Republic*,
7 Oct. 1985), "Black Dignity and the
Common Good" (*First Things*,
June/July 1990), and "Two Paths to
Black Power" (*First Things*, Oct.
1992). He is also the author of the book
*One by One from the Inside Out: Race
and Responsibility in America* (1994).

It is to make a mockery of the ideal
of freedom to hold that, as free men and
women, blacks ought nonetheless passively to wait for white Americans, of
whatever political persuasion, to come to
the rescue. A people who languish in
dependency, while the means through
which they might work toward their own
advancement exist, have surrendered
their claim to dignity, and to the respect
of their fellow citizens. A truly free
people must accept responsibility for
their fate, even when it does not lie
wholly in their hands.

THE HERITAGE FOUNDATION, FEB. 12, 1990

My concern is with the inconsistency
between the broad reliance on quotas by
blacks and the attainment of "true equality." There is a sense in which the
demand for quotas, which many see as
the only path to equality for blacks, con-
cedes at the outset the impossibility that
blacks could ever be truly equal citizens.

IBID.

All blacks, some of our "leaders" seem
proud to say, owe their accomplishments
to political pressures for diversity. And
the effects of such thinking may be seen
in our response to almost every instance
of racially differential performance.
When blacks cannot pass a high school
proficiency test as a condition of obtain-
ing a diploma—throw out the test.
When black teachers cannot exhibit skills
at the same level as whites, the very idea
of testing teachers' skills is attacked. If

black athletes less frequently achieve the minimal academic standard set for those participating in inter-collegiate sports, then let us promulgate for them a separate, lower standard, even as we accuse of racism those suggesting the need for a standard in the first place. If young black men are arrested more frequently than whites for some criminal offense, then let us decry the probability that police are disproportionately concerned about the crimes which blacks commit. If black suspension rates are higher than whites in a given school district—well, let's investigate that district for racist administrative practice. When black students are unable to gain admission at the same rate as whites to the elite public exam school in Boston, let's ask a federal judge to mandate black excellence.

The inescapable truth of the matter is that no judge can mandate excellence. No selection committee can create distinction in black scholars. No amount of circuitous legal maneuvering can obviate the social reality of inner-city black crime, or of whites' and blacks' fear of that crime. No degree of double standard-setting can make black students competitive or comfortable in the academically exclusive colleges and universities. No amount of political gerrymandering can create genuine

sympathy among whites for the interests and strivings of black people. Yet it is to such double standard-setting, such gerrymandering, such maneuvering that many feel compelled to turn.

IBID.

[T]he black poor who are violent must be held responsible for their conduct. Are they not made poorer still when they are not accorded the respect inherent in the equal application of the obligations and expectations of citizenship?

"BLACK POLITICAL CULTURE AFTER THE SIXTIES," IN *SECOND THOUGHTS: FORMER RADICALS LOOK BACK AT THE SIXTIES,* PETER COLLIER AND DAVID HOROWITZ, EDS., 1989

Clare Booth Luce (1903–1987)

*P*laywright, congresswoman, ambassador, and feminist, Clare Booth Luce was a managing editor at *Vogue* (1930) and *Vanity Fair* (1933–1934). She was a U.S. congresswoman from Connecticut (1943–1947), U.S. ambassador to Italy (1953–1957), and a member of the President's Foreign Intelligence Advisory Board

(1973–1977, 1982–1987). Luce wrote the books *Stuffed Shirts* (1933) and *Europe in the Spring* (1940) as well as several plays, including *The Women* (1936), and contributed articles and fiction to magazines. She earned many honors, as when she received the Order of Lafayette, the Dag Hammarskjold medal, the American Statesman medal, and the Fourth Estate award.

If, in an hour of weakness, the moral man does a thing he knows to be wrong, he confesses it, and he "takes his punishment like a soldier." And, if he harms another, even inadvertently, he tries to make restitution. He takes responsibility for his own actions. And if they turn out badly for him, he does not put the blame on others. He does not, for example, yield to the post-Freudian moral cop-out of blaming his follies and failures, his weaknesses and vices, on the way his parents treated him in childhood. Here I cannot resist mentioning the case of Tom Hansen, of Boulder, Colorado, a 24-year-old youth who is living on welfare relief funds. He is presently suing his parents for 350,000 dollars damages because, he claims, they are to blame for lousing up his life, and turning him into a failure. Adam was, of course, the first man to try to shift respon-

sibility for his behavior onto someone else. As there was no Jewish mom to blame, he laid it on to his wife Eve.

HUMAN LIFE REVIEW, SUMMER 1978

All history bears witness to the fact that *there can be no public virtue without private morality*. There cannot be good government except in a good society. And there cannot be a good society unless the majority of individuals in it are at least *trying* to be good people. This is especially true in a democracy, where leaders and representatives are chosen from the people, by the people. The character of a democratic government will never be better than the character of the people it governs. A nation that is travelling the low road is a nation that is self-destructing. It is doomed, sooner or later, to collapse from within, or to be destroyed from without. And not all its wealth, science and technology will be able to save it. On the contrary, a decadent society will use, or rather, misuse and abuse, these very advantages in such a way as to hasten its own destruction.

IBID.

Sex—the procreative urge—is a mighty force. Indeed, it is *the* mightiest force. It is the *life* force. But since the dawn of history, what has distinguished man from the beasts is that he has made *conscious efforts* to control his lustful impulses, and to regulate and direct them into social channels. There is no primitive society known to anthropologists, no civilization known to historians, which has ever willingly consented to give its members full reign—bestial reign—of their sexual impulses. Sex morals, mores and manners have varied enormously from age to age, and culture to culture. But sexual taboos, and no-nos, sex prohibitions (and consequently, of course, inhibitions) are common to all human societies.

Now the fact that mankind has instinctively sensed that there is a right and a wrong way of handling his procreative energies strongly suggests that there may be a universal *sexual* morality. And so there is. And when we examine it, we find that it is this very morality that has made all human progress, and what we call civilization, possible. It is the morality that protects and preserves the basic unit of society—the *family.* The family is the foundation on which mankind has built all his societies. Jean Jacques Rousseau called the family "the most ancient of all societies," and "the first model of political societies."

IBID.

The truth is that very little *can* be done by government to shore up the family, although a great deal can be done and has been done to hasten its collapse.

But the real cause of the breakdown is the abandonment, by millions of people, beginning with husbands, wives and parents of their *interior* devotion to the principles of the universal morality.

IBID.

Thomas Babington Macaulay *(1800–1859)*

*E*nglish writer and statesman Thomas Macaulay was a member of the Supreme Council of India (1834–1835) and secretary of war (1839–1841). He wrote a five-volume *History of England* (1848–1861), *Laws of Ancient Rome* (1842), and numerous essays, biographical sketches, and speeches.

Free trade, one of the greatest blessings which a government can confer on a people, is in almost every country unpopular.

REVIEW, *MITFORD'S HISTORY OF GREECE,* 1824

There is only one cure for the evils which newly acquired freedom produces, and that cure is freedom.

ON MILTON, 1825

If it is admitted that on the institution of property the well-being of society depends, it follows surely that it would be madness to give supreme power in the state to a class which would not be likely to respect that institution.

SPEECH ON THE PEOPLE'S CHARTER, MAY 3, 1842

Men are never so likely to settle a question rightly as when they discuss it freely.

REVIEW, SOUTHEY'S COLLOQUIES ON SOCIETY, 1830

Nothing is so galling to a people, not broken in from the birth, as a paternal, or, in other words, a meddling government, a government which tells them what to read and say and eat and drink and wear.

IBID.

Tibor Richard Machan (1939–)

A libertarian philosophy professor at Auburn University, Tibor Machan holds a doctorate from the University of California at Santa Barbara. He has written a number of books, including *Capitalism and Individualism* (1990), and has edited and written articles in such books as *The Libertarian Alternative: Essays in Social and Political Philosophy* (1974) and *Rights and Regulation* (1983), which he coedited with M. Bruce Johnson.

[M]aking considerateness, compassion, kindness, generosity, and other virtues pertaining to civilized community life matters of government mandate . . . is a fundamental threat to the quality of human community life . . . .

RIGHTS AND REGULATION, 1983

James Madison (1751–1836)

T he fourth president of the United States (1809–1817) and member of the Continental Congress (1780–1783) and the Constitutional Convention (1787), James Madison has influenced conservative thought through his advocacy of individual freedom, capitalism, and limited government. He is also famous for writing, with Alexander Hamilton and John Jay, *The Federalist Papers* (1787–1788), a work explaining and advocating the new Constitution.

The powers delegated by the proposed Constitution to the federal government are few and defined. Those which are to remain in the State governments are numerous and indefinite. The former will be exercised principally on external objects, as war, peace, negotiation, and foreign commerce; with which last the power of taxation will, for the most part, be connected. The powers reserved to the several States will extend to all the objects which, in the ordinary course of affairs, concern the lives, liberties, and properties of the people, and the internal order, improvement, and prosperity of the State.

THE FEDERALIST PAPERS, NO. 45

I believe there are more instances of the abridgement of the freedom of the people by gradual and silent encroachments of those in power than by violent and sudden usurpations.

ADDRESS, VIRGINIA CONVENTION, 1788

No theoretical checks—no form of government, can render us secure. To suppose that any form of government will secure liberty or happiness without any virtue in the people is a chimerical idea.

IBID.

The religion then of every man must be left to the conviction and conscience of every man; it is the right of every man to exercise it as these may dictate.

A MEMORIAL AND REMONSTRANCE, 1784

Jacques Maritain (1882-1973)

A French philosopher and theologian who converted to Roman Catholicism from Protestantism, Jacques Maritain defended traditional religious values, especially those of St. Thomas Aquinas. His works include *True Humanism* (1938), *Man and the State* (1951), and *Moral Philosophy* (1964).

The State is not the supreme incarnation of the Idea, as Hegel believed; the State is not a kind of collective superman; the State is but an agency entitled to use power and coercion, and made up of experts or specialists in public order and welfare, an instrument in the service of man. Putting man at the service of that instrument is political perversion. The human person as an individual is for the body politic and the body politic is for the human person as a person. But man is by no means for the State. The State is for man.

MAN AND THE STATE, 1951

George Mason *(1725-1792)*

*P*lanter and Revolutionary War-
era statesman George Mason
actively opposed the Stamp Act. He
was a member of the Virginia constitutional convention and prepared
Virginia's Declaration of Rights, which
became the basis for the Bill of Rights.
Mason also wrote much of the Virginia
constitution, but he refused to sign the
federal Constitution because of its
compromises on slavery and other
issues.

From the nature of man, we may be
sure that those who have power in their
hands . . . will always, when they can, . . .
increase it.

STATEMENT, FEDERAL CONVENTION, 1787

Government is, or ought to be, instituted for the common benefit, (protection) and security of the people, nation
or community; . . . and . . . whenever
any government shall be found inadequate or contrary to these purposes, a
majority of the community hath an
indubitable, unalienable, indefeasible
right, to reform, alter, or abolish it, in
such manner as shall be judged most
conducive to the public Weal.

VIRGINIA DECLARATION OF RIGHTS, ARTICLE 3,
JUNE 12, 1776

Michael Medved *(1948–)*

A well-known movie critic and
television celebrity, Michael
Medved has written a number of books,
including *What Really Happened to
the Class of '65* (with David
Wallechinsky, 1976), *The Shadow
Presidents* (1979), *The Hollywood Hall
of Shame* (with Harry Medved, his
brother, 1984), and *Hollywood vs.
America: Popular Culture and the War
on Traditional Values* (1992).

[The] . . . association of capitalists
with criminality represents the most
extreme and obvious manifestation of
Hollywood's hostility. The businessmen
who appear week after week on [televi-
sion] network series not only engage in
economic abuses like rent gouging, toxic
waste dumping, union busting, and the
manufacture of dangerous or shoddy
products; they also regularly commit

crimes of violence like murder, rape, assault, and robbery . . . . [I]n contemporary prime time, "although businessmen represented 12 percent of all characters in census-coded occupations, they accounted for 32 percent of the crimes these characters commit . . . 40 percent of the murders and 44 percent of the vice crimes like drug trafficking and pimping . . . ."

Unfortunately, the prevailing vision of vicious tycoons has become so deeply embedded in the popular culture that it is now difficult to imagine any alternative presentation of the captains of industry and finance.

HOLLYWOOD VS. AMERICA, 1992

The days when Hollywood captured the imagination of the entire world with stirring accounts of our heroic history have given way to an era of self-flagellation and irresponsible revisionism—with a series of preachy, politically correct, propagandistic presentations of our country's many crimes and misdemeanors.

IBID.

[T]he common Hollywood assumption [is] that any attempt by viewers to participate in organized efforts to combat violent and sexual excesses in the media is dangerous and fascistic. This viewpoint ignores both history and logic. Nowhere in the Constitution is it written that TV

viewers must sit quietly on their couches and passively accept whatever the industry chooses to place on the air; the right to protest degrading material is not limited to those favored few who are asked to report their viewing on a Nielsen box.

IBID.

In years past, . . . the movie business drew considerable criticism for manufacturing personalities who were larger than life, impossibly noble and appealing individuals who could never exist in the real world. Today, the industry consistently comes up with characters who are *smaller* than life—less decent, less intelligent, and less likable than our own friends and neighbors.

IBID.

Hollywood has not only abandoned larger-than-life heroes, but the industry seems to have lost all vision of the heroic elements in daily life—the selflessness and nobility of which ordinary citizens are consistently capable.

IBID.

The [Hollywood] portrayal of parents as irrelevant—or outright evil—has become so pervasive in every corner of our popular culture that we have begun to take it for granted as a harmless convention of mass entertainment. We blithely assume that our children can absorb innumerable images of inept and idiotic parents in movies, television, and popular songs, while remembering at all times that their own mother and father are completely different.

IBID.

No notion has been more aggressively and ubiquitously promoted in films, popular music, and television than the idea that children know best—that parents are corrupt, hypocritical clowns who must learn decency and integrity from their enlightened offspring.

IBID.

Hollywood no longer reflects—or even respects—the values of most American families.

IBID.

Edwin Meese *(1931–)*

*A*fter going to Yale on a scholarship and graduating in 1953, Ed Meese briefly worked in an iron foundry and then entered Boalt Law School of the University of California at Berkeley. His legal studies, interrupted by a two-year period of army service, were completed in 1958. When working as a deputy district attorney in California's Alameda County, Meese became friends with then-governor Ronald Reagan. Meese served under Reagan in different advisory capacities, ultimately becoming the nation's attorney general during Reagan's second presidential term (1985–1988).

This is a momentous time in the Communist World, quite unlike anything that has occurred since the Bolshevik revolution of 1917. In China, spontaneous demonstrations for democracy have captured the imagination of the world, and even the bloody massacre by the Chinese Army [on 4 June 1989 at Tienanmen Square in Beijing] is unlikely to permanently quell the students and others who are valiantly asserting their desire for freedom.

In Poland, meanwhile, the Solidarity trade union has won its decade-long struggle for democracy. Solidarity candidates won nearly every contested seat in the new Polish Parliament, marking the first election in a communist country in which opposition parties were permitted to organize and campaign. The Soviet Union, too, recently held elections, in which independent candidates dealt embarrassing defeats to scores of party hacks. And in many of its Eastern Europe colonies, the stirrings of liberty are being observed.

These nations are all far from democracy as we know it. But the trend is definitely toward more freedom.

"COMMUNIST NATIONS ARE THIRSTY FOR FREEDOM,"
JUNE 12, 1989

Communist leaders are in an unenviable position: They have been forced to adopt political and economic reforms in order to pull their economies out of the quagmire produced by decades of rigid central planning. But those very reforms have ignited the flame of freedom that threatens to engulf the rulers in Beijing—and that no doubt worries Mikhail Gorbachev as well.

IBID.

There are many lessons to be learned from the events in Beijing. For Gorbachev and other communist rulers, the lesson is that even decades of dreary repression cannot crush the human spirit. Citizens of China, the Soviet Union, and other communist nations are thirsty for freedom, and will not be satisfied in the long run with half measures . . . .

IBID.

The protests in Beijing should . . . be taken as a stinging rebuke of the notion of cultural relativism, and specifically of

the idea that political freedom is a "Western" idea not universally acceptable. In Tienanmen Square, thousands of Chinese have risked and given their lives for the same ideals on which our nation was founded. Indeed, their symbols of democracy are ours—including Thomas Jefferson and the Statue of Liberty.

What is happening in Beijing . . . gives [the] lie to the notion that freedom is divisible—that one can have economic freedom without political freedom, or vice-versa. After all, it was Deng's free-market economic reforms, established out of necessity, that created the political climate which led to the democratic protests.

IBID.

Henry Louis Mencken *(1880–1956)*

*E*ditor and satirist H. L. Mencken, largely self-taught, was known for his skillful and trenchant prose style, in which he often expressed libertarian sentiments. The "sage of Baltimore" was on the staff of several Baltimore newspapers, including the *Evening Sun*. He was a prolific writer who was at various times a reporter, an editor, a literary critic, a social critic, and a student of religion and the American language. *The Smart Set* (1908–1923) contains literary criticism. From 1924–1933, Mencken and George Jean Nathan edited *American Mercury*, which they had founded. He was a contributing editor to the *Nation* and wrote such works as *In Defense of Women* (1917), *The American Language* (1918), *Prejudices* (6 volumes, 1919–1927), *Notes on Democracy* (1926), *Treatise on Right and Wrong* (1934), and the autobiographical *Happy Days, 1880–1892* (1940).

When a new source of taxation is found it never means, in practice, that an old source is abandoned. It merely means that the politicians have two ways of milking the taxpayer where they had only one before.

EVENING SUN, NOV. 13, 1925

A Progressive is one who is in favor of more taxes instead of less, more bureaus and jobholders, more paternalism and meddling, more regulation of private affairs and less liberty. In general, he would be inclined to regard the repeal of any tax as outrageous.

IBID., JAN. 19, 1926

I believe in liberty. In any dispute between a citizen and the government, it is my instinct to side with the citizen . . . . I am against all efforts to make men virtuous by law. I believe that the government, practically considered, is simply a camorra of incompetent and mainly dishonest men, transiently licensed to live by the labor of the rest of us. I am thus in favor of limiting its powers as much as possible, even at the cost of a considerable inconvenience, and of giving every citizen, wise or foolish, right or wrong, the right to criticize it freely, and to advocate changes in its constitution and personnel. In brief, the concept of American "ideals, morals, hopes and institutions" that I subscribe to is substantially the concept that Thomas Jefferson subscribed to. I do not have his confidence in the wisdom and rectitude of the common man, but I go with him in his belief that the very commonest of common men have certain inalienable rights.

AMERICAN MERCURY, SEPT. 1927

I believe that liberty is the only genuinely valuable thing that men have invented, at least in the field of government, in a thousand years. I believe that it is better to be free than to be not free, even when the former is dangerous and the latter safe. I believe that the finest qualities of man can flourish only in free air—that progress made under the shadow of the policeman's club is false progress, and of no permanent value. I believe that any man who takes the liberty of another into his keeping is bound to become a tyrant, and that any man who yields up his liberty . . . is bound to become a slave.

CHICAGO TRIBUNE, JAN. 30, 1927

Frank Straus Meyer *(1909–1972)*

*O*nce a Communist organizer at Oxford and at the University of Chicago, Frank S. Meyer came to lose faith in Communism after reading Hayek's *The Road to Serfdom* and went on to become a prominent member of William F. Buckley's *National Review* circle. Known for attempting to reconcile the traditionalist and libertarian elements of conservative thought, he wrote such works as *In Defense of Freedom* (1962) and *The Conservative Mainstream* (1969), and edited *What is Conservatism?* (1964).

[T]he essential requisite for a good society is such a division of power that no single center will be able to enforce beliefs upon men by force, or to inhibit and destroy other beliefs by force. This principle can be reduced to a simpler maxim: The state must be limited to its proper function of preserving order. But this will only be possible when the person is considered as the central moral entity, and society as but a set of relations between persons, not as an organism morally superior to persons. For if society be given a moral status superior to persons, then it follows both implicitly and logically that society has the right to create an arm to enforce its moral rights. That arm can only be the unlimited Leviathan state. If ultimate moral righteousness rests in society, it is justified in enforcing its righteousness, and the state which is its arm cannot be limited by any rights inherent in individual persons.

IN DEFENSE OF FREEDOM, 1962

Unless men are free to be vicious, they cannot be virtuous.

IBID.

John Stuart Mill *(1806–1873)*

*E*nglish philosopher and economist John Stuart Mill was one of the most influential philosophers in the English-speaking world during the nineteenth century and one of the most effective advocates of individual liberty. Although he wrote on economics, logic (in which he broke new ground), and ethics, his essay *On Liberty* (1859) may be his most enduring work. It is in that work that Mill argues for a limited government to leave room for the flowering of individualism.

[T]he sole end for which mankind are warranted, individually or collectively, in interfering with the liberty of action of any of their number, is self-protection . . . . [T]he only purpose for which power can be rightly exercised over any member of a civilized community, against his will, is to prevent harm to others.

ON LIBERTY, 1859

The spirit of improvement is not always a spirit of liberty, for it may aim at forcing improvements on unwilling people.

IBID.

John Milton *(1608–1674)*

*T*he English poet John Milton is known for not only his many outstanding poems, including the epic *Paradise Lost* (1667), but also his strong beliefs in freedom of speech and the press (expressed in *Areopagitica*, 1644) and in the right of citizens to depose unworthy leaders (*The Tenure of Kings and Magistrates*, 1649), such as England's Charles I.

[A]s good almost kill a man as kill a good book; who kills a man kills a reasonable creature, God's image; but he who destroys a good book, kills reason itself.

AREOPAGITICA, 1644

Give me the liberty to know, to utter, and to argue freely according to conscience, above all liberties.

IBID.

Where there is much desire to learn, there of necessity will be much arguing, much writing, many opinions; for opinion in good men is but knowledge in the making.

IBID.

. . . though all the winds of doctrine were let loose to play upon the earth, so Truth be in the field, we do injuriously by licensing and prohibiting to misdoubt her strength. Let her and Falsehood grapple; who ever knew Truth put to the worse, in a free and open encounter?

IBID.

. . . none can love freedom heartily,
but good men; the rest love not freedom,
but license. . . .

THE TENURE OF KINGS AND MAGISTRATES, 1649

No man who knows aught, can be so
stupid to deny that all men naturally
were born free. . . .

IBID.

Ludwig von Mises *(1881-1973)*

*L*eader of the Austrian school of
economics, Ludwig von Mises
was an important defender of free-
market economics and individual liberty. He wrote such works as *Socialism*
(1922), *Human Action* (1949), and *The
Anti-Capitalistic Mentality* (1956).

Whether Society is good or bad may be
a matter of individual judgment; but whoever prefers life to death, happiness to suffering, well-being to misery, must accept
. . . without limitation or reserve, private
ownership of the means of production.

SOCIALISM, 1922

A nation is the more prosperous
today the less it has tried to put obstacles
in the way of the spirit of free enterprise
and private initiative.

THE ANTI-CAPITALISTIC MENTALITY, 1956

Nobody is needy in the market economy because of the fact that some people
are rich. The riches of the rich are not the
cause of the poverty of anybody. The
process that makes some people rich is, on
the contrary, the corollary of the process
that improves many people's satisfaction.

IBID.

What is wrong with our age is precisely the widespread ignorance of the
role which . . . policies of economic freedom played in the technological evolution of the last two hundred years.

HUMAN ACTION, 1949

It is always the individual who thinks.
Society does not think any more than it
eats or drinks.

IBID.

It is . . . wrong to assume that there
prevails within a market economy, not
hampered and sabotaged by government
interference, a general tendency toward
the formation of monopoly. It is a
grotesque distortion of the true state of
affairs to speak of *monopoly capitalism*

instead of *monopoly interventionism* and of *private cartels* instead of *government-made cartels.*

IBID.

Thomas Molnar *(1921–)*

*H*ungarian-born educator and author, Thomas Molnar has long been a staunch defender of traditional conservative values. He is best known for *Utopia: The Perennial Heresy* (1967).

Passion for equality blinds the utopian to the fact that society, as a whole, is based on inequality of men in two respects: the inventor, the innovator, the exceptional man creates something new and insures continuous progress; the others emulate his work or merely improve their own lot by benefiting from his creativity.

UTOPIA: THE PERENNIAL HERESY, 1967

Marxism would have remained an ideology, and the Marxist intellectuals' writings a file in utopian literature, had the Revolution not taken place in Russia, and a State, claiming to embody Marx's teachings, not been created. Through this historical act, the revolutionary modernization of Russia, the Marxist intellectuals everywhere in the world have become "the elect," servants, masters, and interpreters of the world-historical spirit, and public figures whose words and acts carry weight, often beyond their measure as individuals and intellectuals. No wonder, then, that the existence, the development, the vicissitudes of Soviet Russia as a State and as a revolutionary force (the "workers' fatherland") has been, for the last forty years, one of the most momentous intellectual phenomena, making and breaking careers, bestowing or reviling reputations.

THE DECLINE OF THE INTELLECTUAL, 1962

The Marxist intellectuals' experience and reaction during this period has been characterized by the extraordinary tortuous and tortured relationship they have maintained with the Soviet Union. The land of the proletariat was a fact, and its interests supreme; loyalty to it had precedence over patriotism, friendship, and family ties, because the expected communist society was itself to be a universal homeland, family, and friend. The intellectuals were clinging to these idealized features while the Soviet State itself, making use at once of ideological intransigence and Asian-type despotism, was following the way of all political entities, that is, pursuing its own complex interests. The more these interests demanded cunning, ruthlessness, and ideological leaps, the more baffled the intellectuals became, since the discrepancy did not cease widening between hard reality and the utopian image.

IBID.

This is a passage from Stalin Prize-winner V. Ilenkov's novel, *The Highway* (1949), as quoted by the author of the Esprit article: "For thousands of years, people have suffered because they did not think alike. We, Soviet men, for the first time, we have understood each other . . . we think in an identical fashion on the principal things of life. We are strong with this ideological unity. This is the source of our superiority over other people who are torn and divided by their pluralism of thought."

There is then the fruit of utopian thinking by intellectuals and writers who expect of the State, of an ideology, of philosophy, of literature, of art, to bring about their own destruction for the sake of "transforming reality." This can be done only by denying the existence of problems when they exist; in regimes built on such an attitude there are usually more problems than elsewhere, and the larger their number, the more aggressively are they denied.

IBID.

The anonymous author, victim . . . of the ideology to which he clings and which he believes was betrayed, sums up unwittingly this attitude when he writes: "So that prisons may forever disappear, we have built new ones. So that frontiers between States may crumble, we have surrounded ourselves with a Chinese Wall. So that work may become in the future a rest and a pleasure, we have introduced forced labor. So that not a drop of blood may ever be shed, we have killed, killed, without respite."

No more eloquent funeral oration could be pronounced over the tomb of an ideology that has failed its believers because they despised the true nature of man.

IBID.

Baron de la Brède et de Montesquieu *(1689–1755)*

A French lawyer and political philosopher, an outstanding author and prose stylist, and an important figure of the early French Enlightenment, Montesquieu was counselor of the Bordeaux parliament (1714) and its president (1716). He withdrew from the practice of law to study and write and became well known if not notorious for his satirical attacks on French customs and institutions as well as for *The Spirit of the Laws* (1748), a political work that sold twenty-two editions within two years. While Montesquieu believed in natural law, he held that freedom can flourish only where the constitution sets inviolable limits to governmental activity and where the positive law itself acknowledges individual rights. When laws are just and aim at the common interest, following them, he held, is compatible with liberty.

We must have constantly present in our minds the difference between independence and liberty. Liberty is a right of doing whatever the laws permit.

THE SPIRIT OF THE LAWS, 1748

But constant experience shows us that every man invested with power is apt to abuse it, and to carry his authority as far as it will go.

IBID.

Commerce is a cure for the most destructive prejudices.

IBID.

Peace is the natural effect of trade.

IBID.

Useless laws weaken the necessary laws.

IBID.

Dwight Lyman Moody (1837–1899)

*D*wight Lyman Moody joined the Congregational Church and went to Chicago (in 1856), where he engaged in missionary work and built up a large Sunday school. Joined by Ira D. Sankey in the 1870s, Moody held revival meetings all over the U.S. and Great Britain through nearly the entire remainder of the nineteenth century.

It is better to get ten men to work than to do ten men's work.

QUOTED IN WILLIAM R. MOODY'S *D.L. MOODY*, 1930

Character is what you are in the dark.

QUOTED IN *DRAPER'S BOOK OF QUOTATIONS FOR THE CHRISTIAN WORLD*, 1992

George Edward Moore (1873–1958)

*A*n English philosopher, G. E. Moore taught at Cambridge University (1898–1939) and edited the philosophy journal *Mind* (1921–1947). Moore's views about commonsense beliefs, signs, and the analysis of ordinary language influenced many English and American philosophers. Among other things, he is known for having written *Principia Ethica* (1903).

There is a strong probability in favor of adherence to an existing custom, even if it be a bad one.

PRINCIPIA ETHICA, 1903

Daniel Patrick Moynihan *(1927–)*

*D*aniel Moynihan, neo-conservative Democratic senator from New York, holds a doctorate from the Fletcher School of Law and Diplomacy. He has occupied many academic positions at universities, including Syracuse and Harvard, and written numerous books, including *Maximum Feasible Misunderstanding* (1969), *Coping: On the Practice of Government* (1973), *A Dangerous Place* (1978), *Counting Our Blessings* (1980), *Family and Nation* (1986), *Came the Revolution: Argument in the Reagan Era* (1988), *On the Law*

of Nations (1990), and *Pandaemonium: Ethnicity in International Politics* (1993). Moynihan has also written numerous articles.

[T]here is one unmistakable lesson in American history: a community that allows a large number of young men to grow up in broken families, dominated by women, never acquiring any stable relationship to male authority, never acquiring any set of rational expectations about the future—that community asks for and gets chaos. Crime, violence, unrest, disorder—most particularly the furious, unrestrained lashing out at the whole social structure—that is not only to be expected; it is very near to inevitable.

AMERICA, SEPT. 18, 1965

It [government] cannot provide values to persons who have none or who have lost those they had. It cannot provide inner peace. It can provide outlets for moral energies, but it cannot create those energies.

LOS ANGELES TIMES, FEB. 15, 1969

In a 1992 study entitled *America's Smallest School: The Family*, Paul Barton came up with the elegant and persuasive concept of the parent-pupil ratio as a measure of school quality. Barton, who was on the policy planning staff in the Department of Labor in 1965, noted the great increase in the proportion of children living in single-parent families since then. He further noted that the proportion "varies widely among the states" and is related to "variation in achievement" among them. The correlation between the percentage of eighth graders living in two-parent families and average mathematics proficiency is a solid .74. North Dakota, highest on the math test, is second highest on the family compositions scale—that is second in the percentage of kids coming from two-parent homes. The District of Columbia, lowest on the family scale, is lowest in the test score.

THE AMERICAN SCHOLAR, WINTER 1993

The single most exciting thing you encounter in government is competence, because it's so rare.

NEW YORK TIMES, MAY 2, 1976

Malcolm Muggeridge *(1903-1990)*

*K*nown for his sharp wit and skillful prose style, his conversion to Christianity, and his criticism of Western materialism, Malcolm Muggeridge in the 1950s turned the British humor magazine *Punch* into a superior magazine of controversy and comedy. In the 1970s he published two volumes of memoirs, *Chronicles of Wasted Time*. In many forums, including his friend William F. Buckley's TV show *Firing Line*, Muggeridge came to criticize the West for, in his view, a loss of a sense of the transcendent. Many of his essays are collected in *Things Past* (1978).

Searching in my mind for an appropriate name for the seventies, I settle for The Decade of The Great Liberal Death Wish. It seems to me that this process of death-wishing, in the guise of liberalism, has been eroding the civilization of the West for a century and more, and is now about to reach its apogee.

THINGS PAST, 1978

The liberal mind, effective everywhere, whether in power or in opposition, particularly so during the present period of American world domination, has provided the perfect instrument. Systematically, stage by stage, dismantling our Western way of life, depreciating and deprecating all its values so that the whole social structure is now tumbling down, dethroning its God, undermining all its certainties, and finally mobilizing a Praetorian Guard of ribald students, maintained at the public expense, and ready at the drop of a hat to go into action, not only against their own weak-kneed, bemused academic authorities, but also against any institution or organ for the maintenance of law and order still capable of functioning, especially the police. And all this, wonderfully enough, in the name of the health, wealth and happiness of all mankind.

IBID.

Previous civilizations have been overthrown without by the incursion of barbarian hordes; ours has dreamed up its own dissolution in the minds of its own intellectual élite.

IBID.

Liberalism will be seen historically as *the* great destructive force of our time; much more so than communism, fascism, Nazism, or any of the other lunatic creeds which make such immediate havoc . . . .

IBID.

It is liberalism which makes the Gadarene swine so frisky; as mankind go to their last incinerated extinction, the voice of the liberal will be heard proclaiming the realization at last of life, liberty, and the pursuit of happiness.

IBID.

There is no snobbishness like that of professional egalitarians.

CHRONICLES OF WASTED TIME, 1978

William Murchison *(1942-)*

*W*illiam Murchison is a prominent syndicated columnist for Creators Syndicate. He has also written for several publications, including the *National Review*, *Policy Review*, *Human Events*, and *American Spectator*.

Welfare isn't this country's biggest problem. The problem that makes welfare so deeply troublesome—namely, the demoralization of the citizenry, the general flight from responsibility and personal obligation—is the thing we need most to combat. Most of the time you can't combat it by passing laws. Which leaves our fearless politicians mostly out of the equation . . . .

"WELFARE ISN'T THIS COUNTRY'S BIGGEST PROBLEM," JAN. 9, 1991

Dwight D. Murphey *(1934-)*

A lawyer and college professor, Dwight Murphey has spent many years analyzing and writing about the history of the American liberal intellectual movement. Some of his works are *Burkean Conservatism and Classical Liberalism* (1982), *Socialist Thought* (1983), and *Liberalism in Contemporary America* (1992). In tracing the thought of liberal intellectuals, Murphey underwent the onerous and presumably painful task of reading *every* issue of the *New Republic* from its inception in 1914 to early 1985—almost 200 volumes. He read also about a hundred volumes of the *Nation*.

In recent years . . . "multiculturalism" (enhanced by all the vogue-making mechanisms that the academic and media cultures can muster) has come along to raise the stress on ethnicity to a much higher level. This has become the rage within academic and media circles, and has come to be enforced by irascible taboos that insist on a "politically correct" sensitivity to the needs of the members of "victimized" minorities. This gives us yet another example, on top of the tendencies of the 1930s and later '60s, of just how open the American Left really is to totalitarianism when it feels it has the power (which it does today in important pockets of our society) . . . .

. . . new vistas have opened up with the multiculturalist vision. Ethnic allies can arise from immigration, the growth of the minority populations that are already here, and an intensified self-awareness on the part of each minority (a self-consciousness that the intellectual culture is working hard to create). The members of each group are encouraged to see themselves as the "victims" of "Eurocentric" society . . . . Thus, to the extent the effort succeeds, they are imbued with the intellectuals' own alienation . . . . The idea of assimilation is dropped and "cultural pride and identity" are elevated. This portends an eventual Balkanization within American society.

LIBERALISM IN CONTEMPORARY AMERICA, 1992

Charles Alan Murray *(1943-)*

C harles Murray, who did his doctoral studies in political science at M.I.T. (1974), is best known for his book *Losing Ground: American Social Policy 1950–1980* (1984). He has also written such books as *Safety Nets and the Truly Needy* (1982), *Gaining Ground* (1985), and *In Pursuit: Happiness and Good Government* (1989). His most recent book, *The Bell Curve* (1994), is a controversial work on the nature of intelligence and its social implications. The book was co-written by the late social scientist Richard Herrnstein.

A government's social policy helps set the rules of the game—the stakes, the risks, the payoffs, the tradeoffs, and the strategies for making a living, raising a family, having fun, defining what "winning" and "success" mean. The more vulnerable a population and the fewer its independent resources, the more decisive the effect of the rules imposed from above. The most compelling explanation for the marked shift in the fortunes of the poor is that they continued to respond, as they always had, to the world as they found it, but that we—meaning the not-poor and un-disadvantaged—had changed the rules of their world. Not of our world, just of theirs. The first effect of the new rules was to make it profitable for the poor to behave in the

short term in ways that were destructive in the long term. Their second effect was to mask these long-term losses—to subsidize irretrievable mistakes. We tried to provide more for the poor and produced more poor instead. We tried to remove the barriers to escape from poverty, and inadvertently built a trap.

LOSING GROUND, 1984

The New Deal sponsors of AFDC [Aid to Families with Dependent Children] had intended to help the widow with small children. The support she received would tide her over in the interim between the loss of her husband and the day when the children were old enough to take over her support. AFDC was at the outset the most broadly acceptable of the New Deal innovations in social welfare.

From this innocuous beginning AFDC evolved into the bête noire of the social welfare system. By the fifties it had become embarrassingly, outrageously clear that most of these women were not widows. Many of them had not even been married. Worst of all, they didn't stop having babies after the first lapse. They kept having more. This had not been part of the plan.

IBID.

[F]rom a policy standpoint, it became clear only shortly after the War on Poverty began that henceforth the black lower class was to be the object of a new condescension that would become intertwined with every aspect of social policy . . . .

. . . Before the 1960s, we had a black underclass that was held down because blacks were systematically treated differently from whites, by whites. Now, we have a black underclass that is held down for the same generic reason—because blacks are systematically treated differently from whites, by whites.

IBID.

[T]he intelligentsia and the policy-makers, coincident with the revolution in social policy, began treating the black poor in ways that they would never consider treating people they respected. Is the black crime rate skyrocketing? Look at the black criminal's many grievances against society. Are black illegitimate birth rates five times those of whites? We must remember that blacks have a much broader view of the family than we do—aunts and grandmothers fill in. Did black labor force participation among the young plummet? We can hardly blame someone for having too much pride to work at a job sweeping floors. Are black

high school graduates illiterate? The educational system is insensitive. Are their test scores a hundred points lower than others? The tests are biased. Do black youngsters lose jobs to white youngsters because their mannerisms and language make them incomprehensible to their prospective employers? The culture of the ghetto has its own validity.

IBID.

That the condescension [towards poor blacks] should be so deep and pervasive is monumentally ironic, for the injunction to respect the poor (after all, they are not to blame) was hammered home in the tracts of radical intellectuals. But condescension is the correct descriptor. Whites began to tolerate and make excuses for behavior among blacks that whites would disdain in themselves or their children.

The expression of this attitude in policy has been a few obvious steps— Affirmative Action, minority set-asides in government contracts, and the like . . . . The system *had* to be blamed, and any deficiencies demonstrated by blacks had to be overlooked or covered up—by whites.

. . . the consequences were disastrous for poor people of all races, but for poor blacks especially, and most emphatically for poor blacks in all-black communities—precisely that population that was the object of the most unremitting sympathy.

IBID.

John Courtney Murray (1904-1967)

A Jesuit priest and professor of theology at Woodstock College, John Murray argued for the theory that political liberty cannot exist as a genuine and durable good without moral virtue. That idea is plain in *We Hold These Truths*, a series of political essays published in 1960. Murray also wrote *The Problem of God, Yesterday and Today* (1963) and *The Problem of Religious Freedom* (1965).

[P]art of the inner architecture of the American ideal of freedom has been the profound conviction that only a virtuous people can be free.

WE HOLD THESE TRUTHS, 1960

It is not an American belief that free government is inevitable, only that it is possible, and that its possibility can be realized only when the people as a whole

are inwardly governed by the recognized imperatives of the universal moral law.

IBID.

The American experiment reposes on [Lord] Acton's postulate, that freedom is the highest phase of civil society. But it also reposes on Acton's further postulate, that the elevation of a people to this highest phase of social life supposes, as its condition, that they understand the ethical nature of political freedom. They must understand, in Acton's phrase, that freedom is "not the power of doing what we like, but the right of being able to do what we ought."

IBID.

The people claim this right ["of being able to do what we ought"], in all its articulated forms, in the face of government; in the name of this right, multiple limitations are put upon the power of government. But the claim can be made with the full resonance of moral authority only to the extent that it issues from an inner sense of responsibility to a higher law.

IBID.

In any phase civil society demands order. In its higher phase of freedom it demands that order should not be imposed from the top down, as it were, but should spontaneously flower outward from the free obedience to the restraints and imperatives that stem from inwardly possessed moral principle. In this sense democracy is more than a political experiment; it is a spiritual and moral enterprise. And its success depends upon the virtue of the people who undertake it.

IBID.

Political freedom is endangered in its foundations as soon as the universal moral values, upon whose shared possession the self-discipline of a free society depends, are no longer vigorous enough to restrain the passions and shatter the selfish inertia of men.

IBID.

John Henry Newman *(1801–1890)*

*A*n English churchman who became a Roman Catholic cardinal, John Henry Newman founded the Oxford movement, designed by Anglican clergy at Oxford University to revitalize the Church of England by revising certain Roman Catholic doctrines and rituals. He converted to Catholicism in 1845, was made a cardinal in 1879, and became one of the

most influential English Catholics who ever lived. Cardinal Newman's religious autobiography *Apologia pro Vita Sua* (1864) is famous.

True religion is slow in growth, and, when once planted, is difficult of dislodgement; but its intellectual counterfeit has no root in itself: it springs up suddenly, it suddenly withers.

THE IDEA OF A UNIVERSITY, 1852

Gerhart Niemeyer *(1907–)*

A naturalized American citizen, Gerhart Niemeyer came to the United States in 1937 from Essen, Germany. He attended Cambridge, Munich, and Kiel universities, became a political science professor, and taught at different schools, including Princeton, Oglethorpe, and Notre Dame. Niemeyer was a foreign affairs officer at the Department of State (1950–1953) and a research analyst for the Council on Foreign Relations (1953–1955). He is known especially for his books on Soviet Communism. His books include *Law Without Force* (1941), *An Inquiry into Soviet Mentality*

(1956), *Facts on Communism, Vol.1: The Communist Ideology* (1959), *Handbook on Communism* (1962), *Between Nothingness and Paradise* (1971), and *Aftersight and Foresight* (1988).

Now one of the basic assumptions of morality is an acknowledgement of sameness, or equality, between humans. Martin Buber has insisted that the well-known Biblical commandment should be translated: "and (love) thy neighbor as one like thyself." A realization that we share an ontic or transcendent equality—whether we call it "the human condition," "human nature," a "divine image," or a common "fatherhood of God"—lies at the root of what Bergson has called "absolute morality." This is the attitude of the "open soul," which experiences obligation beyond what is relatively owed to a particular society.

Nothing of this attitude has a place in the Communist mind which, rather than opening the soul, closes it in on a small part of humanity and its "historical mission." All the same, their "narrowing of the soul" has, paradoxically, a moral character[,] for it is motivated by the vision of "human emancipation." Some call it a peculiar "love of mankind." It would seem more correct to speak of a "love for Communism's 'sublime vision' of the future." As far as mankind short of that future is concerned, Communists see in it nothing but a basic and unremediable inequality between the two opposed groups. There can be no rights for the enemies of history, but the Communist party has the historical right to make sure that all others support it unconditionally, for the future's sake.

"COMMUNISM AND THE NOTION OF THE GOOD," IN *THE ETHICAL DIMENSIONS OF POLITICAL LIFE*, 1983

[W]e are thoroughly mistaken if we attribute to communism an advocacy of equality and justice. Marx rejected both principles in his scathing criticism of Proudhon, *The Poverty of Philosophy* (1847), and later, in *The Critique of the Gotha Programme* (1875). There is no need to appeal to authority, though, for the concept of Communist inequality follows logically from a morality centering on history's coming to be and on revolution as the mode of that becoming. In Communist eyes their commitment to two standards has the same moral character as the initial impulse of the revolution. Still, Communists are quite aware that they do not share a common conscience with the rest of humanity, so they feel the need to keep the principle of Communist inequality hidden, and to play publicly on the conscience of "the others." Thus history does make liars of us all.

IBID.

[The Communist] struggle itself, seen in terms of light against darkness, enjoys exemption from all moral restrictions. The "sublimity" of the goal justifies any method required to reach it. Lenin explicitly enjoined on the comrades both violence and trickery, dissimulation and brutal force, concessions and deception. He also succeeded in giving to foreign affairs the color of the class struggle, in which the class enemy has no right to exist. One may say that Communist operations are characterized by moral immorality, immoral practice that is moral in its ultimate justification. The immorality is real, though, while the moral justification is merely implied. After all, the future is not yet. Communist "moral immorality," then, is composed of a moral element amounting to a begged question and an immoral aspect that is consummated practice.

IBID.

Robert A. Nisbet *(1913–)*

*A*n American historian and sociologist, Robert Nisbet earned a doctorate from Berkeley. He was both a professor of history and a professor of sociology and taught at the University of California (at Berkeley and Riverside) and lectured at several other institutions. His works, which have influenced many conservatives, include *The Quest for Community* (1953), *Tradition and Revolt* (1968), *Social Change and History* (1969), *The Degradation of Academic Dogma* (1971), *The Twilight of Authority* (1975), *History of the Idea of Progress* (1980), and *Teachers and Scholars* (1992).

Wherever two or more people associate, there is bound to be some form of hierarchy, no matter how variable, changing from one actor to the other, or how minor. Hierarchy is unavoidable in some degree. Our gravest problem at the present time, in many respects, is the disrepute into which this word, this unavoidable necessity, has fallen as the consequence of the generalized philosophy of egalitarianism . . . . We have seen institution after institution weakened or crippled in the social order as the result of arbitrary power wielded by one or other regulatory agency in the name of a vain and rapid equality. At the present time the ascendant moral philosophy in the West is that which . . . takes what is in effect leveling as the desired norm of justice. How welcome would be [Edmund] Burke's words today: "Believe me, Sir, those who attempt to level never equalize" . . . .

THE TWILIGHT OF AUTHORITY, 1975

We have seen, alas, the appearance of *ressentiment* that Tocqueville and Nietzsche, among others after Burke, predicted: the sense of the greater worthiness of the low, the common, and the debased over what is exceptional, distinctive, and rare, and, going hand in hand with this view, the profound sense of guilt—inscribed in the works of the New Equalitarians—at the sight of the latter. Hierarchy in some degree is . . . an ineradicable element of the social bond, and, with all respect for equality before the law—which is, of course, utterly vital to free society—it is important that rank, class, and estate in all spheres become once again honored rather than, as is now the case, despised or feared by intellectuals. Certainly, no philosophy of pluralism is conceivable without hierarchy—as open as is

humanly possible for it to be but not, in Burke's word, indifferently open.

IBID.

If the functional autonomy of social units is to be respected, if localism, regionalism, and the whole spirit of voluntary association is to flourish, power wielded by government must be distributed into as many hands as possible—not abstract, desocialized *political* hands but those we actually see in the social order, those of workers, enterprises, professionals, families, and neighborhoods . . . . Few things have more grievously wounded the political community in our time than the kind of centralization that has become virtually a passion in the political clerisy during most of this century and that is increasingly becoming but another word for the Federal government today.

IBID.

Richard Milhous Nixon *(1913-1994)*

*T*hirty-seventh president of the United States and vice president under Eisenhower, Richard Nixon wrote a number of books on geopolitics and presidential leadership, including *The Challenge We Face* (1960), *Six*

Crises (1962), *RN: Memoirs of Richard Nixon* (1978), *The Real War* (1980), *Leaders* (1982), *Real Peace* (1983), *No More Vietnams* (1985), *1999: Victory Without War* (1988), *In the Arena: A Memoir of Victory, Defeat and Renewal* (1990), *Seize the Moment: America's Challenge in a One-Superpower World* (1992), and *Beyond Peace* (1994). Because of the Watergate scandal, Nixon resigned from the presidency on August 9, 1974.

The march of civilization cannot and must not be confined merely to economic systems. That is why Mr. Khrushchev's so-called historical analysis in which he traces a line of progress from feudalism to capitalism to communism falls down. History cannot be judged solely in material and economic terms. When we analyze these three systems in terms of freedom for the individual, we find that the change from feudalism to private capitalism was one from less freedom to more freedom. And a change now to communism would be going back rather than forward—exactly the reverse of progress.

THE CHALLENGE WE FACE, 1960

[L]et us broaden this competition to include the higher cultural and spiritual values that characterize the true forward march of our civilization. We reject the idea that the goals and desires of mankind begin and end with material abundance. Our homes, our highways, our motorcars and electronic marvels are not ends in themselves but only the means, the necessary foundations for a life of cultural and spiritual richness. For us this must be a life of individual freedom and human dignity, a life that liberates the human spirit of every restraint beyond its own inherent capability—and then goes on to expand and increase that capability.

IBID.

When Mr. Khrushchev says that our grandchildren will live under communism, our answer should be: we do not fear the outcome, provided they have the freedom to choose the system they want. We do not say in reply that his grandchildren will live under capitalism. The very essence of our belief is that we will not impose it on anyone else; every nation should have the right to choose—free of any outside interferences—the kind of economic and political system which best fits its particular problems.

But this we do believe: that all the people on this earth, including those in the Soviet Union, will inevitably demand and obtain more and more freedom. Because history teaches us that man was made to be free and that freedom, not communism or any other form of dictatorship, is the wave of the future.

IBID.

In assembling a staff, the conservative leader faces a greater problem than does the liberal. In general, liberals want more government and hunger to be the ones running it. Conservatives want less government and want no part of it. Liberals want to run other people's lives. Conservatives want to be left alone to run their own lives . . . . Liberals flock to government; conservatives have to be enticed and persuaded. With a smaller field to choose from, the conservative leader often has to choose between those who are loyal and not bright and those who are bright but not loyal.

LEADERS, 1982

The [Clinton] Administration's ambitious agenda to increase the size and scope of government repeats the domestic policy mistakes of the past. What the U.S. needs is not bigger government but a renewal of its commitment to limited but strong government; economic freedom, which is the only way to assure prosperity and individual liberty; and a moral and cultural system that strengthens the family, personal responsibility and the instincts for civic virtue.

BEYOND PEACE, 1994

Above all, America must rediscover its commitment to the pursuit of excellence for its own sake. In the land of liberty, we have sometimes risked making an obsession out of individual freedom without requiring a concomitant sense of individual responsibility.

IBID.

The Clinton health plan, all 1,342 impenetrable pages of it, is less a prescription for better health care than a blueprint for the takeover by the Federal Government of one-seventh of the nation's economy. If enacted, it would represent the ultimate revenge of the 1960s generation.

IBID.

The debacle in Somalia was a lesson in how not to conduct U.S. foreign policy. What began as a highly popular humanitarian relief program under President Bush became a highly controversial U.N. nation-building project under President Clinton. As the world's richest nation, we should always be generous in providing humanitarian aid to other nations. But we should not commit U.S. military forces to U.N. nation-building projects unless our vital interests are involved, a test that neither Somalia nor Haiti satisfied.

IBID.

No other single factor will have a greater political impact on the world in the century to come than whether political and economic freedom take root and thrive in Russia and the other former communist nations. Today's generations of American leaders will be judged primarily by whether they did everything possible to bring about this outcome. If they fail, the cost that their successors will have to pay will be unimaginably high.

IBID.

Albert Jay Nock *(1870–1945)*

*O*ne of the most eloquent individualists, Albert Jay Nock founded *The Freeman* magazine (1920–1924) and wrote such books as *Jefferson* (1926), *Our Enemy, the State* (1935), and *Memoirs of a Superfluous Man* (1943), an autobiographical work in which he expressed a strong individualism based especially on the ideas of Thomas Jefferson and Herbert Spencer.

The state claims and exercises the monopoly of crime. It forbids private murder, but itself organizes murder on a colossal scale. It punishes private theft, but itself lays unscrupulous hands on anything it wants, whether the property of citizen or of alien.

OUR ENEMY, THE STATE, 1935

I hold it to be a matter of invariable experience that no one can do anything *for* anybody. Somebody may profit by something you do, you may know that he profits and be glad of it, but you do not do it *for* him. You do it, as Augustine says you *must* do it, are bound to do it (*necesse est* is the strong term he uses), because you get more satisfaction, happiness, delight, out of doing it than you would get out of not doing it; and this is egoistic hedonism.

By consequence I hold that no one ever did, or can do, anything *for* "society." When the great general movement towards collectivism set in, about the middle of the last century, "society," rather than the individual, became the criterion of hedonists like Bentham, Hume, J. S. Mill. The greatest happiness of society was first to be considered, because in that the individual would find a condition conducive to his greatest happiness. [Auguste] Comte invented the term *altruism* as an antonym of egoism, and it found its way at once into everyone's mouth, although it is utterly devoid of meaning, since it points to nothing that ever existed in mankind. This hybrid or rather this degenerate form of hedonism served powerfully to invest collectivism's principles with a specious moral sanction, and collectivists naturally made the most of it. It bred a numerous race of energumens, professional doers-of-good; and surrounding these were clusters of amateur votaries whose concern with improving society was almost professional in its intensity. When in the later nineties I first observed this fetishistic exaggeration of society's claims against the individual I regarded it as transparent nonsense, as I still do. I also regarded the activities of its promoters as so ill-conceived and ill-advised as to be in the main pernicious, as the mere passage of time has now shown that they were.

MEMOIRS OF A SUPERFLUOUS MAN, 1943

According to my observations, mankind are among the most easily tamable and domesticable of all creatures in the animal world. They are readily reducible to submission, so readily conditionable (to coin a word) as to exhibit an almost incredibly enduring patience under restraint and oppression of the most flagrant character. So far are they from displaying any over-weening love of freedom that they show a singular contentment with a condition of servitorship, often showing a curious canine pride in it, and again often simply unaware that they are existing in that condition.

IBID.

Considering mankind's indifference to freedom, their easy gullibility and their facile response to conditioning, one might very plausibly argue that collectivism is the political mode best suited to their disposition and their capacities. Under its regime the citizen, like the soldier, is relieved of the burden of initiative and is divested of all responsibility, save for doing as he is told. He takes what is allotted to him, obeys orders, and beyond that he has no care. Perhaps, then, this is as much as the vast psychically-anthropoid majority are up to, and a status of permanent irresponsibility under collectivism would be most congenial and satisfactory to them.

IBID.

- [O]f all political modes a just and generous collectivism is in its nature the most impermanent. Each new activity or function that the State assumes means an enlargement of officialdom, an augmentation of bureaucracy. In other words, it opens one more path of least resistance to incompetent, unscrupulous and inferior persons whom [Edward] Epstean's law has always at hand, intent only on satisfying their needs and desires with the least possible exertion. Obviously the collectivist State, with its assumption of universal control and regulation, opens more of these paths than any other political mode; there is virtually no end of them. Hence, however just and generous an administration of collectivism may be at the outset, and however fair its prospects may then be, it is immediately set upon and honeycombed by hordes of the most venal and untrustworthy persons that Epstean's law can rake together; and in virtually no time every one of the régime's innumerable bureaux and departments is rotted to the core.

IBID.

The idea of a self-limiting or temporary collectivism impresses me as too absurd to be seriously discussed. As long as Newton's law remains in force, no one can fall out of a forty-storey window and stop at the twentieth storey. So, as long as Epstean's law remains in force there can be no such thing as a ten-per-cent collectivist State for any length of time. One might just as sensibly speak of a ten-per-cent mammalian pregnancy.

IBID.

Oliver Laurence North *(1943–)*

A graduate of the U.S. Naval Academy and a decorated Marine officer in the Vietnam War, Lt. Col. Oliver North joined the National Security Council staff under Ronald Reagan in 1981 and eventually was named deputy director of political-military affairs. He is best known for the role he played in helping anti-Communist forces in Central America. In 1994, North ran for a U.S. Senate seat in Virginia. He is the author of *Under Fire* (1991) and the extremely popular *One More Mission* (1993) and is also a columnist for Creators Syndicate and a host of his own radio talk show.

Jerry Brown may not win the Democratic presidential nomination, but he deserves a lot of credit for making the "flat tax" a hot topic of national debate. This is an idea whose time has come . . . .

. . . the fact is that the progressive income tax is straight out of Karl Marx's Communist doctrine. Marx believed that the state ought to confiscate the incomes of successful people in order to subsidize others who would become dependent on the state. The elementary point bears repeating: Communism didn't work; it destroyed incentive and made everybody dependent on the state . . . .

Maybe Gov. Brown doesn't go far enough with a flat tax. A case can be made that the federal income tax ought to be abolished entirely. After all our government functioned quite nicely before the 16th amendment was ratified in 1913. At the very least, the federal income tax ought to be simplified. The simplest way to go is to pass a flat tax.

"SIMPLEST WAY TO GO IS TO PASS A FLAT TAX,"
APRIL 15, 1992

Most of Eastern Europe has now embraced the ideals of freedom and democracy, and Communism has shown itself to be the fatally flawed system that Ronald Reagan always insisted it was. I remember watching on television as the Berlin Wall came down. I had tears in my eyes, and Dornin, our youngest daughter, ran upstairs to say, "Mom, what's wrong with Daddy?"

Daddy was fine, of course; I was just overwhelmed by the moment. While I had known that these changes would come, I didn't really expect to witness them in my lifetime. I felt that way again in 1990, when, for the second time in

eleven years, the people of Nicaragua rejected a brutal and corrupt regime. And yet again in August 1991, watching Boris Yeltsin stop a Soviet tank during the second Russian Revolution.

UNDER FIRE, 1991

Michael John Novak (1933-)

A religion educator, author, and columnist, Michael Novak has taught at Harvard, Stanford, SUNY at Westbury, and other institutions, including Syracuse, where he was a professor of religion from 1977 to 1979. His writings on traditional religious values and democratic capitalism have appealed to many conservatives. His books include *Belief and Unbelief* (1965), *The Experience of Nothingness* (1970), *All the Catholic People* (1971), *The American Vision* (1978), *The Spirit of Democratic Capitalism* (1982), and *The New Consensus on Family and Welfare* (1987).

Socialists seem to think that humans should feel envy, even if they don't. For socialism, the fundamental evil is the conflict between classes . . . .

. . . Under democratic capitalism, inequalities of wealth and power are not considered evil in themselves. They are in tune with natural inequalities which everyone experiences every day. Nature itself has made human beings equal in dignity before God and one another. But it has not made them equal to one another in talent, personal energy, luck, motivation, and practical abilities. On the other hand, inequalities of every sort are potential sources of evil and abuse. Human beings are insecure. Often, even as little children, they engage in petty rivalries and tear one another down. Long before the rise of democratic capitalism, even in biblical times, envy was potent. Nature itself generates inequality of looks, stature, intellect, and heart.

THE SPIRIT OF DEMOCRATIC CAPITALISM, 1982

Any society which does not promote and support its best natural leaders punishes itself and weakens its probabilities of survival and progress.

IBID.

Democratic capitalism does not promise to eliminate sin. It certainly does not promise equality of results (an outcome which, in any case, would run counter both to nature and to justice). It does not even promise that all those who have wealth or who acquire wealth will do so according to moral merit. Its sense of meritocracy is not a judgment upon individuals but is based upon the system qua system.

IBID.

It is, so to speak, the chief virtue of democratic capitalism that, in giving rein to liberty, it allows tares to grow among the wheat. Its political economy is not designed for saints. Whereas socialists frequently promise, under their coercive system, "a new socialist man" of a virtuous sort the world has never seen before, democratic capitalism (although it, too, depends upon and nourishes virtuous behavior) promises no such thing. Its political economy, while depending upon a high degree of civic virtue in its citizens (and upon an especially potent moral-cultural system separated from the state), is designed for sinners. That is, for humans as they are.

IBID.

A confidence in the workings of talent over time leads the democratic capitalist to expect that, under conditions of equal opportunity and open social mobility, . . . families which acquire wealth will invest it wisely or lose it, and that elites will circulate as new families producing wealth in new ways replace older elites. "Concentrations of economic power" are, on the one hand, limited. On the other, they have a way of dissolving over time under the dynamics of economic change.

IBID.

Wealth . . . is safest in a free, growing society and most at risk in a decaying society. Thus the wealthy have a real and abiding interest in the economic, political, and social health of their societies. Under democratic capitalism, the wealthy have incentives to be public-spirited, civic-minded, and philanthropic. This is true not only of the Carnegies, Mellons, Rockefellers, and Fords, with their libraries, art galleries, and foundations, but of lesser-known families of wealth in every locality, with their gifts to hospital wings, college dormitories, city orchestras, and the like. It is in their interest not to use their own wealth narrowly. When they do not recognize this interest, a free society brings many institutional resources to their correction. Not only wealthy families but great corporations and entire industries rise and fall—the whaling industry, the railroads,

even nuclear energy—under quite natural rhythms, rhythms related to their own perspicacity and social vision. Unenlightened management of wealth invites its own punishment. The democratic capitalist, then, need not play God.

IBID.

Western civilization is possible because it has triumphed over envy. It did so largely through the invention of the market. Exchange in markets requires trust—trust in society's future, trust in the stability of the currency, trust in credit extended, and trust in goods received. It also requires information about the needs of others, for each exchange is other-regarding as well as self-regarding. Where markets exist, information about the needs of others is direct and simple. Where markets do not exist, distant authorities must speculate about needs and assign them rankings. Exchange relations are more fully human than relations of dependency. For this reason, markets take for granted (and promote) elementary equalities and, where such equalities do not exist, slowly generate them. Democratic socialists conclude from this slowness that markets should be abridged in favor of governmental action.

IBID.

The Marxist stencil applied to poverty begins by suggesting that the poverty of some is due to the wealth of others. An alternative theory suggests that cultures differ from one another in the mental and emotional disciplines in which they instruct their young, in their economic proclivities, and in other respects significant for economic and political competition . . . .

. . . [In addition, a] population with a median age of twenty-four should, other things being equal, have a lower average income than a population whose median age is thirty, since younger workers tend to make less money. Populations disproportionately concentrated in lower-income regions of the nation, like rural areas or the South, will show a lower average income than populations concentrated in higher-income regions (thus Irish-Americans, in the Northern states, have higher average incomes than Irish-Americans in the South). Finally, populations with larger average numbers of children, or with a higher proportion of female-headed households, will have lower average incomes than those whose family status includes fewer children, and those in which husband and wife are together, both of whom may be working.

IBID.

[T]o see improvement in the lot of all the poor, including the black poor . . . the private sector must be the point of concentration, since about 90 percent of all new jobs are created by small businesses and relatively modest corporations.

IBID.

Markets have amazing capacities for invention. Keen eyes may discern needs no one else is meeting. Adjustments and experiments with the minimum wage for teenagers may open up new possibilities for those whose economic skills are not high. Within communities where the unemployed live, buildings need repair, businesses need to be built. There is no lack of work to be done. Workers to do it are available. But to match laborers to labor so that income results is a task for intelligence and wit. Under current conditions, it cannot be said that such communities lack capital. Many beginning with less capital have made much more from it. Some catalyst is necessary. The spirit of democratic socialism, with its litany of statist solutions, seems designed to prevent such a catalyst from ever emerging.

IBID.

Robert Novak

(See Rowland Evans, Jr.-Robert Novak entry.)

Robert Nozick *(1938–)*

A libertarian philosophy professor at Harvard, Robert Nozick has written numerous articles and a number of books, including *Anarchy, State, and Utopia* (1974), *The Examined Life* (1989), and *The Nature of Rationality* (1993).

[N]o end-state principle or distributional patterned principle of justice can be continuously realized without continuous interference with people's lives.

ANARCHY, STATE, AND UTOPIA, 1974

The minimal state best reduces the chances of . . . takeover or manipulation of the state by persons desiring power or economic benefits . . . .

IBID.

Michael Oakeshott *(1901–1990)*

A n English philosopher whose critique of rationalism epitomizes the conservative's rejection of abstract political thinking, Michael Oakeshott is the author of such works as *Experience and Its Modes* (1933) and *Rationalism in Politics and Other Essays* (1962).

To be conservative . . . is to prefer the familiar to the unknown, to prefer the tried to the untried, fact to mystery, the actual to the possible, the limited to the unbounded, the near to the distant, the sufficient to the superabundant, the convenient to the perfect, present laughter to utopian bliss. Familiar relationships and loyalties will be preferred to the allure of more profitable attachments; to acquire and to enlarge will be less important than to keep, to cultivate and to enjoy; the grief of loss will be more acute than the excitement of novelty or promise. It is to be equal to one's own fortune, to live at the level of one's means, to be content with the want of greater perfection which belongs alike to oneself and one's circumstances.

RATIONALISM IN POLITICS AND OTHER ESSAYS, 1962

[T]he man of conservative temperament draws some appropriate conclusions. First, innovation entails certain loss and possible gain; therefore, the onus of proof, to show that the proposed change may be expected to be on the whole beneficial, rests with the would-be innovator. Secondly, he believes that the more closely an innovation resembles growth (that is, the more clearly it is intimated in and not merely imposed upon the situation) the less likely it is to result in a preponderance of loss. Thirdly, he thinks that an innovation which is a response to some specific defect, one designed to redress some specific disequilibrium, is more desirable than one which springs from a notion of a generally improved condition of human circumstances, and is far more desirable than one generated by a vision of perfection. Consequently, he prefers small and limited innovations to large and indefinite [ones]. Fourthly, he favours a slow rather than a rapid pace, and pauses to observe current consequences and make appropriate adjustments. And lastly, he believes the occasion to be important; and, other things being equal, he considers the most favourable occasion for innovation to be when the projected change is most likely to be limited to what is intended and least likely to be corrupted by undesired and unmanageable consequences.

IBID.

Patrick Jake O'Rourke *(1947–)*

*H*umorist P. J. O'Rourke has been a writer for *National Lampoon* (since 1973) and *Rolling Stone* (since 1981), for which he has also served as foreign affairs desk chief. He is the author of such books as *Republican Party Reptile* (1987), *Parliament of Whores* (1991), and *Give War a Chance* (1992).

The federal government of the United States of America takes away between a fifth and a quarter of all our money every year. That is eight times the Islamic zakat, the almsgiving required of believers by the Koran; it is double the tithe of the medieval church and twice the royal tribute that the prophet Samuel warned the Israelites against when they wanted him to anoint a ruler.

PARLIAMENT OF WHORES, 1991

The three branches of government number considerably more than three and are not, in any sense, "branches" since that would imply that there is something they are all attached to besides self-aggrandizement and our pocketbooks. I never determined how many sections there really are to the federal system. It probably can't be done. Government is not a machine with parts; it's an organism. When does an intestine quit being an intestine and start becoming [a rectum] . . . ? Nor did I ever determine any valuable rule for examining the branches of government, except one: If you want to know what an institution does, watch it when it's doing nothing.

IBID.

Federal spending is determined by a simple mathematical formula:
$X - Y = $ A Huge Stink. X is what we want from the government, which is everything in the world. Y is how much we're willing to pay for this in taxes . . . .

IBID.

The budget grows because, like zygotes and suburban lawns, it was designed to do nothing else.

IBID.

[A]ll tax revenue is the result of holding a gun to somebody's head. Not paying taxes is against the law. If you don't pay your taxes, you'll be fined. If you

don't pay the fine, you'll be jailed. If you try to escape from jail, you'll be shot.

IBID.

The great danger of special interests is not . . . that a minority of some kind will get fat at our nation's expense. The great danger is that our nation will discover a special interest to which a majority of us belong.

IBID.

The Bill of Rights protects freedom of speech, freedom of religion and freedom of assembly, of course. You could hardly call yourself free without those freedoms. But even more important, the Bill of Rights protects your money, car, house and stereo. The Fifth Amendment says, " . . . nor shall private property be taken for public use, without just compensation." . . .

In fact, most day-to-day freedoms are material freedoms. Your career, your home, your workout at the gym, shopping, traveling, entertainment, recreation, any buying and selling . . . are all matters of property rights.

"WHY I BELIEVE WHAT I BELIEVE," *ROLLING STONE,*
JULY 1995

When those who are against conservative policies don't have sufficient opposition arguments, they call the love of freedom selfish. Of course it is—in the sense that breathing's selfish.

IBID.

Charity is one of the great responsibilities of freedom . . . . But [that responsibility] must proceed from the bottom up, from the individual outward, never from the top down . . . .

You have to take care of yourself to the best of your ability to do so. Your family has to take care of you. Friends have to take care of your family. Neighbors have to take care of those friends. And a community has to take care of its neighbors. Government, with its power of coercion, red tape and inevitable unfamiliarity with the specifics of the case, is a last and a desperate resort.

IBID.

There is no virtue in compulsory government charity. And no virtue in advocating it. A politician who commends himself as "caring" and "sensitive" because he wants to expand the government's charitable programs is merely saying that he's willing to try to do good with other people's money. Who isn't? A voter who takes pride in supporting such programs is telling us that he'll do good with his own money—if a gun is held to his head.

IBID.

When government . . . becomes the principal source of aid and assistance in our society, [it is] proof that we're jerks, since we've decided that politicians are wiser, kinder and more honest than we are and that they, not we, should control the dispensation of eleemosynary goods and services.

IBID.

A conservative could have told you: If you want something done right, do it yourself.

IBID.

José Ortega y Gasset *(1883–1955)*

S panish philosopher, author, and statesman José Ortega y Gasset wrote a number of books but is particularly well known for *The Revolt of the Masses* (1930). In it, he argued that culture is so insecure that it can lapse into barbarism unless achievement-oriented persons, a distinct minority, exercise constant effort.

The most radical division that it is possible to make of humanity is that which splits it into two classes of creatures: those [responsible creatures] who make great demands on themselves, piling up difficulties and duties; and those who demand nothing special of themselves, but for whom to live is to be every moment what they already are, without imposing on themselves any effort towards perfection; mere buoys that float on waves.

THE REVOLT OF THE MASSES, 1930

Eric Partridge *(1894–1979)*

*N*ew Zealand-born Eric Partridge attended both Queensland and Oxford universities. After teaching school for three years, he served as a private in the Australian infantry in the First World War. In 1921, he was appointed Queensland Travelling Fellow at Oxford and later a lecturer at the universities of Manchester and London. Partridge was known for his many dictionaries and other books on English, including *Origins: A Short Etymological Dictionary of Modern English* (1958), *Usage and Abusage* (1942), and *The Gentle Art of Lexicography* (1963).

Since the war of 1939–1945 and partly because of it, there has arisen a Do-It-Yourself cult, affecting not only the practicalities of life but also its embellishments and enhancements and consolations: music and the arts, literature and the drama, all show an undermining by the levelling process. Those for whom "anything goes" have yet to learn that ultimately, for them, nothing goes; lacking a worthwhile ambition, a compulsive aspiration, a genuine integrity, they are easily satisfied with mediocrity and by the mediocre. For them, Bedlam is as musical as Bach or Beethoven; a daub indicates genius; a dead-level of uninspired and almost formless monotony, and the I.Q. of an idiot, are superior to a controlled imagination and a high intelligence; and the kitchen sink possesses a validity and a beauty they deny to the other parts of a dwelling.

For them, the speech of an illiterate is preferable to that of an educated, cultured person. Subtlety and suppleness, distinctions and variety, eloquence and ease, clarity of phrasing and perspicuity of sentence, all these are suspect, for they imply superiority of mind and spirit. That ambiguity and tedium and a drab parochialism inevitably result from such an attitude seems to have eluded the little-minded, for they are stultified by envy. No wonder mediocrity flourishes in literature and, indeed, at all levels of writing, for its only vehicle, language, has been slowed down by the slow-minded and the sluggish-hearted, by the dull and the indifferent. Anyone who believes in civilization must find it difficult to approve, and impossible to abet, one of the surest means of destroying it. To degrade language is finally to degrade civilization.

USAGE AND ABUSAGE, ADDENDUM TO 1973 EDITION

Norman Vincent Peale *(1898–1994)*

A minister of the Reformed Church in America and founder of *Guideposts* magazine (ca.1942), Norman Vincent Peale was most famous for his book, *The Power of Positive Thinking*, a perennial best seller since 1952. His other books include *Enthusiasm Makes the Difference* (1967), *You Can If You Think You Can* (1974), *The Power of the Plus Factor* (1987), and *The American Character* (1988).

We may hear and see sensational accounts of mendacious, duplicitous, corrupt politicians and double-dealing, unscrupulous business operators. These,

however, are the exception. The rule is honesty. Because long after the crooks and cheats have faded from our memories, we will recall the pervasiveness of principle. We will remember the people who showed integrity when it wasn't convenient, who did the right thing when it would have been easier (and perhaps more profitable) to do the wrong, who were honest when they didn't *have* to be.

THE AMERICAN CHARACTER, 1988

Initiative—the bold, resourceful spirit of enterprise—is a hallmark American trait. After all, wasn't this the essential characteristic that fueled America's discovery, exploration, and settlement? Surely, it was. Just as surely, it was this same spontaneous quality that energized the fantastic accomplishments of America's premier inventors, scientists, industrialists, and developers. Those famous men and women became world leaders and world beaters by seizing the initiative and determinedly achieving their goals in the face of daunting obstacles.

IBID.

Kevin Price Phillips *(1940–)*

K evin Phillips, who was special assistant to Richard Nixon's campaign manager in 1968, special assistant to the attorney general of the United States from 1969 to 1970, and a syndicated newspaper columnist from 1970 to 1983, is the author of several books, including *The Emerging Republican Majority* (1969), *Electoral Reform and Voter Participation* (1975), *Mediacracy* (1975), *Boiling Point: Democrats, Republicans, and the Decline of Middle-Class Prosperity* (1993), and *Arrogant Capital: Washington, Wall Street, and the Frustration of American Politics* (1994).

Over the last half century, a Washington swollen by expansions in peace and war has become what ordinary citizens of the 1780s and even some architects of the U.S. Constitution feared—a capital city so enlarged, so incestuous in its dealings, so caught up in its own privilege that it no longer seems controllable or even swayable by the general public.

ARROGANT CAPITAL, 1994

Awareness of . . . America's need to reawaken the radical spirit of the Declaration of Independence has grown in the last few years. Signs are everywhere— in grassroots movements and coalitions, in the unusual new alliances for purging the

capital and empowering ordinary Americans, and in the demand . . . for res- urrecting the boldness and antiestablish- ment insurgency of the founding fathers.

IBID.

Aging great-power capitals often become parasitic cultures. The term "para- site" was frequently used in seventeenth- and eighteenth-century criticisms of the Spanish and Dutch capitals. Washington, in different ways, is beginning to resemble those wayward governmental centers of previous declining empires, from Greece and Rome to Hapsburg Madrid and The Hague . . . . The lessons of history could not be more relevant. Too much of what happened then is happening again now.

IBID.

[T]he outsider groups and grassroots movements that snap and snarl at 1990s Washington exemplify a mindset unmatched in any preceding great power: a revolutionary awareness and tradition that was quickly reworked during the nineteenth century into a uniquely suc- cessful style of national politics. Whether the insurgent groups of the 1990s can still play yesteryear's essential renewal role—whether another bloodless political revolution is possible—will tell us a lot about America's place in the new century.

IBID.

Plato *(427?–347B.C.)*

*T*he Greek philosopher Plato, Socrates' most famous student, founded a university, the Academy, where he taught philosophy to young men, the most famous of whom was Aristotle. His emphasis on justice, truth, and virtue and his suspicion of tyrannical majorities have appealed to many conservatives.

Until philosophers are kings, or the kings and princes of this world have the spirit and power of philosophy, and political greatness and wisdom meet in one, and those commoner natures who pursue either to the exclusion of the other are compelled to stand aside, cities will never have rest from their evils . . . .

REPUBLIC

The people have always some champion whom they set over them and nurse into greatness . . . . This and no other is the root from which a tyrant springs; when he first appears he is a protector.

IBID.

Our object in the construction of the State is the greatest happiness of the whole, and not that of any one class.

IBID.

A tyrant . . . is always stirring up some war or other, in order that the people may require a leader.

IBID.

Norman Podhoretz *(1930–)*

*E*ditor of *Commentary* and an influential neo-conservative, Norman Podhoretz is the author of a number of books, including *Breaking Ranks* (1979), a book that explains why he broke ranks with liberals.

The main emphasis in the case for capitalism, then, is not that it reduces inequality—although under certain political conditions it certainly does, and probably to a greater degree than socialism; it is, rather, that capitalism improves the lot of everyone. Rich and poor alike grow richer under capitalism. Indeed, in capitalist societies the very idea of what constitutes poverty undergoes a change from absolute to relative deprivation.

Thus, life even at the bottom of capitalist societies is amazingly prosperous by the standards of the pre-capitalist past as well as by those of the socialist present. Material possessions such as cars, television sets, and appliances, which are taken for granted even in less-developed capitalist countries like Taiwan, remain luxuries even in highly developed communist countries like the Soviet Union.

HARVARD BUSINESS REVIEW, MARCH/APRIL 1981

Far from being grateful defenders of the system from which they have profited, the children of capitalism tend to turn against it. Thus it is that radicals and even revolutionaries almost always stem from the middle and upper classes rather than the working class or the poor, in whose name they presume to speak. And thus it is that what is called liberalism today is increasingly identified with the more, rather than the less, prosperous sectors of American society.

IBID.

Even as early as 40 years ago, Joseph Schumpeter noted "the extent to which the bourgeoisie, besides educating its own enemies, allows itself to be educated by them. It absorbs," he pointed out, "the slogans of current radicalism, and seems quite willing to undergo a process of conversion to a creed hostile to its very existence."

This paradoxical process has acceler-

ated since Schumpeter's day with vast increase in both the numerical size and the cultural weight of the class of persons hostile to capitalism—the "new class," as it has come to be known.

IBID.

[Irving] Kristol includes in the new class "scientists, teachers, and educational administrators, journalists and others in the communication industries, psychologists, social workers, those lawyers and doctors who make their careers in the expanding public sector, city planners, the staffs of the larger foundations, the upper levels of the government bureaucracy, and so on."

These people are not, most of them, radicals, but they are adversaries of capitalism and the values associated with it. Because of the ways in which they make their living, they also stand to gain in power and influence from the expansion of state control over the operations of the marketplace. Hence, partly out of conviction and partly out of self-interest, they have conducted a relentless ideological campaign which has cut deeply into the self-confidence of a business community that today more than ever before "seems quite willing to undergo a process of conversion to a creed hostile to its very existence."

IBID.

[In the 1930s] the two leading liberal weeklies in America, *The Nation* and *The New Republic*, became loyal apologists for Stalin, constantly printing pieces that praised his many accomplishments and denouncing as reactionaries and fascists anyone who called those accomplishments into question or tried to expose the bloodiness and repression behind the smiling facade. No one today denies that Stalin murdered millions of peasants who resisted his plan to expropriate their land and organize them into collective farms where they would all become employees of the state. But the fellow-traveling liberals (not to mention the "liberals in a hurry") of the 1930s denied it and vilified as liars and worse those who tried to tell the world what was happening. Nor does anyone today deny that the Soviet Union under Stalin was a police state in which all political opponents were either murdered or imprisoned in the Gulag Archipelago, a vast network of concentration camps that . . . eventually offered gruesome hospitality to an estimated sixty million people. Yet the fellow travelers of the 1930s denied this too and denounced reports of it as fascist propaganda.

BREAKING RANKS, 1979

[A] great many people, liberals as well as radicals, had at first seen Castro as a hero— "the first and greatest hero to appear in the world since the Second War," according to Norman Mailer—and had taken him at his word when he claimed to be fighting to replace the military dictatorship of Batista with a system of "Jeffersonian" democracy. Even after Castro had come to power in 1959 and had begun establishing a dictatorship of his own, and one moreover in which the Communist party was playing a larger and larger role all the time, a great effort was made to deny or apologize for these developments. There was no Communist influence in Cuba, it was said; the whole idea was a right-wing myth . . . . He represented an alternative to capitalism on the one side and "authoritarian socialism" on the other—a "new humanist socialism" which might yet prove a model for the entire underdeveloped world.

IBID.

Where then does radicalism now live? Exactly where it has always lived: not primarily in doctrines and not in the outward signs of manner and dress, but in self-hatred and self-contempt. It was out of an infection of self-hatred and self-contempt—disguised, to be sure, by the various gospels of expanding human possibility preached by early prophets like Norman O. Brown, Norman Mailer, and

Paul Goodman—that the radicalism of the sixties was born; and as it grew and spread, the infection grew and spread until it reached the proportions of an epidemic. The young were especially vulnerable. They had been inoculated against almost every one of the physical diseases which in times past had literally made it impossible for so many to reach adulthood. But against a spiritual plague like this one they were entirely helpless. Indeed, so spiritually illiterate had the culture become that parents were unable even to recognize the disease when it struck their children, and so confused were they that they went on insisting, even when the evidence of sickness and incapacity stared them full in the face, that the children were models of superior health.

IBID.

In the case of the white young [of the 1960s], the contemptuous repudiation of everything American and middle-class was mistaken for a form of idealism when it really represented a refusal to be who they were and to assume responsibility for themselves by taking their place in a world of adults. The case of the black young was more complicated because unlike their white counterparts they had real external oppressions to contend with. But this only made it easier to mistake

the plague for health when it struck them in the form of a refusal to accept any responsibility whatever for their own condition—to trace its ills entirely to the actions of whites and to look entirely to external forces for the cure.

IBID.

In the case . . . of the intellectuals . . . [of the 1960s], self-hatred took the form of a repudiation not so much of who as of what they were. To be an intellectual—a scholar, a thinker, an artist, a writer—was not good enough. Not even "the production of literary masterpieces" was good enough: one had to change the world. Nor was it even good enough to be, as Shelley had said the poets were, the unacknowledged legislators of the world: they had to be acknowledged, they had to exercise actual political power.

IBID.

James Danforth Quayle *(1947–)*

*V*ice president of the United States under George Herbert Walker Bush (1989–1993), Dan Quayle received his J.D. from Indiana

University (1974). He has been an associate publisher, and a general manager, of the *Huntington [Ind.] Herald*; a member of the consumer protection division of the office of the attorney general of Indiana; a U.S. congressman of the 95th and 96th Congresses; and a U.S. senator from Indiana (1981–1989).

The intergenerational poverty that troubles us so much today is predominantly a poverty of values. Our inner cities are filled with children having children, with people who have not been able to take advantage of educational opportunities, with people who are dependent on drugs or the narcotic of welfare.

SPEECH, COMMONWEALTH CLUB, MAY 19, 1992

Right now the failure of our families is hurting America deeply. When families fail, society fails. The anarchy and lack of structure in our inner cities are testament to how quickly civilization falls apart when the family foundation cracks.

IBID.

Ultimately, . . . marriage is a moral issue that requires cultural consensus, and the use of social sanctions. Bearing babies irresponsibly is, simply, wrong. Failing to support children one has fathered is wrong.

We must be unequivocal about this. It doesn't help matters when prime time TV has Murphy Brown—a character who supposedly epitomizes today's intelligent, highly paid, professional woman—mocking the importance of fathers by bearing a child alone and calling it just another "lifestyle choice."

IBID.

I know it is not fashionable to talk about moral values, but we need to do it. Even though our cultural leaders in Hollywood, network TV, the national newspapers routinely jeer at them. I think that most of us in this room know that some things are . . . [right], and other things are wrong.

Now it's time to make the discussion public. It's time to talk again about family, hard work, integrity and personal responsibility. We cannot be embarrassed out of our belief that two parents, married to each other, are better in most cases for children than one.

IBID.

Ayn Rand *(1905–1982)*

*T*he views of Russian-born author Ayn Rand have been

described as representing "radical individualism" because of her unwavering defense of laissez-faire capitalism and individual liberty and responsibility. Rand's critiques of communism, socialism, and the modern welfare state have endeared her to many libertarians and the libertarian wing of conservatism. She was the editor of *The Objectivist* (1962–1971) and the author of such books as *Atlas Shrugged* (1957) and *The Virtue of Selfishness* (1964). Her philosophy is well represented in not only her novels but also in *Philosophy: Who Needs It* (1982), a collection of previously published essays.

The only proper purpose of a government is to protect man's rights, which means: to protect him from physical violence. A proper government is only a policeman, acting as an agent of man's self-defense, and, as such, may resort to force *only* against those who *start* the use of force.

FOR THE NEW INTELLECTUAL, 1961

We are on strike, we, the men of the mind. We are on strike against self-immolation. We are on strike against the creed of unearned rewards and unrewarded duties. We are on strike against the dogma that the pursuit of one's happiness is evil. We are on strike against the doctrine that life is guilt.

ATLAS SHRUGGED, 1957

The motive [of egalitarianism] is not the desire to help the poor, but to destroy the competent. The motive is hatred of the good for being the good—a hatred focused specifically on the fountainhead of all goods, spiritual or material: the men of ability.

"EGALITARIANISM AND INFLATION" (1974) IN PHILOSOPHY, WHO NEEDS IT, 1982

Two world wars, three monstrous dictatorships—in Soviet Russia, Nazi Germany, Red China—plus every lesser variant of devastating socialist experimentation in a global spread of brutality and despair, have not prompted modern intellectuals to question or revise their dogma. They still think that it is daring, idealistic and unconventional to denounce the rich. They still believe that money is the root of all evil—except government money, which is the solution to all problems. The intellectual Establishment is frozen on the level of those elderly "leaders" who were prominent when the system of governmental "encouragement" took hold. By controlling the schools, the "leaders" perpetuated their dogma and gradually silenced the opposition.

"THE ESTABLISHING OF AN ESTABLISHMENT" (1973), *IBID.*

The new "theory of justice" [from philosopher John Rawls] demands that men counteract the "injustice" of nature by instituting the most obscenely unthinkable injustice among men: deprive "those favored by nature" (i.e., the talented, the intelligent, the creative) of the right to the rewards they produce (i.c., the right to life)—and grant to the incompetent, the stupid, the slothful a right to the effortless enjoyment of the rewards they could not produce, could not imagine, and would not know what to do with.

"AN UNTITLED LETTER" (1972), *IBID.*

It is at a time like this, in the face of an approaching economic collapse, that the intellectuals are preaching egalitarian notions. When the curtailment of government spending is imperative, they demand more welfare projects. When the need for men of productive ability is desperate, they demand more equality for the incompetents. When the country needs the accumulation of capital, they demand

that we soak the rich. When the country needs more savings, they demand a "redistribution of income." They demand more jobs and less profits—more jobs and fewer factories—more jobs and no fuel, no oil, no coal, no "pollution"—but, above all, more goods for free to more consumers, no matter what happens to jobs, to factories, or to producers.

"EGALITARIANISM AND INFLATION" (1974), *IBID.*

Ronald Wilson Reagan *(1911-)*

*T*he fortieth president of the United States and a former governor of California, Ronald Reagan has been known for his articulate expression of a belief in limited government, economic freedom, and personal responsibility. He is doubtless one of the most popular and charismatic conservative leaders of the twentieth century

I suggest to you there is no left or right, only an up or down. Up to the maximum of individual freedom consistent with law and order, or down to the ant heap of totalitarianism, and regardless of their humanitarian purpose, those who would sacrifice freedom for security have, whether they know it or not, chosen this downward path.

SPEECH, ELECTION-EVE, 1964

Today there is an increasing number who can't see a fat man standing beside a thin one without automatically coming to the conclusion the fat man got that way by taking advantage of the thin one.

IBID.

But the truth is that outside of its legitimate function, government does nothing as well or as economically as the private sector of the economy.

IBID.

The greatest good for the greatest number is a high-sounding phrase but contrary to the very basis of our Nation, unless it is accompanied by recognition that we have certain rights which cannot be infringed upon, even if the individual stands out-voted by all of his fellow citizens. Without this recognition, majority rule is nothing more than mob rule.

IBID.

It matters little that you hold the title to your property or business if govern-

ment can dictate policy and procedure and holds life and death power over your business. The machinery of this power already exists.

IBID.

This must be an agenda that opens the gates of freedom so all people can go as far as their God-given talents will take them. For every legal and economic action we consider, I ask: Will this serve to liberate and empower the individual; will it encourage us to reach for the stars, or will it weaken us and drag us down into submission and dependence?

ADDRESS TO THE AMERICAN BAR ASSOCIATION, ATLANTA, 1983

Let us have the courage to speak the truth: Policies that increase dependency and break up families are not progressive; they're reactionary, even though they are invariably promoted, passed, and carried out in the name of fairness, generosity, and compassion.

IBID.

We . . . must never turn our back on our basic industries—we will always need them. But neither must we attempt to prop up industries employing outmoded means of production. We must encourage our firms to retool and our workers to retrain. And we should allow market incentives to encourage the flow of resources—labor and capital—into modern methods of production and new industries.

RESPONSES TO QUESTIONS SUBMITTED BY *BUNTE MAGAZINE* (FEDERAL REPUBLIC OF GERMANY), 1983

The years ahead will be good ones for our country, for the cause of freedom, and for the spread of civilization. The West will not contain communism; it will transcend communism. It will not bother to denounce it; it will dismiss it. There is a sad, bizarre chapter in human history whose last pages are now being written.

COMMENCEMENT ADDRESS, NOTRE DAME, 1981

In an ironic sense Karl Marx was right. We are witnessing truly a great revolutionary crisis—crisis where demands of the economic order are colliding with those of the political order. But the crisis is happening not in the free, non-Marxist West, but in the home of Marxist-Leninism, the home of the Soviet Union . . . . What we see here is a political structure that no longer corresponds to its economic base, a society where productive forces are hampered by political ones.

ADDRESS TO THE BRITISH PARLIAMENT, JUNE 1982

This isn't a Keynesian Recovery produced by big-spending bureaucrats tinkering with aggregate demand. In fact, I don't know of a single Keynesian who predicted it. Instead, this recovery was created by the incentives of tax rate reductions, which shifted resources away from government back to American producers, savers, and investors.

SIGNING A MESSAGE TO CONGRESS, 1984

If we can control spending and shave a few points off the inflation rate, we can do more good for the poor, the elderly, and the finances of state and local government than any package of Federal programs ever could.

SIGNING DOCUMENTS TRANSMITTING BUDGET REVISIONS TO THE CONGRESS, 1981

We don't have a trillion dollar debt because we haven't taxed enough; we have a trillion dollar debt because we spend too much.

ADDRESS TO THE NATIONAL ASSOCIATION OF REALTORS, 1982

Why is it inflationary if the people keep their own money, and spend it the way they want to [but] not inflationary if the government takes it and spends it the way it wants to?

WHITE HOUSE RECEPTION FOR BUSINESS AND GOVERNMENT LEADERS, 1981

What specifics can be given to support the repeated charge that our tax cut favors the wealthy? Seventy-four percent of the tax savings goes to the lower- and middle-class who presently pay 72 percent of the tax. May I just say, in the request for economic literacy, high tax rates don't soak the rich, they only create more tax shelters or an outright capital drain. Reducing high tax rates provides incentives to get more people paying taxes again. Just as important, we preserve one of the few systems left on Earth where people at the bottom of the ladder can still get rich. That's what America should be all about. From now on, more of what people earn belongs to them.

ADDRESS TO THE CHAMBER OF COMMERCE OF THE UNITED STATES, 1982

The Soviet empire is faltering because it is rigid—centralized control has destroyed incentives for innovation, efficiency, and individual achievement. Spiritually, there is a sense of malaise and resentment.

ADDRESS, EUREKA COLLEGE, EUREKA, ILL., 1982

In the 1960s black unemployment fell from 10.7 percent to 6.4 percent. In the 1970s it increased from 6.4 percent to 11.3 percent. What is more, relative to the white unemployment rate, black unemployment fell more in the 1960s but rose more in the 1970s. The declining economy has cut black family income. From 1959 to 1969, the median family income of blacks, after adjusting for inflation, rose at 5 percent per year, but from 1969 to 1979, income actually dropped.

Now, these are hard economic facts which are hard to take, because they show massive amounts of government aid and intervention have failed to produce the desired results.

ADDRESS TO THE NATIONAL ASSOCIATION FOR THE ADVANCEMENT OF COLORED PEOPLE, DENVER, CO., 1981

The Government can provide subsistence, yes, but it seldom moves people up the economic ladder . . . . You have to get on the ladder before you can move up on it.

IBID.

I believe many in Washington, over the years, have been dedicated to making needy people government-dependent rather than independent. They've created a new kind of bondage, because regardless of how honest their intention in the beginning, those they set out to help soon became clients essential to the well-being of those who administered the program.

IBID.

Controlling crime in American society is not simply a question of more money, more police, more courts, more prosecutors; it's ultimately a moral dilemma, one that calls for a moral or, if you will, a spiritual solution . . . [I]n the end, the war on crime will only be won when an attitude of mind and a change of heart takes place in America, when certain truths take hold again and plant their roots deep in our national consciousness, truths like: right and wrong matters; individuals are responsible for their actions; retribution should be swift and sure for those who prey on the innocent.

ADDRESS TO THE INTERNATIONAL ASSOCIATION OF THE CHIEFS OF POLICE, NEW ORLEANS, LA., 1981

It's time to face the truth. Advocates of more and more government interference in education have had ample time to make their case, and they've failed. Look at the record. Federal spending on education soared eightfold in the last 20 years, rising much faster than inflation. But during the same period, scholastic aptitude test scores went down, down, and down.

ADDRESS, SETON HALL UNIVERSITY, SOUTH ORANGE, N.J., 1983

We support and endorse a program of tuition tax credits, so that our independent schools and our country as a whole will prosper. We need diversity and excellence. As economist Thomas Sowell has suggested, these tuition tax credits are especially important "to those who are mentioned the least: the poor and the working class." As the cost of education has skyrocketed, it is these groups that have been particularly hard hit by the double burden of supporting private and public schools.

And let me add here that far from being a threat to the public school system, these tax credits will serve only to raise the standards of the competing school systems. As a *New York Times* editorial pointed out recently, the mere threat of tax credits "served to jolt public education out of its lethargy. In New York and other places, public schools now show encouraging signs of improvement."

ADDRESS TO THE KNIGHTS OF COLUMBUS, 1982

The size of the Federal budget is not an appropriate barometer of social conscience or charitable concern.

ADDRESS TO THE NATIONAL ALLIANCE OF BUSINESS, 1981

It's time to reject the notion that advocating government programs is a form of personal charity. Generosity is a reflection of what one does with his or her own resources and not what he or she advocates the government to do with everyone's money.

ADDRESS TO THE CONCRETE AND AGGREGATE INDUSTRIES ASSOCIATIONS, CHICAGO, 1984

There is no institution more vital to our Nation's survival than the American family. Here the seeds of personal character are planted, the roots of public virtue first nourished. Through love and instruction, discipline, guidance and example, we learn from our mothers and fathers the values that will shape our private lives and our public citizenship.

PROCLAMATION 4845, FATHER'S DAY, 1981

You won't get gun control by disarming law-abiding citizens. There's only one way to get real gun control: Disarm the thugs and the criminals, lock them up, and if you don't actually throw away the key, at least lose it for a long time.

"SALUTE TO THE PRESIDENT" DINNER, LONG BEACH, CA., 1983

Ralph E. Reed, Jr. *(1961-)*

*R*alph Reed has served as executive director (since 1989) of the Christian Coalition, a one-million-member pro-family organization. He holds a Ph.D. in American history from Emory University (1991) and since 1976 has worked on several congressional and statewide campaigns to become one of the nation's leading grass-roots political strategists. Reed is the author of *Politically Incorrect* (1994).

The only true solution to crime is to restore the family. Young males raised in homes with male authority will emulate their fathers in marriage and procreation. Through their families, they will have a personal stake in creating a moral climate for their own children.

POLICY REVIEW, SUMMER 1993

The pro-family movement will realize many of its objectives if it can begin to speak to the issues that concern the voters. The Bible admonishes to "divide your portion to seven, or even to eight, for you do not know what misfortune may occur on the earth." Diversifying one's investments applies to political capital as well as financial capital. Building a political agenda around a single issue is a risky proposition, because when progress lags on that issue, as it inevitably will, the viability of the entire movement is threatened.

IBID.

Education is another issue that church-going voters view primarily through the eyes of their children. Many observers mistakenly believe that the abortion issue gave rise to the Religious Right. In fact the spark that ignited the modern pro-family movement was the fear of increased government regulation of church schools. When the government begins to threaten their children, evangelicals will pour into the civic arena like a flood, albeit reluctantly. The first goal of education policy should be to make schools safe . . . .

In part because of the breakdown in discipline in public schools, churchgoing voters strongly support choice in education.

IBID.

rights, which are the basis of political freedom, than about schemes to control traffic and housing developments; more concerned about freedom than in accomplishing social goals at the expense of freedom; more concerned about freedom than about some fool being corrupted by what he reads or sees.

Basically, what it means to be free is to be let alone. People have a right to be let alone. They have an obligation to leave others alone. They do not have a right to subsidies, to be liked or approved, or granted favors. Just let alone. Nor do they have an obligation to like, approve or grant favors to others. Just to leave them alone.

"FREEDOM DEMANDS BETTER PEOPLE," JULY 6, 1992

Charley Reese *(1937–)*

*C*harley Reese is a prominent syndicated columnist for King Features Syndicate.

A true son or daughter of the American Revolution will be more concerned about freedom than about making it easier for the police to catch criminals; more concerned about property

William Hubbs Rehnquist

(1924–)

*W*illiam Rehnquist replaced Warren Burger in September 1986 to become the sixteenth chief justice of the Supreme Court. He had clerked for Supreme Court Justice Robert Jackson (1952), was in private law practice in Phoenix (1953–1969), served as an assistant attorney general

(1969–1971), and became an associate justice of the Supreme Court in 1971.

The Supreme Court has on occasion been referred to as the conscience of the country, but I think this description has a considerable potential for mischief. If no more is meant by it than that the Supreme Court insofar as it upholds the principles of the Constitution is the conscience of the country, it is of course quite accurate. But the phrase is also subject to the more sweeping interpretation that the justices of the Supreme Court are to bring to bear on every constitutional question the moral principles found in each of their individual consciences. Yet to go beyond the language of the Constitution, and the meaning that may be fairly ascribed to the language, and into the consciences of individual judges, is to embark on a journey that is treacherous indeed. Many of us necessarily feel strongly and deeply about the judgments of our own consciences, but these remain only personal moral judgments until in some way they are given the sanction of supreme law.

THE SUPREME COURT, 1987

It has always seemed to me that [the] . . . presumption of constitutionality

makes eminent good sense. If the Supreme Court wrongly decides that a law enacted by Congress is constitutional, it has made a mistake, but the result of its mistake is only to leave the nation with a law duly enacted by the popularly chosen members of the House of Representatives and the Senate and signed into law by the popularly chosen president. But if the Supreme Court wrongly decides that a law enacted by Congress is not constitutional, it has made a mistake of considerably greater consequence; it has struck down a law duly enacted by the popularly elected branches of the government not because of any principle in the Constitution, but because of the individual views of desirable policy held by a majority of the nine justices at that time.

IBID.

Every time a claim of constitutional right is asserted by an individual or a group against a legislative act, the principle of majority rule and self-government is placed on one side of the judicial scale, and the principle of the individual right is placed on the other side of the scale. The function of the Supreme Court is, indeed, to hold the balance true between these weights in the scale, and not to consciously elevate one at the expense of the other.

IBID.

[F]ar more important than the fact that the Court has on occasion made rather demonstrable errors of both omission and commission . . . is the fact that it and the country have survived these mistakes and the Court as an institution has steadily grown in authority and prestige. In the light of the temptations that naturally beset any human being who becomes a judge of the Supreme Court, the truly remarkable fact is not that its members may have on infrequent occasions succumbed to these temptations, but that they have by and large had the good judgment and common sense to rise above them in the overwhelming majority of the cases they have decided.

IBID.

The framers of our system of government may indeed have built perhaps better than they knew. They wanted a Constitution that would check the excesses of majority rule, and they created an institution to enforce the commands of the Constitution. But wary of unchecked power in the judiciary as in all other branches of government, they gave the president with the consent of the Senate the power to appoint members of the Court, and the people by extraordinary majority the right to amend the Constitution. They limited

the Court to deciding actual cases and controversies that were brought before it, and they left it partially dependent upon the popularly elected branches of government for the enforcement of its mandates. Two hundred years of experience now tell us that they succeeded to an extraordinary degree in accomplishing their purpose.

IBID.

We cannot know for certain the sort of issues with which the Court will grapple in the third century of its existence. But there is no reason to doubt that it will continue as a vital and uniquely American institutional participant in the everlasting search of civilized society for the proper balance between liberty and authority, between the state and the individual.

IBID.

Paul Craig Roberts III *(1939–)*

*A*n economics educator and consultant, Paul Craig Roberts earned a doctorate in economics and taught economics at Virginia Polytechnic Institute and the University of New Mexico. He became the assistant secretary of treasury for economic policy in the Department of Treasury and has been the William E. Simon Professor of Political Economy at the Georgetown University Center for Strategic and International Studies. He has also been an adjunct scholar at the Cato Institute. His columns are nationally syndicated, and he is also a contributing editor to the *National Review*. His books include *Alienation and the Soviet Economy* (1971), *The Supply-Side Revolution* (1984), and *Meltdown: Inside the Soviet Economy* (1990).

February 7, 1990, marked a turning point in world history. On that day the Communist Party repudiated Article 6 of the Soviet Constitution and stripped itself of its monopoly on power. The same party conference endorsed the principle of private property. As stated in the party platform, "the C.P.S.U. believes the existence of individual property, including ownership of the means of production, does not contradict the modern stage in the country's economic development."

This shift signifies the end of the totalitarian state. Communism, said Soviet foreign minister Eduard Shevardnadze, "has been destroyed by the will of peoples who wished no longer to tolerate coercion." The communists learned that Leninism dissolved the natural conduits of society and made life irrational and inhumane. Voluntary society is reemerging in the Soviet Union. Under Gorbachev's encouragement, independent organizations are springing up; religion is encouraged; traditional morality is sanctioned; art, literature, and the media are regaining their independence; and Marxism is even being edited out of school textbooks. Another dictator could arise, but he would be a mere authoritarian, restrained by law and voluntary associations.

MELTDOWN: INSIDE THE SOVIET ECONOMY, 1990

The dream of Marxist utopia, which caused the deaths of millions in the 20th century, has been expelled from the Soviet Union. Its last refuge is in American church groups and academic faculties. Abandoned by a Soviet regime that is embracing the economic institutions and human values of Western civilization, our alienated intellectuals have no Marxist societies left to defend. It remains to be seen whether they will rediscover the virtues of a free society or become more fanatical in their attack on Western civilization.

IBID.

Whether in China, the Soviet Union, socialist Europe, statist America, or the government-devastated economies of the Third World, no one outside the ruling nomenklaturas any longer views government as the instrument of social progress . . . . The reemergence of private property and economic freedom out of communism is the greatest victory that liberal society has ever achieved.

IBID.

Whatever else it does, the demise of Marxism-Leninism will cause a renaissance in Western scholarship. For decades we have explained ourselves in terms of power, profit, and economic interests. Marx's view—that the character of individuals and the nature of society are determined by economic interests—permeates the study of history and society and has made almost every Western achievement and institution seem illegitimate. Moreover, to the extent that we have been influenced by them, the Marxian explanations have worsened our character as a people, because, as the old

saying goes, "a person becomes what he thinks he is."

Never before has the world seen such a privileged and powerful organization as the Communist Party of the Soviet Union. If material interests are the determining force in history, why is the Communist party giving up its own? Its consent to its own demise proves that good will can prevail over material interest; and this will revive idealistic explanations dismissed by Marx as fantasy. As our explanations of our free society become less denunciatory and more positive, the West will become a better example for those countries struggling to regain a humane existence.

IBID.

Marion Gordon (Pat) Robertson *(1930–)*

*C*hristian Broadcasting Network-founder Pat Robertson has been the host of the *700 Club* television show since 1968. He is also the founder of CBN University (now Regent

University). In the 1988 U.S. presidential campaign, Robertson ran for the Republican Party's nomination. He holds an M.Div. from New York Theological Seminary and a J.D. from Yale University Law School and is the author of such books as *The Secret Kingdom* (1982), *Answers to 200 of Life's Most Probing Questions* (1984), *The New World Order* (1990), and *The New Millenium* (1991).

"Can one be both Christian and Marxist?" There is no way that one can hold simultaneously to philosophies from God and the enemy of God. Marxism, at its base, is an atheistic system that has a view of history based solely on materialism. Marxism is in itself a religion, and it demands the allegiance of people everywhere. The Leninist model of Marxism demands allegiance at the point of a gun and the violent overthrow of legitimate governments.

ANSWERS TO 200 OF LIFE'S MOST PROBING QUESTIONS, 1984

It is ludicrous to think that Christianity can be believed along with a system that calls religion "the opium of the people" and a falsehood. In every instance where Marxists have taken control, they have suppressed the church. They have outlawed the Bible, forbidden the instruction of the young in religious values, and persecuted believers. Communists are always enemies of Christianity. Why the Western governments and many people still cannot see that, after all these years, is a mystery to me.

IBID.

"You cannot serve God and mammon." You cannot serve Christ and Belial, and there is no way a Christian can serve Jesus Christ and Karl Marx.

IBID.

Although capitalism can be abused and abusive, it is the economic system most conducive to freedom, most in accord with human nature, and most closely related to the Bible . . . .

. . . [T]he basis of free enterprise is very biblical. We read in the Old Testament that in the millennial time, everyone will sit under his own vine and under his own fig tree on his own property. There we have an idealized concept of the private ownership of property.

In the early days of our country, the Massachusetts Bay Colony attempted a primitive form of socialism. Land was owned jointly, everyone was to work together, and then the produce was to be divided to each according to his need.

This experiment failed miserably. The people began to starve to death because there was not enough incentive to work. It was only after the land was divided into acre plots and given to individual families that the people began to prosper. That was because they were now working for enlightened self-interest and giving to one another out of their increase.

God has given each human being a healthy personal self-interest. Jesus said, "You shall love your neighbor as yourself." This is something we all can relate to. There are few so altruistic that they will give up all they have produced for the good of other people. A person may love others as well as he loves himself, but he will not love them to the exclusion of himself.

IBID.

[T]he profit motive is *not* evil; it is a creative force. It is based on self-interest, to be sure, but from this has come technology, creativity, the tremendous explosion of the scientific method, and other things that have made our world a better place in which to live. The profit motive has also produced tremendous social initiatives that have provided millions of dollars to help the poor, to care for the sick and needy, and to build hospitals, schools, and charitable institutions.

Yes, unbridled capitalism must be restrained, or people will get too much money and too much power and will use it to oppress others. But at the same time, government must allow people the freedom to create, to own property, and to develop the potential God has placed within them.

IBID.

Murray Newton Rothbard

(1926–1995)

A prominent libertarian, Murray Rothbard wrote several essays and a number of books defending free markets and a minimal state. His works include *Man, Economy, and State* (2 vols., 1962), *Power and Market* (1970), *For a New Liberty* (1973), and *The Ethics of Liberty* (1982).

[C]ontrol of the police and the army is particularly important in enforcing and assuring all of the State's other powers, including the all-important power to extract its revenue by coercion.

For there is one crucially important power inherent in the nature of the State apparatus. *All other* persons and groups in society (except for acknowledged and sporadic criminals such as thieves and bankrobbers) obtain their income voluntarily: *either* by selling goods and services to the consuming public, *or* by voluntary gift . . . . *Only* the State obtains its revenue by coercion, by threatening dire penalties should the income not be forthcoming. That coercion is known as "taxation" . . . . Taxation is theft, purely and simply, even though it is theft on a grand and colossal scale which no acknowledged criminals could hope to match.

THE ETHICS OF LIBERTY, 1982

William Allen Rusher *(1923–)*

*P*ublisher of the *National Review* from 1957 to 1988, William Rusher has been a radio and television personality, a syndicated columnist, a professional lecturer, and a political activist. Educated at Princeton University and Harvard Law School, he served as associate counsel to the Senate Internal Security Subcommittee (1956–1957), chaired the American Conservative Union, served as a member of the National News Council (1973–1980), and became a senior fellow of the Claremont Institute for the Study of Statesmanship and Political Philosophy in 1989. His books include *The Making of the New Majority Party* (1975), *How to Win Arguments* (1981), *The Rise of the Right* (1984), and *The Coming Battle of the Media* (1988).

Reagan's victory can be said to mark the point at which the conservative movement achieved a political maturity equal to the intellectual maturity it already possessed. In one sense, it just doesn't matter whether conservatism wins or loses some particular future election: The point is that conservatism is unmistakably on the playing field at last, as one of the two major contestants. It has numerous candidates for public office eager to expound its views; it has seasoned political managers ready to manage their campaigns; it has formidable research institutions developing its analyses of every conceivable issue; it has "public interest" lawyers testing its contentions in the courts; it has columnists, radio and television commentators, and authors of all sorts, pleading its causes; and slowly but steadily young conservative journalists and academicians, in growing numbers that cannot be resisted forever, are entering and rising through those long-hostile ranks.

THE RISE OF THE RIGHT, 1984

Contemplating the generation of young conservatives that is coming along after my own, I am sometimes reminded of Ripley's dramatic formulation for the growth of the population of China: If the Chinese people were to march, four abreast, past a given point, they would march on forever.

IBID.

William Safire *(1929-)*

*N*ew York Times columnist William Safire has been a special assistant to President Nixon and a 1978 winner of the Pulitzer Prize. He is the author of such books as *Plunging Into Politics* (1964), *The New Language of Politics* (1968, 1979), *On Language* (1980), and *What's the Good Word?* (with Leonard Safir, 1982).

Economists and orators might ponder these Ten Commandments of profit:

1. *Thou shalt have no political gods before me.* No golden idols called "the public interest," dictated by elitist goo-goos, shall replace the individual decisions of people in the marketplace.

2. *Thou shalt keep the Sabbath day and other fringe benefits.* Corporations must remember that labor's profit is not only expressed in dollars but in job satisfaction and in more leisure time more creatively spent.

3. *Thou shalt not take the name of profits, thy system, in vain.* Before anybody denounces capitalism as the institutionalization of greed, he ought to consider with what other incentives—or coercion—it would be replaced.

4. *Honor thy father and mother, and other dependents, but not one food stamp to an able-bodied loafer.* Countercyclical benefits improve the free enterprise system, but when we remove incentives for productivity, we kill the goose that lays the golden eggs, which is not to be confused with a golden idol.

5. *Thou shalt not steal thy competitor's secrets, not kill his markets, nor covet his stockholders lists; neither shalt thou bribe local politicians nor pay off foreign customers,* as business morality varies from place to place and changes from time to time.

6. *Whosoever eschews risk shall forgo profit.* The businessman who seeks loan guarantees or wage and price controls should be driven from his corporate tent with shouts of "Abomination!"

7. *Thou shalt not adulterate thy product nor unduly pollute thy environment, nor fail to disclose thy every weakness* (nor continue to ten commandments when space permits but seven).

NEW YORK TIMES, FEB. 19, 1976

The lust to make money, the desire to get ahead, the shame of failure, the pride of achievement—this amalgam of motives, some of them ignoble, powers a system that produces more public good with personal freedom than any other.

That personal freedom is the political soul of our body politic. It is what the profit system puts first and what socialism—the nonprofit system—puts second, well after material things.

IBID.

George Santayana *(1863–1952)*

A poet and a philosopher, George Santayana taught philosophy at Harvard (1889–1912) and wrote several volumes of verse and philosophical works, including *The Life of Reason* (1905–1906), *Winds of Doctrine* (1913), *Character and Opinion in the United States* (1920), and *Soliloquies in England and Later Soliloquies* (1922).

Liberalism had been supposed to advocate liberty; but what the advanced parties that still call themselves liberal now advocate is control, control over property, trade, wages, hours of work, meat and drink, amusements . . . and it is only on the subject of marriage . . . that liberalism is growing more and more liberal.

WINDS OF DOCTRINE, 1913

Benevolence was one of the chief motives in liberalism in the beginning, and many a liberal is still full of kindness in his private capacity; but politically, as a liberal, he is something more than kind. The direction in which many, or even most, people would like to move fills him with disgust and indignation; he does not at all wish them to be happy, unless they can be happy on his own diet; and being a reformer and a philanthropist, he exerts himself to turn all men into the sort of men he likes, so as to be able to like them. It would be selfish, he thinks, to let people alone. They must be helped, and not merely helped to what they desire—that might really be very bad for them—but helped onwards, upwards, in the *right* direction.

CHARACTER AND OPINION IN THE UNITED STATES, 1920

The liberal system, which sought to raise the individual, has degraded the masses; and this on so vast a scale and to so pitiable a degree, that the other element in liberalism, philanthropic zeal, has come again to the fore. Liberty go hang, say the new radicals; let us save the people. Liberal legislation, which was to have reduced government to the minimum of police control, now has undertaken public education, social reform, and even the management of industry.

SOLILOQUIES IN ENGLAND AND LATER SOLILOQUIES, 1922

Ideal society is a drama enacted exclusively within our imagination.

THE LIFE OF REASON, 1905–1906

Antonin Scalia *(1936–)*

A justice on the Supreme Court of the United States, Antonin Scalia has an A.B. degree from Georgetown University (1957) and an L.L.B. degree from Harvard University (1960). From 1960 to 1967, he practiced law in Cleveland and then taught at the University of Virginia Law School. From 1971 to 1974, Scalia held some governmental positions, including head of the Justice Department's Office of Legal Counsel, and from 1977 to 1982, he taught at the University of Chicago Law School. He was a judge on the U.S. Court of Appeals (1982–1986) before being nominated associate justice by Ronald Reagan. Scalia is known for his erudition as well as his strict constructionist view of the Constitution, which places a premium on the exact wording of the Constitution and the "original intent" of its framers. Scalia believes strongly that his judicial philosophy minimizes the chance of his functioning as an unauthorized legislator.

There is nothing new in the realization that the Constitution sometimes insulates the criminality of a few in order to protect the privacy of all.

MAJORITY OPINION IN 6-3 RULING THAT REFUSED TO EXPAND POLICE POWERS TO SEARCH OR SEIZE EVIDENCE THAT IS THOUGHT STOLEN, MARCH 3, 1987

The Court today completes the process of converting [Title VII of the Civil Rights Act of 1964] from a guarantee that race or sex will not be the basis for employment determinations, to a guarantee that it often will.

<small>DISSENTING OPINION IN 6-3 RULING THAT EMPLOYERS MAY SOMETIMES FAVOR WOMEN AND MEMBERS OF MINORITIES OVER BETTER-QUALIFIED MEN AND WHITES IN HIRING AND PROMOTING IN ORDER TO ACHIEVE BETTER BALANCE IN THEIR WORK FORCES, MARCH 25, 1987</small>

Ever so subtly, without even alluding to the last obstacles preserved by earlier opinions that we now push out of our path, we effectively replace the goal of a discrimination-free society with the quite incompatible goal of proportionate representation by race and by sex in the workplace.

IBID.

Phyllis Stewart Schlafly (1924–)

*K*nown for her emphasis on the value of the family and tradition, Phyllis Schlafly has been an outspoken critic of many liberal causes, especially those espoused by some feminists. She is a lawyer and has written on a number of legal issues, such as the Equal Rights Amendment, from a conservative viewpoint. She writes a syndicated column and has written several books, including *The Betrayers* (1968) and *The Power of the Positive Woman* (1977). She has received ten honorary awards from the Freedoms Foundation, and has been voted one of the ten most admired women in the world in a *Good Housekeeping* poll.

The first requirement for the acquisition of power by the Positive Woman is to understand the differences between men and women. Your outlook on life, your faith, your behavior, your potential for fulfillment, all are determined by the parameters of your original premise. The Positive Woman starts with the assumption that the world is her oyster. She rejoices in the creative capability within her body and the power potential of her mind and spirit. She understands that men and women are different, and that those very differences provide the key to her success as a person and fulfillment as a woman.

THE POWER OF THE POSITIVE WOMAN, 1977

The women's liberationist . . . is imprisoned by her own negative view of herself and of her place in the world around her. This view of women was most succinctly expressed in an advertisement designed by the principal women's liberationist organization, the National Organization for Women, . . . and run in many magazines and newspapers as spot announcements on many television stations. The advertisement showed a darling curlyheaded girl with the caption: "This healthy, normal baby has a handicap. She was born female."

This is the self-articulated dog-in-the-manger, chip-on-the-shoulder, fundamental dogma of the women's liberation movement. Someone—it is not clear who, perhaps God, perhaps the "Establishment," perhaps a conspiracy of male chauvinist pigs—dealt women a foul blow by making them female. It becomes necessary, therefore, for women to agitate and demonstrate and hurl demands on society in order to wrest from an oppressive male-dominated social structure the status that has been wrongfully denied to women through the centuries.

IBID.

By its very nature . . . the women's liberation movement precipitates a series of conflict situations—in the legislatures, in the courts, in the schools, in industry—with man targeted as the enemy. Confrontation replaces cooperation as the watchword of all relationships.

Women and men become adversaries instead of partners.

IBID.

The Positive Woman spends her time, ingenuity, and efforts seizing her opportunities—not whining about past injustices.

IBID.

The real liberator of women in America is the free enterprise system, which has produced remarkable inventors who have lifted the drudgery of housekeeping from women's shoulders . . . .

. . . The American free enterprise system has stimulated inventive geniuses to pursue their talents with the knowledge that they could keep the fruits of their labor and ideas. All Americans reap the profits, but women most of all. The great heroes of women's liberation are not the straggly haired women on television talk shows and picket lines, but Thomas Edison, who brought the miracle of electricity to our homes to give light and to run all those labor-saving devices—the equivalent, perhaps, of a half-dozen household servants for every American woman. Or Elias Howe, who gave us the sewing machine that resulted in ready-made clothing. Or Clarence Birdseye, who invented the process for freezing foods. Or Henry Ford, who mass-produced the automobile so that it came within the price reach of every American, man or woman.

IBID.

A major occupation of women in other countries is doing their daily shopping for food, which requires carrying their own containers and standing in line at dozens of small shops. They buy only small portions because they can't carry very much and have no refrigerators or freezers to keep a surplus. Our American free enterprise system has given us the gigantic food and packaging industry and beautiful supermarkets, which provide an endless variety of foods, prepackaged for easy carrying, a minimum of waiting in line, and a minimum of cooking.

IBID.

The woman's allocation of career priorities necessarily limits the range of her financial return. There is no way, for example, that a married woman lawyer who puts in a forty-hour week or less and who opts out of her career for several years to have babies can ever earn the same income or achieve the same status in the professional world as a topflight lawyer, who typically devotes sixty hours a week to acquiring, serving, and retaining clients. There is nothing discrimina-

tory about this differential. It is simply a matter of personal choice based on the different scales of male and female values. The situation should not cause "remedial" legislation or court action to abolish "discrimination," or whining complaints about how few lawyers or judges are female, but a mature acceptance of the different goals of men and women.

IBID.

Supporting the Equal Rights Amendment is like trying to kill a fly with a sledge hammer. You don't kill the fly, but you end up breaking the furniture . . . . We cannot reduce women to equality. Equality is a step down for most women.

BOSTON GLOBE, JUNE 16, 1974

Robert Harold Schuller *(1926–)*

A minister of the Reformed Church in America and popular television evangelist, Robert Schuller graduated from Western Theological Seminary in 1943 and went on to host the *Hour of Power* television show (since 1970) and to write such positive works as *Move Ahead with Possibility Thinking* (1967), *Power*

Ideas for a Happy Family, (1971), *The Greatest Possibility Thinker that Ever Lived* (1973), and *Self-Esteem: The New Reformation* (1982).

The United States of America is in the gravest danger of falling from the spreading rot of social immorality. Moral character is the skeletal system of a personality, an individual, an institution, a nation.

When the Ten Commandments are violated, openly, you can expect collapse.

POWER IDEAS FOR A HAPPY FAMILY, 1971

What is morality? It is making a decision on what is *right*, not on what is *pleasurable*. The moral person never acts upon "What would I like to do?" rather on "What is the right thing to do?"

Teach your children morality and they will surely be successful persons.

IBID.

An inheritance is not a gift—it is a trust. A trust is something that is given to you to take care of and pass on to others . . . .

. . . Apply this principle of inheritance to your citizenship. You are a citizen of the United States of America; you have inherited the freedom to think and talk and work . . . . Assume your responsibility to keep your country alive by protecting it from dangers from without and within.

IBID.

Roger Scruton *(1944–)*

A British philosopher, Roger Scruton has written many books on many subjects, from art to sex, from politics to the philosophical thought of Kant and Spinoza. He wrote *The Meaning of Conservatism* (1980) and edited *Conservative Texts: An Anthology* (1991).

Conservatives are increasingly hostile . . . to the welfare state, arguing against its extension in broadly three ways. First, the idea of "social justice" on which the welfare state is founded—where social justice is supposed to be something other than charity, a "right" of the recipient rather than a virtue of the one who gives—seems to sponsor and condone a corruption of the moral sense. Secondly, the welfare state that is built upon this conception seems to move precisely away from the conservative conception of authoritative and personal government, towards a labyrinthine, privilege-sodden structure of anonymous power, nurturing a citizenship that is increasingly reluctant to answer for itself, increasingly void of personal responsibility, and increasingly parasitic on the dispensations of a bureaucracy towards which it can feel no gratitude.

The third argument—more familiar, perhaps, but of less central ideological concern—is that the welfare state promises more than it can provide, grows like a cancer in the economic order, and finally threatens the process of wealth-creation itself. If the lot of the poor is changed by the welfare state, it is because something else changes also— namely, the productive capacity upon which the welfare state depends, and which it also threatens to extinguish.

INTRODUCTION, *CONSERVATIVE TEXTS*, 1991

Hans F. Sennholz *(1922–)*

*G*erman-born Hans Sennholz, president of the Foundation of Economic Education, immigrated to the U.S. in 1949 and was naturalized in 1955. Holding doctorates both in political science and economics, Sennholz was

chair of the economics department at Grove City College, Pennsylvania, for thirty-seven years and has been a trustee for the Federation for Economic Education (F.E.E.) at Irvington-on-Hudson, New York, since 1969. (The F.E.E., which Sennholz chaired from 1982 to 1985, publishes data defending and explaining the virtues of the free market, private property, and limited government.) Sennholz contributed to the anthologies, *Gold is Money* (1975) and *The Morality of Capitalism* (1992), and has written several books, including *How Can Europe Survive?* (1955), *The Great Depression* (1969), *Age of Inflation* (1979), and *Money and Freedom* (1985).

Ethical statism is advancing slowly and steadily in the hearts and minds of many people and eroding their moral fiber. Many Americans now rate entitlement income and security more highly than individual freedom, self-reliance, and personal dignity. What they call "freedom" is more often than not merely license, arbitrariness, laziness, or political favor. Choice and decision-making are shifting from the individual, the family, and the group to political institutions. The power of government is growing, but the sense of community is dying. This is clearly visible in the activities of demagogues and lobbyists who are turning politics into a fine art of political burglary, channeling other people's income into the pockets of their favorite groups. All along, government is losing public esteem and moral authority, or worse, is becoming an object of contempt and corruption.

INTRODUCTION TO *THE MORALITY OF CAPITALISM*,
MARK HENDRICKSON, ED., 1992

Robert Sheaffer *(1949–)*

*R*obert Sheaffer has written articles for such diverse publications as *Astronomy*, the *Skeptical Inquirer*, and *Spaceflight*. He is the author of such books as *The UFO Verdict: Examining the Evidence* (1980) and *Resentment Against Achievement: Understanding the Assault upon Ability* (1988).

Socialism is that scheme that seeks to harness and exploit the superior achiever for the benefit of the inferior. Of course, the superior achiever seeks to escape this servitude if he can. Hence a "brain drain"

is suffered by partly socialist countries, while the Berlin Wall becomes a necessity where resentment's triumph has been complete . . . . When a society becomes mired in socialism, no class—neither rich nor poor—actually benefits. Achievers derive little advantage from their exertions and hence gradually stop trying, while the resentful find that there remains practically no achievement left in that society to exploit . . . .

RESENTMENT AGAINST ACHIEVEMENT, 1988

[W]hile we are fortunate that our political liberties remain largely intact, the once ironclad protection of property rights, which the Founding Fathers wrote into the Constitution, has been eroded by two centuries of covetous assault by the politics of resentment, turning what was once a magnificent edifice for the protection of achievement into a scheme for milking it. When achievement-oriented values prevail, people may keep what they hold and what they earn, except for a small self-assessed fee for the common defense against resentment, foreign and domestic. However, when we see achievers being milked like cows, it is a clear sign that proletarian theft-oriented values have infected the body politic.

IBID.

William Edward Simon (1927–)

*A*n investment banker and former secretary of the treasury
(1974–1977), William E. Simon holds a
B.A. in government and law from
Lafayette College and several honorary
degrees. Before becoming secretary of
the treasury, he was the administrator
(or "czar") of the Federal Energy Office
(1973–1974). His awards and honors,
which include the 1974 Outstanding
Citizen of the Year award, are so
numerous that they would take up an
entire page to list. An uncompromising
defender of capitalism and critic of governmental intervention in the economy,
Simon is the author of *A Time for Truth*
(1978) and *A Time for Action* (1980).

During my tenure at Treasury I
watched with incredulity as businessmen
ran to the government in every crisis,
whining for handouts or protection from
the very competition that had made this
system so productive . . . . And always,
such gentlemen proclaimed their devotion to free enterprise and their opposition to the arbitrary intervention into
our economic life by the state.

A TIME FOR TRUTH, 1978

[T]he reason for discussing economic
issues is not to inspire a national passion
for bookkeeping, but to inspire a
national awareness of the connection
between economic and political freedom. The conclusion is real and
unbreakable. To lose one is to lose the
other. In America we are losing both in
the wake of the expanding state. That
was my constant thesis as Secretary of
the Treasury . . . . There is no surer sign
of the danger we face than the fact that
so cardinal a truth—that the state itself
is a threat to individual liberty—should
be classified today as "controversial."

IBID.

I have . . . come to realize that of all
the aspects of political freedom guaranteed to us by our Constitution, freedom
of action—most particularly, freedom of
productive action or free enterprise—is
the least understood. For years, in
Washington, I have been watching the
tragic spectacle of citizens' groups, businessmen, politicians, bureaucrats, and
media people systematically laying waste
to our free enterprise system and our freedom even as they earnestly—and often
sincerely—proclaimed their devotion to
both. Again, this widespread incompre-
hension is largely due to the fact that
freedom of action, including freedom of

productive action, is simply a subdivision of freedom; it, too, is an *absence* rather than a *presence*—an absence of governmental constraint. By whatever name one wishes to call this category of free human action—free enterprise, the free market, capitalism—it simply means that men are free to produce. They are free to discover, to invent, to experiment, to succeed, to fail, to create means of production, to exchange goods and services, to profit, to consume—all on a voluntary basis without significant interference by the policing powers of the state. In the most fundamental sense, the right to freedom in this entire chain of productive action adds up to the right to life—for man, by his nature, is a being who must produce in order to live.

IBID.

The United States, in changing with relative speed into a social democracy, has undergone an alteration that is more fundamental than any other nation's. It has actually repudiated its own *identity* . . . . America was born a capitalist nation, was created a capitalist nation by the intent of its founders and the Constitution, and developed a culture and a civilization that were capitalist to the core. But this capitalist, or free enterprise, identity is true of no other nation. Only America

was invented from scratch by libertarian philosophers! . . . America *is* tied to its original political and economic arrangements because they were the *definition* of America. And an American who is hostile to individualism, to the work ethic, to free enterprise, who advocates an increasing government takeover of the economy or who advocates the coercive socialization of American life is in some profound sense advocating that America cease being America. He is advocating values that are not American and are philosophically antithetical to America itself.

IBID.

The actual number of federal programs for transferring producer's income to nonproducer's pockets [has] proliferated. In 1960, at the end of the Eisenhower years, there were approximately 100 federal programs. By 1963 there were 160 such programs. By 1976 there were more than 1000.

IBID.

Since the sixties the vast bulk of the regulatory legislation passed by Congress and the hundreds of thousands of elaborations in the forms of regulatory rulings have been largely initiated by a powerful new political lobby that goes by the name of the Public Interest movement. This movement represents neither of the conventional economic divisions of the past—*i.e.*, business or labor. It claims, instead, to speak only for the People and concentrates on the well-being of "consumers," "[the] environment," and "minorities." These terms, too, are chosen so that one cannot with any comfort challenge them. No one, after all, wishes to be perceived as hostile to such worthy entities. But the terms, on close examination, are meaningless: *Every* group in America, including business and labor, is the People; *everyone*, including the biggest producers, is a "consumer"; *everything* that exists, including factories, is the "environment"; and in America's pluralistic society *everyone* is a member of one or another "minority." What, then, are the real purposes of the various public interest groups? One discovers them readily enough if one identifies, not the fictitious entities for which they pretend to speak, but the actual groups which are their targets and which they seek to control through the power of the state. In practice, the target of the "consumer" movement is *business*, the target of the "environmentalists" is *business*, and the target of the "minorities," at least where employment is concerned, is *business*. In sum, the Public Interest movement is a lobby, not for the People, but for expanding police powers of the state over American producers. There have been few more consistently and vehemently anticapitalist groups in the history of America.

IBID.

The overriding principle to be revived in American political life is that which sets individual liberty as the highest political value.

IBID.

The ethics of egalitarianism must be repudiated. Achievers must not be penalized or parasites rewarded if we are to aspire to a healthy, productive and ethical society.

IBID.

Our government has not been warring on poverty; it has been creating poverty by attacking every value and every institution on which the generation of wealth depends.

IBID.

Protectionism is not patriotism. Protectionism is pure and total folly, because it always fails, always provokes retaliation, raises prices and wrecks economic growth.

"THE CHALLENGE FOR BUSINESS LEADERSHIP IN THE 90s,"
SPEECH IN HONOLULU, 1987

The genius of the capitalist system is that it is *not* based on the treasure of specific things like oil or gold, but on the treasure of *ideas*.

"THE ENTREPRENEURIAL SPIRIT,"
SPEECH, SIMON GRADUATE SCHOOL OF BUSINESS,
UNIVERSITY OF ROCHESTER, 1987

Once government dominates an economy to the point where it becomes the single, largest employer, consumer and borrower, it will inevitably control and imperil many of the personal decisions of its citizens.

SPEECH, TEMPLETON COLLEGE,
OXFORD UNIVERSITY, 1987

History is littered with the wreckage of countries which foolishly sought security by sacrificing their economic freedoms, only to see all their freedoms—economic, personal and political—buried in a common grave.

IBID.

Our nation's free enterprise system has given America the greatest prosperity, the highest standard of living, and most important, the greatest individual freedom in the history of mankind.

REMARKS AT THE GLANDEY CENTER, 1993

If America is so fearful that we bury our head in the sand today, then we will condemn our children to a world where freedom and prosperity are buried tomorrow.

"AMERICA AT THE CROSSROADS," SPEECH,
ADELPHI UNIVERSITY, 1992

[O]ur personal, political and economic freedoms are inextricably linked—and when nations permit their economic freedoms to disappear, their personal and political freedoms do not long survive.

IBID.

The countries today where growth rates are strongest, inflation the lowest and prosperity most secure are not those dominated by the heavy hand of government, but [those] invigorated by the incentives of low tax rates, rising competition, sound money and free trade.

IBID.

Let us remember the proper role of government—it's not to control our lives, but to create conditions for ours and the global economy to grow without inflation—for new jobs to be created, businesses to expand and people to produce, save and invest for their future, and their children's future.

IBID.

But permit government to continue exceeding [its] . . . mandate in the name of doing good—creating programs we cannot afford based on revenues that are not there, keeping tax rates on risk capital higher here than any other industrial nation—and we will end up hurting those who need help the most, impoverishing every taxpayer, fatally weakening the financial moorings of this country, and losing the very freedoms we hold most dear.

IBID.

Adam Smith *(1723–1790)*

A Scottish economist and professor of logic (1751) and of moral philosophy (1752–1764), Adam Smith won a reputation with his *Theory of Moral Sentiments* (1759). Smith established theories of division of labor, money, prices, wages, and distribution. His classic work, *Inquiry into the Nature and Causes of the Wealth of Nations* (1776), laid a foundation for a science of political economy and has exerted worldwide influence. His work is enormously important to conservatives, libertarians, and all defenders of liberty.

The property which every man has in his own labor, as it is the original foundation of all other property, so it is the most sacred and inviolable.

THE WEALTH OF NATIONS, 1776

Without any intervention of law, . . . the private interests and passions of men naturally lead them to divide and distribute the stock of every society, among all the different employments carried on in it, as nearly as possible in the proportion which is most agreeable to the interest of the whole society.

IBID.

It is not from the benevolence of the butcher, the brewer, or the baker, that we expect our dinner, but from their regard to their own interest.

IBID.

By preferring the support of domestic to that of foreign industry, he [every individual] intends only his own gain, and he is in this, as in many other cases, led by an invisible hand to promote an end which was no part of his intention. Nor is it always the worse for the society that it was no part of it. By pursuing his own interest, he frequently promotes that of the society more effectually than when he really intends to promote it. I have never known much good done by those who affected to trade for the publick good.

IBID.

There is no art which one government sooner learns of another than that of draining money from the pockets of the people.

IBID.

The market price of every particular commodity is regulated by the proportion between the quantity which is actually brought to market, and the demand of those who are willing to pay the natural price of the commodity or the whole value of the rent, labor and profit which must be paid in order to bring it thither.

IBID.

Every man, as long as he does not violate the laws of justice, is left perfectly free to pursue his own interest in his own way, and to bring both his industry and capital into competition with those of any other man, or order of man.

IBID.

The real price of everything, what everything really costs to the man who wants to acquire it, is the toil and trouble of acquiring it.

IBID.

Robert Anthony Snow *(1955–)*

*T*he director of speechwriting at the White House from 1991 to 1992, and deputy assistant for media affairs to the president from 1992 to 1993, Tony Snow has been a staff writer for several newspapers, including the *Greensboro Record*, *Virginian-Pilot*, *Detroit News*, and *Washington Times*. Since 1993, he has been a columnist for *USA Today*, a commentator for National Public Radio, and a frequent guest host on Rush Limbaugh's radio show.

Who creates the good life? Postwar liberalism advanced the notion that government fosters virtue and safeguards the blessings of liberty by assuming responsibility for the important things: job security, income, charity—even the connubial bliss of spotted owls.

But no one looks to government for moral regeneration anymore. Uncle Sam, revered as a great liberator during the civil-rights revolution, has become the great suffocator. Regulations grow like kudzu. Bureaucracies like the Environmental Protection Agency have given themselves to the dark arts of superstition and torture.

And millions of Americans have come to share our founders' understanding that big government is divisive, intrusive and endlessly expensive.

"DELIVERANCE," NOVEMBER 14, 1994

People don't want to turn the federal Leviathan over to management consultants. They want to send a wrecking ball swinging through the Washington establishment.

IBID.

[President] Clinton likes to console himself with comparisons to Harry Truman, who suffered a congressional massacre in 1946 only to win re-election in 1948. But Truman ran as a liberal just as the welfare state was beginning to take shape. Clinton, in contrast, finds himself dragging the corpse of Trumanism across the country at the precise moment Americans have lost their hunger for presidents who feel their pain.

IBID.

Joseph Sobran *(1946–)*

A long-time senior editor of the *National Review* and a con-

tributing editor to the *Human Life Review*, Joseph Sobran writes a column that is syndicated by Universal Press Syndicate. He has been a frequent contributor to the *Center Journal* (of the Center for Christian Studies at Notre Dame) and has written *The Conservative Manifesto* (1984) and *Single Issues* (1983).

The essence of the overclass [people who either work for the government or receive government grants or subsidies] is that we are forced to pay them whether we want their services or not. And when even the government decides they aren't needed, they resist layoffs and cutbacks with a fury. Nominally they may be public servants, but this hardly squares with their imperious attitude toward the public.

"WASHINGTON IS THE MECCA OF THE GREEDY,"
DEC. 5, 1991

Unlike private business, the overclass doesn't have to turn a profit or please the customers. Its responsibilities can be devilishly hard to pinpoint and there is simply no real test of its efficiency. Evasiveness is its hallmark. When private schools outperform public schools, for example, the overclass insists that this is only because the private schools serve a privileged clientele.

IBID.

Generally speaking, a man on the public payroll is a man whose services we could easily do without. There are exceptions (police and garbage collectors come to mind)[,] but this statement is far truer than it used to be. The very fact that the government pays him often means that nobody else would. Yet we don't call people "greedy" for expecting to be paid more than their market value. In fact we consider it desirable for the government to "create jobs" (with money that might otherwise have created jobs). But all the government can really create is an unproductive class of white-collar Bolsheviks.

IBID.

The difference between Wall Street and Washington can be summed up simply and vividly. If the stock market crashed, the whole country would be impoverished. But if the federal government suddenly went poof, most Americans would be immediately enriched. The only losers would be the overclass.

IBID.

Alexander Solzhenitsyn *(1918–)*

A Russian novelist and world-famous dissident, Alexander Solzhenitsyn described his labor camp experience in *One Day in the Life of Ivan Denisovich* (1962). He also wrote *The First Circle* and *Cancer Ward* (both 1968), as well as *August 1914* (1971) and *The Gulag Archipelago* (1973–76). He accepted the 1970 Nobel Prize for Literature by letter and when he was expelled from the Soviet Union and criticized Western decadence, he drew worldwide publicity.

I have spent my whole life under a Communist regime, and I will tell you that a society without any objective legal scale is a terrible one indeed. But a society with no other scale than the legal one is not quite worthy of man, either.

<small>COMMENCEMENT ADDRESS, HARVARD UNIVERSITY, 1978</small>

[I]t is time to remember that the first thing we belong to is humanity. And humanity is separated from the animal world by thought and speech and they should naturally be free. If they are fettered, we go back to being animals.

LETTER TO THE WRITERS' UNION, MOSCOW
QUOTED IN THE *NEW YORK TIMES*, NOV. 15, 1969

It is characteristic that Communism is so devoid of arguments that it has none to advance against its opponents . . . . Communism has never concealed the fact that it rejects all absolute concepts of morality, it scoffs at any consideration of "good" and "evil" as indisputable categories . . . . Communism is anti-humanity.

ADDRESS, AFL-CIO, NEW YORK CITY, JULY 1978

(1987), and *Compassion Versus Guilt and Other Essays* (1987).

"Equal opportunity" laws and policies require that individuals be judged on their qualifications as individuals, *without regard* to race, sex, age, etc. "Affirmative action" requires that they be judged *with regard* to such group membership, receiving preferential or compensatory treatment in some cases to achieve a more proportional "representation" in various institutions and occupations.

CIVIL RIGHTS: RHETORIC OR REALITY?, 1984

Thomas Sowell *(1930–)*

A highly influential black columnist, Thomas Sowell received a Ph.D. in economics from the University of Chicago (1968) and is a senior fellow at the Hoover Institution, Stanford University. Especially well known for his work on the economic movements of ethnic groups in the U.S. and other countries, he is the author of such books as *Ethnic America* (1981), *Civil Rights* (1984), *A Conflict of Visions*

Deep thinkers who look everywhere for the mysterious causes of poverty, ignorance, crime, and war need look no further than their own mirrors. We are all born into this world poor and ignorant, and with thoroughly selfish and barbaric impulses. Those of us who turn out any other way do so largely through the efforts of others, who civilized us before we got big enough to do too much damage to the world or ourselves. But for these efforts, we might well be on welfare or in the penitentiary.

We owe gratitude for those efforts,

not guilt for those who didn't get them. We certainly cannot make it up to those without values by easing standards and letting them become a burden and a threat to others.

Those who want to share their good fortune can share the sources of that good fortune—the skills, values, and discipline that mean productivity. Those who want to ease their burden of guilt should seek professional help, at their own expense—not make policy at everyone else's expense.

COMPASSION VERSUS GUILT AND OTHER ESSAYS, 1987

One of the curious features of the modern welfare state is how often its unskilled and so-called "menial" work is done by foreigners . . . . Despite much fashionable talk that suggests that today jobs are plentiful only for people with hi-tech skills, the cold fact is that thousands of poorly educated Mexicans cross the border every week and go right to work. How can people new to the country and its language constantly keep finding jobs that elude native-born Americans?

IBID.

[M]any of the deep thinkers in our universities, editorial offices, and social organizations talk as if people are "enti-

tled" to what others have worked for, and should not be forced to take "menial" jobs. It doesn't seem to bother them that others are forced to work to support the idle.

Welfare state spending is sold politically as "compassion" for the unfortunate. But these vast expenditures do not protect people from hunger so much as they protect their egos from having to earn their own food by doing whatever work matches their capabilities . . . .

. . . The real culprits are those who created a system that makes it dangerous to work and safe to loaf, those who have turned honest work into a shame and made being a parasite respectable.

Such labels as "menial" and "dead-end" jobs disparage the very necessary work of keeping things clean, growing food, or tending children. For young workers especially, the things you can learn on such jobs—responsibility, cooperation, punctuality—can be lifelong assets in many other occupations. Insulating people from such realities is one of many cruelties perpetrated under the banner of compassion.

IBID.

Wherever the government sets prices below the market level, shortages are virtually guaranteed. It may take the form of gasoline lines, as it did in the 1970s here, food lines as in Eastern Europe, waiting lists for automobiles in India, or interminable searches for apartments in cities with rent control—whether in America, Europe or Asia. Government-imposed prices created shortages under the Emperor Diocletian in the days of the Roman Empire. Prices imposed to make food "affordable" to the masses created widespread hunger instead when the French did it in the 1790s, when the Russians did it after the Bolshevik Revolution, and in numerous African countries in our own time.

IBID.

The classic rule of propaganda is that people will believe any lie, if it is repeated often enough, loud enough, and long enough. One of the major "facts" of our time has been created in this way—the claim that a woman receives only 59 percent of what a man receives for doing the same work.

. . . Among people who remain single, women earn 91 percent of the income of men. Nor can the other 9 percent automatically be called "discrimination." There are physically demanding and well-paid fields that women seldom enter—mining, lumberjacking and con-

struction work, for example. There are other well-paying fields that require a mathematics background that most women do not have . . . .

Married women are far more likely to work part-time, to stop working altogether for various periods of time, or to take jobs whose hours and duties do not conflict with their responsibilities at home—even if these are not the highest paying jobs they could get . . . .

While married women work less than single women, especially when there are children, married men work more than single men—also especially when there are children . . . . The net result is that there are huge differences between the incomes of married women and married men . . . .

. . . As women began having more babies, they began having fewer high-level careers. When the birth rate began to fall in the 1960s, women's representation rose in many high-level fields.

IBID.

Herbert Spencer *(1820–1903)*

*E*nglish philosopher Herbert Spencer first came to prominence when he wrote *Social Statics* (1851), in which he advocated individualism.

Thereafter Spencer applied the doctrine of evolution to sociology and wrote a number of works, including *Principles of Ethics* (1892, 1893) and *The Man versus the State* (1884).

An argument fatal to the communist theory, is suggested by the fact . . . that a desire for property is one of the elements of our nature.

SOCIAL STATICS, 1851

Liberty of each, limited by the like liberties of all, is the rule in conformity with which society must be organized.

IBID.

Feudalism, serfdom, slavery, all tyrannical institutions, are merely the most vigorous kind of rule, springing out of, and necessary to, a bad state of man. The progress from these is in all cases the same—less government.

IBID.

A man's liberties are none the less aggressed upon because those who coerce him do so in the belief that he will be benefited.

IBID.

Society exists for the benefit of its members; not the members for the benefit of society.

PRINCIPLES OF ETHICS, 1892, 1893

All socialism involves slavery.

THE MAN VERSUS THE STATE, 1884

Lysander Spooner *(1808–1887)*

A libertarian lawyer, Lysander Spooner was an ardent individualist who strongly condemned slavery, as in his abolitionist book, *The Unconstitutionality of Slavery* (1845). He not only wrote essays defending a minimal state but also lived his convictions, as when he rejected the government's monopoly of the mails by establishing an independent postal service from Boston to New York—at a lower price than the government rate. Although he was compelled to retire from that undertaking because of government prosecution, Spooner's efforts did result in lower government rates.

Constitutions are utterly worthless to restrain the tyranny of governments, unless it be understood that the people will by force compel the government to keep within constitutional limits. Practically speaking, no government knows any limits to its power except the endurance of the people.

AN ESSAY ON THE TRIAL BY JURY, 1852

All restraints upon man's natural liberty, not necessary for the simple maintenance of justice, are of the nature of slavery, and differ from each other only in degree.

IBID.

Shelby Steele *(1946–)*

A black critic of the civil rights establishment, Shelby Steele is an English professor who strongly rejects the proposition that race, class, religion, and even law can fully deprive people of either individual choice or moral obligations. He is particularly well known for the highly acclaimed book, *The Content of Our Character* (1990), which is a collection of his essays.

Personal responsibility is the brick and mortar of power. The responsible person knows that the quality of his life is something that he will have to make inside the limits of his fate. Some of these limits he can push back, some he cannot, but in any case the quality of his life will pretty much reflect the quality of his efforts. When this link between well-being and action is truly accepted, the result is power. With this understanding and the knowledge that he is responsible, a person can see his margin of choice. He can choose and act, and choose and act again, without illusion. He can create himself and make himself felt in the world. Such a person has power.

THE CONTENT OF OUR CHARACTER, 1990

James Fitzjames Stephen

(1829–1894)

A famous English judge, James Stephen wrote *General View of the Criminal Law of England* (1863), the first attempt made since that of Blackstone to explain the principles of English law. He also wrote *Liberty, Equality, Fraternity* (1873) and *History of the Criminal Law* (1883).

Philanthropic pursuits have many indisputable advantages, but it is doubtful whether they can be truly said to humanize or soften the minds of those who are most addicted to them . . . . The grand objection to them all is that people create them for themselves . . . . Benevolence is constantly cultivated by philanthropists at the expense of modesty, truthfulness, and consideration for the rights and feelings of others; for by the very fact that a man devotes himself to conscious efforts to make other people happier and better than they are, he asserts that he knows better than they what are the necessary constituent elements of happiness and goodness. In other words, he sets himself up as their guide and superior.

"DOING GOOD" (1859) IN *LIBERTY, EQUALITY, FRATERNITY*, 1873

Leo Strauss *(1899–1973)*

*A*n educator and author, Leo Strauss earned a doctorate from the University of Hamburg in 1921. He left Germany in 1938 to come to the United States, where he was naturalized in 1944. Strauss was a lecturer and an associate professor of political science and philosophy at the New School for

Social Research in New York City (1938–1948) and a professor of political philosophy at the University of Chicago (1949–1968). He wrote such books as *The Political Philosophy of Hobbes* (1936), *On Tyranny* (1950), *Natural Right and History* (1950), *Persecution and the Art of Writing* (1952), *What Is Political Philosophy?* (1959), *The City and Man* (1964), and *Liberalism[:] Ancient and Modern* (1968).

"We hold these truths to be self-evident, that all men are created equal, that they are endowed by their Creator with certain unalienable Rights, that among these are Life, Liberty, and the pursuit of Happiness." . . . Does this nation in its maturity still cherish the faith in which it was conceived and raised? Does it still hold those "truths to be self-evident?" About a generation ago, an American diplomat could still say that "the natural and the divine foundation of the rights of man . . . is self-evident to all Americans." At about the same time a German scholar could still describe the difference between German thought and that of Western Europe and the United States by saying that the West still attached decisive importance to natural right, while in Germany the very terms "natural right" and "humanity" "have now become almost incomprehensible . . . and have lost altogether their original life and color." . . . What was a tolerably accurate description of German thought twenty-seven years ago would now appear to be true of Western thought in general.

NATURAL RIGHT AND HISTORY, 1950

Liberal relativism has its roots in the natural right tradition of tolerance or in the notion that everyone has a natural right to the pursuit of happiness as he understands happiness; but in itself it is a seminary of intolerance.

IBID.

[A]bsolute tolerance is altogether impossible; the allegedly absolute tolerance turns into ferocious hatred of those who have stated clearly and most forcefully that there are unchangeable standards founded in the nature of man and the nature of things.

LIBERALISM[:] ANCIENT AND MODERN, 1968

William Graham Sumner

(1840–1910)

---

*A*n American economist and sociologist and a professor of politi-cal and social science at Yale (1872–1910), William Graham Sumner was a strong advocate of free trade, sound currency, and laissez-faire capitalism. He wrote a number of influential essays, many of which are included in *The Forgotten Man and Other Essays* (1919). Sumner also wrote a number of books, including *A History of American Currency* (1874), *What Social Classes Owe to Each Other* (1883), and *Folkways* (1907).

The type and formula of most schemes of philanthropy or humanitarianism is this: A and B put their heads together to decide what C shall be made to do for D. The radical vice of all these schemes . . . is that C is not allowed a voice in the matter . . . . I call C the Forgotten Man.

WHAT SOCIAL CLASSES OWE TO EACH OTHER, 1883

We must not overlook the fact that the Forgotten Man is not infrequently a woman.

IBID.

Rights should be equal, because they pertain to chances, and all ought to have equal chances so far as chances are provided or limited by the action of society.

This, however, will not produce equal results, but is right just because it will produce unequal results—that is, results which shall be proportioned to the merits of individuals.

IBID.

It is an especially vicious extension of ... false doctrine ... that criminals have some sort of a right against or claim on society.

IBID.

The men who have not done their duty in this world never can be equal to those who have done their duty more or less well. If words like wise and foolish, thrifty and extravagant, prudent and negligent, have any meaning in language, then it must make some difference how people behave in this world.

IBID.

The danger of minding other people's business is twofold. First, there is the danger that a man may leave his own business unattended to; and, second, there is the danger of an impertinent interference with another's affairs. The "friends of humanity" almost always run into both dangers. I am one of humanity, and I do not want any volunteer friends. I regard friendship as mutual, and I want to have my say about it.

IBID.

There is a sense in which it may be said that it is easy to provide a precept for the abolition of poverty. Let every man be sober, industrious, prudent, and wise, and bring up his children to be so likewise, and poverty will be abolished in a few generations. If it is answered that men, with the best intentions, cannot fulfill this precept, because they make innocent mistakes, and fall into errors in judgment, then the demand is changed, and we are not asked for a means of abolishing poverty, but for a means of abolishing human error. If it be objected, again, that sober, industrious, and prudent men meet with misfortune, then the demand is for a means of abolishing misfortune.

ESSAYS, 1934, VOL. I

We are told what fine things would happen if every one of us would go and do something for the welfare of somebody else; but why not contemplate also the immense gain which would ensue if everybody would do something for himself?

IBID.

Wherever collective standards, codes, ideals, and motives take the place of individual responsibility, we know from ample experience that the spontaneity and independent responsibility which are essential to moral vigor are sure to be lost.

IBID.

When we are told that the state would do all things better, if we would give it more things to do, the answer is that there is nothing which the state has not tried to do, and that it has only exceptionally performed anything well, even war or royal marriages.

IBID., II

The reason why I defend the millions of the millionaire is not that I love the millionaire, but that I love my own wife and children, and that I know no way in which to get the defense of society for my hundreds, except to give my help, as a member of society, to protect his million.

IBID., I

If this country, with its population, its resources, and its chances, is not prosperous by the intelligence, industry, and thrift of its population, does any sane man suppose that politicians and stump orators have any devices at their control for making it so?

IBID., II

The way to minimize the dangers to democracy, and from it, is to reduce to the utmost its functions, the number of its officials, the range of its taxing power, the variety of its modes of impinging on the individual, the amount and range of its expenditures, and, in short, its total weight.

IBID.

[W]e should regard . . . every cent of tax as needing justification . . . . All taxation, beyond what is necessary for an economical administration of good government, is either luxurious or wasteful.

IBID.

We are born into no right whatever but what has an equivalent and corresponding duty right alongside it. There is no such thing on this earth as something for nothing. Whatever we inherit of wealth, knowledge, or institutions from the past has been paid for by the labor and sacrifice of preceding generations.

IBID., I

Responsibility rises up by the side of liberty, correlative, commensurate, and inevitable.

IBID.

The notion is accepted as if it were not open to any question that if you help the inefficient and vicious you may gain something for society or you may not, but that you lose nothing. This is a complete mistake. Whatever capital you divert to the support of a shiftless and good-for-nothing person is so much diverted from some other employment, and that means from somebody else. I would spend any conceivable amount of zeal and eloquence if I possessed it to try to make people grasp this idea.

IBID.

It is especially incompatible with our form of democratic republic to charge the state with many and various functions, for our state should be simple to the last possible degree. It should handle as little money as possible; it should encourage the constant individual activity of its citizens and never do anything to weaken individual initiative. But the tendency to-day is all the other way.

IBID., II

Now, who is the Forgotten Man? He is the simple, honest laborer, ready to earn his living by productive work. We pass him by because he is independent, self-supporting, and asks no favors. He does not appeal to the emotions or excite the sentiments. He only wants to make a contract and fulfill it, with respect on both sides and favor on neither side.

IBID., I

Such is the Forgotten Man. He works, he votes, generally he prays—but he always pays—yes, above all, he pays . . . . He is the clean, quiet, virtuous, domestic citizen, who pays his debts and his taxes and is never heard out of his little circle. Yet who is there in the society of a civilized state who deserves to be remembered and considered by the legislator and statesman before this man?

IBID.

Charles J. Sykes *(1954–)*

A stalwart defender of personal responsibility and an enemy of political correctness, Charles Sykes has written *Profscam: Professors and the Demise of Higher Education* (1988), *The Hollow Men: Politics and Corruption in Higher Education* (1990), and *A Nation of Victims: The Decay of the American Character* (1992). He has also written the *National Review College Guide* (1991).

The politicized culture of victimization often confuses difference with inequity and oppression, while common sense reminds us that difference is often, well, just being different. Most of us can discern between making a mistake and being victimized; between excelling and oppressing someone. All of us experience unfairness and injustice, but that does not mean we need to turn them into all-purpose alibis.

Most important, our common sense, and the human tradition it reflects, reminds us that we are all fallible, all beset with human foibles and limitations. Any movement that fails to take those into account, or that overlays our frailties and our humanity with ideology, misunderstands what our lives are about—and diminishes us as human beings. Ultimately, common sense is the stumbling block that victimism may not be able to overcome. At some level of our being, we all know that something is required of us, however much we may try to shake it off. Instinctively and rationally, we know our responsibilities; we know that we are not sick when we are merely weak; we know that others are not to blame when we have erred; we know that the world does not exist to make us happy.

A Nation of Victims, 1992

Thomas S. Szasz *(1920–)*

*H*ungarian by birth, Thomas Szasz moved to the United States in 1938, where he earned a medical degree (1944). A libertarian psychiatrist, he has won many awards and honors and also provoked much controversy, as by his second book, *The Myth of Mental Illness* (1961). Szasz has written over 20 books, has argued for a minimal government, and has opposed psychiatric coercion and attenuation of personal responsibility. In 1990, a collection of his thoughts—*The Untamed Tongue*—was published.

The proverb warns that "You should not bite the hand that feeds you." But perhaps you should, if it prevents you from feeding yourself.

THE UNTAMED TONGUE, 1990

Formerly, men wanted to *do* a good job; from that desire arose craftsmanship. Today, they *want* a good job; from that desire arise unions and affirmative action programs.

IBID.

If you don't value your family, you will not have a family that values you. If you don't value money or health or liberty, you will have no money or health or liberty. If you don't value knowledge and competence and self-reliance, no one, including yourself, will value you—and no amount of psychiatric treatment will remedy your failure to value what is worthy.

IBID.

Cal Thomas *(1942–)*

A columnist for the Los Angeles Times Syndicate and host of a television talk show on CNBC, Cal Thomas was with NBC-TV News from 1973 to 1977. He has won the AMY Writing Award and AP and UPI Spot News Awards. A strong advocate of traditional values, he is the author of *Public Persons and Private Lives: Intimate Interviews* (1979), *Uncommon Sense* (1990), and *Things That Matter Most* (1994).

The country must not be stampeded into another round of spending on programs that don't work. We should regu-larly reassess race relations and reach out to minorities to help them with their special problems. But their biggest problem is not lack of money, it is lack of family. No federal program will have a greater impact on crime and other antisocial behavior than the return of the black man as husband to his wife and father to his children. Since 1965, the number of out-of-wedlock births has more than tripled. It is now a cliché that more young black men are in prison than in college.

Lawrence Mead of New York University has observed, "What matters for success is less whether your father was rich or poor than whether you knew your father at all." Nothing will substitute for or have the same effect in the rearing of a child than a man who keeps his promises to his wife and loves his children.

"VIOLENCE WASN'T ABOUT CIVIL RIGHTS," MAY 7, 1992

Clarence Thomas *(1948–)*

A U.S. Supreme Court associate justice (since 1991), Clarence Thomas received his J.D. from Yale University (1974) and went on to serve as an assistant to the attorney general of

Missouri (1974–1977), legislative assistant to Senator John C. Danforth (1979–1981), assistant secretary for civil rights at the Department of Education (1981–1982), chair of the Equal Employment Opportunity Commission (1982–1990), and a judge of the U.S. Court of Appeals (1990–1991).

There is a tendency among young upwardly mobile, intelligent minorities today to forget. We forget the sweat of our forefathers. We forget the blood of the marchers, the prayers and hope of our race. We forget who brought us into this world. We overlook who put food in our mouths and clothes on our backs. We forget commitment to excellence . . . . We subdue, we seduce, but we don't respect ourselves, our women, our babies. How do we expect a race that has been thrown into the gutter of socio-economic indicators to rise above these humiliating circumstances if we hide from responsibility for our own destiny?

SAVANNAH STATE COLLEGE, JUNE 9, 1985

I was raised to survive under the totalitarianism of segregation, not only without the active assistance of government but with its active opposition. We were raised to survive in spite of the dark oppressive cloud of governmentally sanctioned bigotry. Self-sufficiency and spiritual and emotional security were our tools to carve out and secure freedom. Those who attempt to capture the daily counseling, oversight, common sense, and vision of my grandparents in a governmental program are engaging in sheer folly. Government cannot develop individual responsibility, but it certainly can refrain from preventing or hindering the development of this responsibility.

THE HERITAGE FOUNDATION, JUNE 18, 1987

I often felt that the media assumed that, to be black, one had to espouse leftist ideas and Democratic politics. Any black who deviated from the ideological litany of requisites was an oddity and was to be cut from the herd and attacked. Hence, any disagreement we had with black Democrats or those on the Left was exaggerated. Our character and motives were impugned and challenged by the same reporters who supposedly were writing objective stories. In fact, on numerous occasions, I have found myself debating and arguing with a reporter, who had long since closed his notebook, put away his pen, and turned off his tape recorder.

IBID.

Without . . . a notion of natural law, the entire American political tradition, from Washington to Lincoln, from Jefferson to Martin Luther King, would be unintelligible. According to our higher law tradition, men must acknowledge each other's freedom, and govern only by the consent of others. All our political institutions presuppose this truth. Natural law of this form is indispensable to decent politics. It is the barrier against the "abolition of man" that C. S. Lewis warned about in his short modern classic.

This approach allows us to reassert the primacy of the individual, and establishes our inherent equality as a God-given right.

IBID.

Walden, or Life in the Woods (1854). His famous essay, *Civil Disobedience* (1849), advocated peaceful opposition to unjust laws. From his journals, letters, and manuscripts, his friends published *The Writings of Henry David Thoreau* (20 vols., 1906).

I heartily accept the motto, "That government is best which governs least"; and I should like to see it acted up to more rapidly and systematically. Carried out, it finally amounts to this, which also I believe— "That which is best which governs not at all"; and when men are prepared for it, that will be the kind of government which they will have.

CIVIL DISOBEDIENCE, 1849

Henry David Thoreau *(1817–1862)*

*O*ne of America's most famous individualists, Henry David Thoreau graduated from Harvard, taught school in Concord, Massachusetts, and often associated with Ralph Waldo Emerson, in whose home Thoreau lived for a few years. Although he was a prolific writer, he published only two books, namely, *A Week on the Concord and Merrimack Rivers* (1849) and

Alexis Charles Henri Maurice Clérel de Tocqueville *(1805–1859)*

*F*rench political thinker Alexis de Tocqueville is admired for his concern for personal freedom, fear of majoritarian tyranny, and desire for limited government. He wrote the classic *Democracy in America* (2 volumes, 1835, 1840).

Americans are so enamored of equality that they would rather be equal in slavery than unequal in freedom.

DEMOCRACY IN AMERICA, 1835

The nations of our time cannot prevent the conditions of men from becoming equal; but it depends upon themselves whether the principle of equality is to lead them to servitude or freedom, to knowledge or barbarism, to prosperity or to wretchedness.

IBID.

Within these limits the power vested in the American courts of justice of pronouncing a statute to be unconstitutional forms one of the most powerful barriers that have ever been devised against the tyranny of political assemblies.

IBID.

In order to enjoy the inestimable benefits that the liberty of the press ensures, it is necessary to submit to the inevitable evils that it creates.

IBID.

The man who asks of freedom anything other than itself is born to be a slave.

THE OLD REGIME AND THE FRENCH REVOLUTION, 1856

You defend the conservative principles on which our ancient system of society in Europe is founded, and the liberty and the individual responsibility attendant upon it; you defend especially the institution of property. You are quite right; you can hardly conceive life without these primary laws . . . .

LETTER TO MRS. GROTE, JULY 24, 1850

R. Emmett Tyrrell, Jr. *(1943–)*

R. Emmett Tyrrell, Jr., is the founder and editor-in-chief of *American Spectator*. Known for his witty, sardonic style, he is the author of *The Liberal Crack-Up* (1984), *The Conservative Crack-Up* (1992), and other books.

Liberalism's most deeply held political value—in fact its only steadfastly observed political value—is that item mentioned early in most criminal codes, to wit, the misdemeanor of disturbing the peace. This explains the peculiarity of Liberal tolerance, which is almost never extended across the board but almost always extended to those fantasticos further to the left of Liberalism. Tolerating leftist zanies is tremendously disturbing to ordinary Americans; ipso facto Liberals tolerate them chivalrously and go aflutter over their every wild-eyed scheme.

THE CONSERVATIVE CRACK-UP, 1992

Liberalism has elevated disturbing the peace to the level of a metaphysical imperative. A review of nearly a century of Liberal policy reveals Liberals undertaking many ambitious projects and promoting a multitude of humane values only to revise these projects and values once the bourgeoisie no longer objects. Thus the Liberal tolerates talk of a guaranteed annual income, and if that does not shake up the guy next door the Liberal thumps for the system of taxation favored by the late Mao Tse-tung. The Liberal favored a color-blind society, then black militancy, then quotas. He will support nudity on the beach and, once the bourgeoisie acquiesces to nudity on the beach, he will urge it in the shopping mall or across the street from the old people's retirement home.

IBID.

Critical as I am of the Liberalism of the New Age and of those Liberals who would not resist the New Age, I have always willingly admitted that the earlier liberalism of the New Deal had comprehensible and even defensible ideas. What is more, its proponents had the courage to defend them. They believed in the planned society. They believed in Keynesian economics and progressive education. They believed that social problems were susceptible to social reforms. Possibly, as my grandfathers always insisted, these ideas were erroneous and corrupting; but they were at least arguable.

By the 1980s, however, Liberals had been seduced ever further towards the left—that is to say towards the infantile, self-absorbed left of the New Age. Had they been candid, the Liberals of the New Age would have declared themselves socialists, so atrophied was their regard for property rights and so vast had become their vision of state power. They agreed with most of socialism's propositions. They were in open sympathy with socialists all over the world (even violent socialists). Yet not many New Age Liberals ever came right out and called themselves socialists.

IBID.

As political systems go, socialism was too exacting for the child of the New Age. Socialism required action, decisiveness, resistance to vested interests, the cracking of a few heads every now and then. It demanded active governance, and the only act of governance that the New Age Liberal was capable of was raising taxes. He believed in taxing the middle class to the utmost reaches of the tolerable, though even here he was tentative. He denoted the middle class as "the rich" and he preferred to tax them surreptitiously through tax bracket creep. To Liberals in the New Age, reality could be fudged. Words, it was presumed, had no consequences beyond their idiotic music and actions were but empty poses. Ideas became vaporous collections of complaints . . . . In the 1980s Liberals and neoliberals did not truly believe in much of anything other than personal advancement.

IBID.

By the 1970s American Liberalism had become distinctive for petulance, moral preciousness, and an amplitude of exigent causes, most of which have been comic when not downright pernicious. In a review of New Age Liberal writing the English political philosopher Maurice Cranston notes that American Liberalism has transformed itself into a kind of girlish socialism fraught with a multitude of contradictions.

THE LIBERAL CRACK-UP, 1984

However we may judge it, all civilized observers will agree that Liberalism lacks coherence and no longer follows such maxims as David Spitz laid down for it in *The Real World of Liberalism:* "Esteem liberty above all other values," he wrote in the late 1970s, "even over equality and justice." Then he died. Had Spitz lived he would have grimly joined the cause to "desex" English or some such New Age fanaticism, or he would have been marked down as a Black Shirt. Now Liberalism was juddering along the path foreseen for it long ago by Kenneth Minogue in that wise and eloquent book, *The Liberal Mind.* New Age Liberalism was by the 1970s obsessed with searching out what Minogue called "suffering situations"— that is to say the aggrieved: aggrieved classes, aggrieved sexes, and the aggrieved in such idiotic categories as flora (rights for trees!) and fauna (farm animals! laboratory animals! the Hollywood Ten!).

IBID.

The socialist theory is a fable. The socialist reality is a very uncomfortable place to live: political tyrants having replaced the bosses of yore; coercion having vanquished liberty; shortages and want having replaced economic growth and self-reliance. Greed remains, but long ago it was surpassed in popularity and maliciousness by envy. Where there once was optimism there is now pessimism. The citizen who once hoped to be an entrepreneur now queues up like everyone else for a new pair of socks or a feast of moldy state-issued potatoes.

IBID.

Wherever socialism has slithered into power there is either unspeakable cruelty or slow economic decomposition. Russia, the Socialist Motherland, offers its citizens both. The decrepitude of Britain, upon whose wealth the sun could not set four decades ago, is evidence of socialism's knack for despoiling an economy. More recently we have witnessed the amazing impoverishment of Germany under the Social Democrats and the almost instantaneous economic collapse of France's theretofore robust economy under François Mitterand's Socialists.

IBID.

The intelligent quest is for the free society with equality of opportunity. The quest for equality of result is the path to the widest inequality of all: despotism.

IBID.

By ascribing ignoble values so widely throughout our society, they [the Liberals] gravely damaged all faith in institutions, in individuals, even in the future; and without faith societies begin to fall apart. The Liberals' problem was that they had come into the world as idealists, and every idealist exits a cynic. Better it is to be a realist facing up to the world as it is than to fall into the stupidity of the cynic.

IBID.

After the New Age Liberal had had his say women did not trust the marriage bed, blacks did not trust whites, no one trusted a producer of any kind. Many doubted the arrival of tomorrow. Doctors, lawyers, businessmen, scientists—in fact, experts in almost every walk of life—saw their authority evaporate. As in decadent societies of old, morale sagged. The reward for doing right was abuse or disbelief. The smart fellow was encouraged to cut corners. That is the legacy that the moral hams of the New Age brought into American life, and whether America could ever recover what the founding fathers called its Republican virtue would be in doubt for years to come.

IBID.

Ernest van den Haag (1914–)

*B*orn in The Hague, Netherlands, Ernest van den Haag came to the United States in 1940 and became naturalized in 1947. He received his doctorate in 1952 from New York University, where he taught social philosophy (1946–1975). Until 1980, he was a lecturer in sociology and psychology at the New School for Social Research in New York City. Van den Haag has written many articles and books, including *Political Violence and Civil Disobedience* (1972), *Punishing Criminals* (1975), *Capitalism: Sources of Hostility* (1979), and *The U.N.: In or Out?* (with John P. Conrad, 1987).

. . . I think what we really have to do is to establish that the purpose of punishment . . . is basically retributive and deterrent. That is, that you're not so much interested in the man you put in prison as you are interested in restraining other men who may not want to go to prison from committing the crime that got the first one into prison; and furthermore that you are interested in keeping society's threat—if you do such and such, you will be punished—credible by actually punishing people. Now, as long as people believe . . . in rehabilitation as the purpose, indeed they will be perfectly willing to give up prisons. So what we have constantly to explain is that rehabilitation is not the purpose of punishment at all. It is possibly a desirable, incidental result. So far it hasn't occurred. We haven't found a good way of doing it.

BILL BUCKLEY'S FIRING LINE ON PBS,
"CRIME AND CRIMINALS," NOV. 22, 1975

Richard Art Viguerie (1933–)

*R*ichard Viguerie, former publisher of the *Conservative Digest* (1975–1985) and former director of Young Americans for Freedom, is the author of *The New Right: We're*

Ready to Lead (1980) and *The Establishment vs. the People* (1983).

[The elite] are civil rights leaders more concerned about getting upper-class blacks into Harvard Medical School than making sure poor blacks can read or walk down neighborhood streets in safety. They are ministers more concerned with organizing protests against the Reagan Administration than with saving souls. They are television reporters who try to make the world conform to their own narrow leftwing ideology. They are Big Business, Big Banks, Big Media, Big Unions, Big Government, and their allies.

THE ESTABLISHMENT VS. THE PEOPLE, 1983

What they [the elite] have in common is support for the concentration of power in the hands of a few. They oppose efforts to transfer decision-making . . . [resisting] the notion that decisions should be made at the level closest to the people and that, ideally, people should decide for themselves how to live as long as they do not violate the equal rights of others to do so.

IBID.

The elite fears any private institution strong enough to challenge the absolute authority of the central government. Private schools, churches, businesses, colleges, theaters, libraries, labor unions, and charitable organizations must be regulated into submission.

IBID.

The unspoken assumption of the welfare bureaucracy is that poor people just don't have enough sense to use money for food unless it comes to them in the form of food stamps; that they aren't smart enough to use money to pay their rent unless it is given to them in the form of housing subsidies; and so forth.

IBID.

It is not just the poor whom the government assumes to be stupid. How many government regulations exist to prevent us from doing harm to ourselves? Herbert Spencer had the perfect response to government paternalism: "To protect men from their own folly is to people the world with fools."

With government regulation of everything from milk prices to whether automobiles must have airbags, the question must be asked: Who's in charge here? Do we run the government, or does the government run us?

IBID.

The special interests who are the real beneficiaries of [government programs] . . . believe that there is a limit to the amount of wealth that society can produce, and that we have reached that limit. In their view, which runs counter to the whole of human history, there are only so many products that can be made, so many factories that can be built, and so many jobs that can be created. Their concern is how to divide society's wealth, not how to produce more for everyone.

IBID.

[The special interests'] philosophy divides America into competing interest groups, with each group fighting for its share of a stagnant economy. They would pit old against young (for example, the Social Security bailout), North against South (proposals to prohibit companies from moving factories without government permission), and black against white (racial quotas). They care less about increasing the standard of living of society as a whole than about ensuring that misery is fairly distributed.

IBID.

Marilyn vos Savant (1946–)

*M*arilyn vos Savant is listed in the Guinness Hall of Fame for having the highest officially measured IQ—228. Her column, "Ask Marilyn," is featured weekly in *Parade*. She has written a number of books, including *Ask Marilyn* (1992), *The World's Most Famous Math Problem* (1993), and *I've Forgotten Everything I Learned in School!* (1994).

In addition to buying votes, what's wrong with government doing the spending instead of our doing the spending ourselves? Consider this: When you spend your own money on yourself (such as buying yourself a tie or a handbag), you do an excellent job of keeping the cost down and getting exactly what you want. But when you spend your own money on someone else (such as buying a gift tie and handbag for your parents), you still keep the cost down, but you don't get them what they'd choose themselves. (Think about all the gifts you've ever received: What percentage of them would you have chosen yourself?)

Even worse, when you spend a third party's money on someone else, you not only don't get the recipient what he or she would choose, there's also no pressure to keep the cost under control. (Imagine being allowed to charge that gift tie and handbag to the "taxpayers" instead of to your own account: Would you worry about the cost?) This is what the government does, and in a massive way, every single day.

"ASK MARILYN," *PARADE*, OCT. 9, 1994.

George Washington *(1732–1799)*

*T*he first president of the United States, George Washington began his political life as a member of the Virginia House of Burgesses (1759–1774) and became one of the leaders of the colonial opposition to British policies in America. He was a member of the First and Second Continental Congresses (1774–1775) and was elected to command all Continental armies on June 15, 1775. Near the end of 1783, he resigned his commission and retired to Mount Vernon, from which he was called from retirement to preside at the federal con-

vention in Philadelphia (1787). He was unanimously chosen president of the United States under the new constitution and took his official oath on April 30, 1789. He was unanimously re-elected in 1793 and later declined a third term.

[T]he preservation of the sacred fire of liberty and the destiny of the republican model of government are justly considered, perhaps, as deeply, as finally, staked, on the experiment entrusted to the hands of the American people.

FIRST INAUGURAL ADDRESS, APRIL 30, 1789

It is a maxim founded on the universal experiences of mankind that no nation is to be trusted farther than is bound by its interest.

LETTER TO HENRY LAURENS, 1778

The basis of our political system is the right of the people to make and to alter their constitutions of government.

FAREWELL ADDRESS, 1796

Happily the Government of the United States, which gives to bigotry no sanction, to persecution no assistance, requires only that they who live under its protection should demean themselves as good citizens in giving it on all occasions their effectual support.

LETTER TO THE JEWISH CONGREGATION OF NEWPORT, RHODE ISLAND, 1790

Every man, conducting himself as a good citizen, and being accountable to God alone for his religious opinions, ought to be protected in worshipping the Deity according to the dictates of his own conscience.

LETTER TO THE UNITED BAPTIST CHAMBER OF VIRGINIA, MAY 1789

A free people ought to be armed, but disciplined.

MESSAGE TO CONGRESS, 1790

James Gaius Watt *(1938–)*

*A*fter having earned business and law degrees from the University of Wyoming, James Watt served in various governmental and political positions during several presidential administrations. He served three years as secretary of the interior in the Reagan administration. Watt is the author (with Doug Wead) of *The Courage of a Conservative* (1985).

As laws mandating higher minimum wages have been passed, black youth unemployment has risen from 25.3 percent in 1966 to 47.3 percent in the 1980s.

THE COURAGE OF A CONSERVATIVE, 1985

Conservatives are so sure that a reduced minimum wage would give jobs to millions of untrained, nonunion black workers that they have even tried to get a summer experimental program through the Congress. This would give the country one summer to see if the conservative theorists are right. And with black youth unemployment so staggeringly high, it would certainly be worth the try.

Not so, says the liberal Establishment. Out of one corner of its mouth, it tells blacks that they don't have to settle for lower wages. Meanwhile, almost half of black youth get no wages at all. Out of the other corner of its mouth, it tells white union workers not to worry. Their jobs are protected. Frustrated conservatives point out that this is the very rationalization used in South Africa to keep blacks out of the white work force, but the irony is conveniently ignored. Carlton Pearson points out this cruel discriminatory cycle: "You can't get work without a union card, and you can't get a union card if you have no work experience."

IBID.

Another possible answer to the problems of black economic inequality is enterprise zones. By lowering the tax rates and, in some cases, eliminating them altogether, inner-city ghettos could be transformed. Restaurants, shops, businesses, and factories would pour in, and with them, thousands of jobs.

At first, liberals were dubious and warned that the value of land would increase. Renters would be forced out. One of their studies worried that life in the inner cities would be "disrupted."

Conservatives did their homework, however, on this issue. Our think tanks show convincingly that jobs would multiply at a much faster rate than prices. A few city governments have made the concept work, reviving their inner cities .... Conservatives are offended at the sanctimonious way that liberals refer to "disruption of life" in the ghettos, as if crime-ridden and fire-trap tenement houses were historic

landmarks in need of preservation in their present state.

IBID.

There was a tragic reason why the black divorce rate had reached twice that of whites, and why 55 percent of the nation's illegitimate births were to black mothers. Quite simply, it was the fault of the well-intended but often distorted federal program called Aid to Families with Dependent Children. This program literally induced fathers of poor families to leave home. If the head of a household with children would simply disappear, the federal government would provide his wife with monthly checks, based on the number of those dependent children. In other instances, the program had the effect of encouraging young girls to get pregnant out of wedlock so that they could secure public housing and AFDC payments.

IBID.

Within one generation, the black family unit, which had survived slavery and ugly racial discrimination, was nearly decimated. Many black fathers, who wanted to be strong role models for their children and wanted to spend their lives with the women they loved, were at a loss. The government had shut them out of most small business enterprises with excessive regulations and licensing procedures that favored already established businesses. White labor unions, with powerful Washington lobbies and hypocritical protection by liberal politicians, shut them out. With the rising minimum wage, even menial jobs began disappearing. For many, welfare was the only real alternative, and it was a trap. Regulations required that savings must be spent. It was difficult, if not impossible, to gather the capital to launch any kind of enterprise to break free of government dependency.

IBID.

We conservatives have, from the beginning, challenged the whole idea of a crime-poverty connection. America's crime rate has risen with her wealth. Her crime rate has grown many times higher than that of India, for instance, even though the difference in wealth between our two countries is staggering. Why would a beggar on the streets of Calcutta starve to death rather than steal food to live, even when his punishment would mean only a jail sentence with regular meals? Because being poor does not in itself force him to crime.

IBID.

A shrewder liberal position, and one that has endured to this day, is that crime breeds among the disenfranchised. It is the people who have been discriminated against, liberals insist, or the people to whom society has been unfair who are more likely to violate the law, if they have to, to "get even."

We conservatives, however, challenge this thesis. We simply don't believe that the rise of crime can be blamed on the American system, which liberals would have us believe is flawed and filled with inequities. After forty years when liberal power has been brought to bear on these alleged causes of crime, with every opportunity for experiments by government agencies, with redistribution of wealth and with liberal federal courts, the crime rate has increased. If fairness were indeed the issue, and a liberal program did indeed redress it, then crime should have been going down, not up. Sometime around the 1930s, and again in the 1960s, crime should have begun to decrease as the champions of liberalism saw their legislation passed and their court appointments confirmed. However, the very opposite occurred.

IBID.

Ben J. Wattenberg *(1933–)*

*A*uthor and journalist Ben Wattenberg is a former Democratic Party strategist who now writes for the *Washington Times*. He was an assistant to President Johnson (1966–1968) and an aide to Vice President Humphrey (1970). He has been associated with several leading think tanks, including the Hudson Institute and the American Enterprise Institute. Wattenberg became well known as the host of a series of PBS television specials called *In Search of the Real America* (1977–1978). He returned to PBS in 1990 as host of *Wattenberg—Trends in the '90s*, a news and public affairs series. Wattenberg has been a professor at Mary Washington College and at United States International University. He is the author of such books as *The Real Majority* (1970), *The Good News Is the Bad News Is Wrong* (1984), *The Birth Dearth* (1987), and *The First Universal Nation* (1991).

Reagan's real language should be obvious to historians: . . . he pushed America to think publicly about big things that were not on the anvil before he arrived . . . . Was big government out of hand? Were we overtaxed? Were civil rights initiatives going awry? Was commercial innovation being smothered? . . .

He refocused the national dialogue. Agree with him or disagree, that is the hallmark of a man who has changed his times.

THE FIRST UNIVERSAL NATION, 1991

Environmentalism is the nice crisis. It's the one that a civilization arrives at when there is no war, when the totalitarian threat is shriveling, when the economy is doing pretty well.

Environmentalism is the residual crisis. So, thanks environmentalists. Thanks for a crisis that is never-ending, never provable or disprovable, perennially partially conquerable, and psychologically necessary when there is no other game in town.

"THANKS, ENVIRONMENTALISTS," NOVEMBER 1, 1989

Richard M. Weaver *(1910–1963)*

*A*merican political theorist Richard Weaver, an important defender of traditional conservative values, is best known for his *Ideas Have Consequences* (1948). He is also the author of a collection of essays, *Visions of Order* (1964), and various books on writing and language.

The truth is that if the culture is to assume form and to bring the satisfactions for which cultures are created, it is not culturally feasible for everyone to do everything "any way he wants to."

VISIONS OF ORDER, 1964

The propaganda of egalitarianism encourages belief that any society embodying distinctions must necessarily be torn with envy and hatred.

IBID.

Man is constantly being assured today that he has more power than ever before in history, but his daily experience is one of powerlessness. If he is with a business organization, the odds are great that he has sacrificed every other kind of independence in return for that dubious one known as financial. Modern social and corporate organization makes independence an expensive thing; in fact, it may make common integrity a prohibitive luxury for the ordinary man.

IDEAS HAVE CONSEQUENCES, 1948

Daniel Webster *(1782–1852)*

A lawyer and politician famous for his oratory, Daniel Webster won national recognition in the Supreme Court case *McCullough v. Maryland* (1819). He was a Federalist and represented New Hampshire in the House of Representatives (1813–1817). After he moved to Boston, he served in the House (1823–1827) and Senate (1827–1841, 1845–1850). Webster was secretary of state under presidents Harrison (1841–1843) and Fillmore (1850–1852).

An unlimited power to tax involves, necessarily, the power to destroy.

ARGUMENT IN *McCULLOUGH V. MARYLAND,* SUPREME COURT, 1819

In the nature of things, those who have no property and see their neighbors possess much more than they think them to need, cannot be favorable to laws made for the protection of property. When this class becomes numerous, it becomes clamorous. It looks on property as its prey and plunder, and is naturally ready, at times, for violence and revolution.

ADDRESS, MASSACHUSETTS CONVENTION, 1820

Whatever government is not a government of laws, is a despotism, let it be called what it may.

SPEECH, AUG. 25, 1825

Paul Michael Weyrich (1942-)

A political organizations executive, Paul Weyrich has been a newscaster and a political reporter. He was an assistant to U.S. Senator Gordon Allott of Colorado (1966–1973) and U.S. Senator Carl Curtis of Nebraska (1973–1977). He was the founder and original president of the Heritage Foundation (1973–1974), the largest conservative think tank. He has also been the national chair of the Free Congress PAC and president of the Free Congress Foundation. Recipient of a number of awards, including the Documentary of the Year Award for Wisconsin TV (1965), Weyrich is the president of National Empowerment Television. He is the author of *The Role of Rails* series (1964), an editor of *Future 21: Directions for America in the 21st Century* (with Connaught Marshner, 1984) and a contributor to *The New Right Papers* (Robert W. Whitaker, editor, 1982).

Collectivism, which is what the Left is ultimately advocating in a thousand guises, is an error.

"BLUE COLLAR OR BLUE BLOOD?"
IN *THE NEW RIGHT PAPERS*, 1982

It is time for changes that will once again empower voters themselves to shape the American agenda.

"THE REFORM OF DEMOCRATIC INSTITUTIONS"
IN *FUTURE 21*, 1984

It is time to do a better, more thoughtful job of defining moral issues. It is time to reach out to people everywhere and show them how important moral issues are in their lives, how moral problems are at the root of the growing dissatisfaction with life in the United States.

"BUREAUCRACY: AN INHERENT EVIL?" IN *FUTURE 21*, 1984

The question is, do our institutions— our government, our companies, our military services, our schools, and so on— reward moral or immoral behavior? . . .

. . . My fear is that we are becoming more and more like the Soviet Union— not because we are becoming communist, but because we are becoming bureaucratic, and bureaucracies everywhere tend to reward evil and punish good.

IBID.

Whether in Russia or in the United States, bureaucracy rewards immoral behavior and punishes the honest man. And so it works to turn the honest man into a liar and a cheat. That is not an accident. It is a part of the soul of bureaucracy.

IBID.

Aaron B. Wildavsky *(1930–1993)*

*A*aron Wildavsky was a professor of political science and public policy as well as a member of the Surrey Research Center at the University of California at Berkeley. The editor of several works, he also wrote *How to Limit Government Spending* (1980), *A History of Taxation*

and Expenditure in the Western World (with Carolyn Webber, 1986), *Presidential Elections* (with Nelson Polsby, 7th edition, 1988), *Searching for Safety* (1988), *The Deficit and the Public Interest* (with Joseph White, 1989), and *Assimilation Versus Separation* (1993).

Why don't I like big government? It breeds dependency, which is bad for the moral fiber of the citizenry. It breaks down, which brings disrespect. When the rate of return on government securities is higher than in the stock market, which it has been for some time, thinking of government as one's main source of support is as understandable as it is unfortunate. In falling, as it were, by its own weight, big government threatens to take a free society with it. The liberty we prize is compromised when it appears to result in government that does too much and accomplishes too little. The disrepute of democracy is the high price we pay for elephantiasis of the political organs.

HOW TO LIMIT GOVERNMENT SPENDING, 1980

There was a time, no later than the 1950s, when liberals lusted after federal expenditure to do good. If only there were billions for higher education or for mass transportation or for mental health, on and on, what wonders would be performed! Now we know better. Government is an inadequate and expensive replacement for the family. Deep-seated behavior, requiring the cooperation of the convert, is difficult to change at any price. Those who used to argue that federal money would not bring federal effort to control education, like I did as a college student, have had their naiveté exposed. It is not that public policy is good for nothing, but that it is not good for everything. And the more that is done, the more programs like disaster insurance and Medicaid lead to huge, unanticipated costs, the less we understand or are able to alter them. Thus it is reasonable for us to reconsider what has been done over the decades with a view to perfecting our preferences about what we ought to want. But reconsidering and revamping public policy cannot be carried on seriously while government is expanding on all cylinders and in every sector.

IBID.

Donald Ellis Wildmon *(1938–)*

*O*rdained a United Methodist minister in 1964, Donald Wildmon, the former pastor of First United Methodist Church, Southhaven, Miss. (1976–1977), is the founder (in 1977) of both the influential National Federation for Decency (N.F.D.), which changed its name to the American Family Association (A.F.A.) in 1987, and the Coalition for Better Television (1981–1982). Through the A.F.A. and its *AFA Journal*, the Reverend Donald Wildmon has crusaded for higher-quality television programming. He is also the author of numerous books, including *Thoughts Worth Thinking* (1968), *Stand Up to Life* (1975), and *Words of Gold* (1975).

We [the N.F.D.] don't mess around with the FCC or the government. If you want to change TV, you change it through the pocketbook.

PEOPLE, Nov. 27, 1978

[Television] is a medium that has the potential to be one of the most constructive forces in history . . . , and it's going to the gutter.

IBID.

It has taken fifty years or longer to reduce our culture to its present sorry state. We are just beginning to swing the pendulum back the other way . . . .

QUOTED IN *CONSERVATIVE DIGEST*, MARCH 1988

The demand for sex and violence, for porn and titillation, has always been there. But for our nation's first 180 years or so, we had the good sense to keep it under wraps where it belongs. Until 1950, until television.

QUOTED IN THE *WALL STREET JOURNAL*, APRIL 7, 1989

George Frederick Will *(1941-)*

S yndicated columnist, contributing editor for *Newsweek*, and commentator on ABC's *This Week* television program, George Will is the winner of a Pulitzer Prize in commentary (1977) and the author of such books as *The Pursuit of Happiness and Other Sobering Thoughts* (1979), *Statecraft as Soulcraft: What Government Does* (1983), *Men at Work* (1990), and *Restoration* (1992).

The recent lowering of academic standards reflects, in part, the same collapse in standards, and the same celebration of self-expression as a self-justifying process of "liberation." Thus it is considered "elitist," and hence disreputable, to think that some achievements, and hence some achievers, are better than others. Anti-elitism is the natural consequence of liberalism that celebrates "liberation" through "self-expression" of a spontaneously formed "self." Given this idea, education is less a matter of putting something into people than of letting something out of them. That something can be let out only by "liberation" of the individual from his own inhibitions, and from society's standards, which are externally "imposed" and hence repressive. The transformation of the word "elite" into an epithet is a symptom that society no longer understands that the political question is always which elites shall rule, not whether elites shall rule. The use of "elite" as an epithet is symptomatic of a society in which standards of excellence are regarded as a form of aggression, an offense against the egalitarian principle that all desires are created equal in moral worth.

STATECRAFT AS SOULCRAFT, 1983

At a time when society needs all the excellence and discipline it can muster, the idea of excellence is regarded as faintly illiberal, and discipline is regarded as an unjustifiable impediment to spontaneity. The novelist Peter De Vries was caricaturing such liberalism when he wrote of a girl "who sometimes spelled the same word two different ways in the same paragraph, thereby showing spontaneity."

IBID.

The essence of childishness is an inability to imagine an incompatibility between one's appetite and the world. Growing up involves, above all, a conscious effort to conform one's appetites to a crowded world.

IBID.

World War II was the last government program that really worked.

WASHINGTONIAN, JULY 1975

The best use of history is as an inoculation against radical expectations, and hence against embittering disappointments.

THE PURSUIT OF HAPPINESS AND OTHER SOBERING THOUGHTS, 1979

The ambition of the modern mind is to spare itself a chilling sight, that of the cold blank stare of personal evil. The modern program is squeamishness dressed up as sophistication. Its aim is to make the reality of evil disappear behind a rhetorical gauze of learned garbage.

Until relatively recently in most societies, people who did what the "wilding" boys [30 young persons who brutally assaulted and raped a female jogger in New York City] did would have been punished swiftly and with terrible severity.

Punishment in this case will be interminably delayed and ludicrously light . . . . A society that flinches from the faces of evil will flinch from the act of punishment. I should not wonder why it does not feel safe.

WASHINGTON POST, APRIL 30, 1989

Armstrong Williams *(1960–)*

*H*ost of the nationally syndicated talk show, *The Right Side*, and one of America's most influential black conservatives, Armstrong Williams has been a legislative aide to Senator Strom Thurmond (1980), Congressman Carroll Campbell (1981), and Congressman Floyd Spence (1981). He was also a legislative analyst at the U.S. Department of Agriculture (1981–1983) and a confidential assistant to Clarence Thomas during part of Thomas's tenure at the U.S. Equal Employment Opportunity Commission. The CEO of the international public relations firm, the Graham-Williams Group, Williams was honored as one of the thirty most influential young black Americans by *Ebony Magazine* (1985) and was voted Youth of the Year by the Congressional Black Caucus (1982–1983). He is the author of *Beyond Blame* (1995), a book based on letters Williams wrote to a young black man who was involved in crime and other antisocial behavior.

Today the "civil rights establishment" is all about what kind of special treatment America owes blacks as a result of its racist past, rather than about what we can do to get beyond that. We push for a legalized racial spoils system called affirmative action, which, in principle, is just another shade of the old Jim Crow laws.

BEYOND BLAME, 1995

We talk about "reparations." From whom? People who never held slaves. For whom? People who never were slaves.

IBID.

[W]e set up our own children for bitter disappointment by trying to fill them up with empty self-esteem. We think that if we teach kids to feel good about themselves, perhaps real accomplishments will follow. That approach is exactly backward. Both Malcolm X and Dr. King would have agreed that each of us should understand our own inherent worth as beloved children of God. Beyond that, both would measure a man or woman by how hard he or she struggles to follow God's laws and improve himself or herself. Esteem is a high reward or opinion for someone. Real self-esteem comes from making oneself worthy to be esteemed, but today it is in fashion to teach young people that just showing up is enough. Our children are in for an awful shock if we send them into the world with a baseless high regard for themselves.

IBID.

Walter E. Williams (1936–)

*W*alter Williams, an economist at George Mason University, is a black critic of the civil rights establishment. His political and economic thought largely reflects a libertarian perspective, from which he resists demands for "economic rights" that go beyond those rights guaranteed by the Constitution. Williams has written many articles, as well as such books as *The State Against Blacks* (1982) and *All It Takes Is Guts* (1987). He is also a frequent guest host on Rush Limbaugh's radio show.

Years ago, there was far more pride and self-respect in America. Someone who had two or three illegitimate children was seen as their own worst enemy. Today, we blame society. People who refused to work were considered bums; today they're helpless "victims" of society, and you and I must be taxed for their indiscretions and sustain them in their mistaken lifestyle.

"TODAY, WE BLAME SOCIETY," APRIL 26, 1989

It's about time we recognize that the government cannot provide the basic ingredients for upward mobility. Child-rearing practices in which parents make children do their homework, behave in school, and go to bed on time are beyond government policy. Personal pride, ambition, perseverance,

and self-respect can't be given by government; but they can be weakened by handout programs. Government is no match for the family, church, and civic organizations for instilling success-oriented values.

IBID.

On measures of self-esteem, compared to most other industrial nations, American students rank quite high. However, so far as academic performance, our youth rank among the lowest. That's because self-esteem, instead of self-discipline, has become part of our educational creed.

IBID.

Children are precious not only to parents but to the future of our nation. Our children are not materially poor; however, they are spiritually impoverished. They've been led to believe that life's disappointments and challenges are violations of human rights; gratification is never to be postponed; ethics and values depend on the person and the situation; and honesty and morality are only for chumps. Not all youngsters have this vision of the world, but enough have it so that the future of our country stands in jeopardy.

"GET THE 'EXPERTS' OUT OF OUR LIVES," OCT. 2, 1991

Garry Wills *(1934–)*

A professor of classics and of American culture and public policy, syndicated columnist Garry Wills is the author of several works, including *Chesterton* (1961), *Inventing America* (1978), *Confessions of a Conservative* (1979), *Reagan's America* (1987), *Explaining America* (1980), and *Under God* (1990). He also contributed "The Convenient State" in *What is Conservatism?* (1964).

If you want to find the jealous embrace of attained power, go to the Liberal idealogue, who must have total power in order to achieve his total reform, his rapid creation of Utopia.

WHAT IS CONSERVATISM?, 1964

James Quinn Wilson *(1931–)*

A n author and a U.C.L.A. professor of management, James Q. Wilson has served on various presiden-tial task forces and national advisory commissions on crime, law enforcement, and drug abuse prevention. He has also written numerous books, including *Political Organizations* (1973), *Thinking about Crime* (1975), *The Investigators: Managing the FBI and Narcotics Agents* (1978), *Crime and Human Nature* (with Richard Herrnstein, 1985), and *The Moral Sense* (1993).

There are no more liberals . . . . They've all been mugged.

TIME, JAN. 21, 1985

Private property, though the enemy of equality, is the ally of equity. It gives men the motive to supply contributions of efforts and a yardstick to judge the allo-cation of rewards. Ownership leads to disputes, but property individually held produces fewer disputes than property commonly held. Property rights supply a basis for settling disputes that is fairer than the feasible alternative, which is brute force, whether that force is the mailed fist of a monarch or the velvet glove of the legislature.

THE MORAL SENSE, 1993

Political liberty, which is one of the greatest gifts a people can acquire for themselves, is threatened when social order is threatened. It is dismaying to see how ready many people are to turn to strong leaders in hopes that they will end, by adopting strong measures, the disorder that has been the product of failed or fragile commitments. Drug abuse, street crime, and political corruption are the expression of unfettered choices. To end them, rulers, with the warm support of the people, will often adopt measures that threaten true political freedom. The kind of culture that can maintain reasonable human commitments takes centuries to create but only a few generations to destroy. And once destroyed, those who suddenly realize what they have lost will also realize that political action cannot, except at a very great price, restore it.

IBID.

Mankind's moral sense is not a strong beacon light, radiating outward to illuminate in sharp outline all that it touches. It is, rather, a small candle flame, casting vague and multiple shadows, flickering and sputtering in the strong winds of power and passion, greed and ideology. But brought close to the heart and cupped in one's hands, it dispels darkness and warms the soul.

IBID.

Wicked people exist. Nothing avails except to set them apart from innocent people. And many people, neither wicked nor innocent, but watchful, dissembling, and calculating of their chances, ponder our reaction to wickedness as a clue to what they might profitably do. Our actions speak louder than our words. When we profess to believe in deterrence and to value justice, but refuse to spend the energy and money required to produce either, we are sending a clear signal that we think that safe streets, unlike all other great public goods, can be had on the cheap. We thereby trifle with the wicked, make sport of the innocent, and encourage the calculators. Justice suffers, and so do we all.

THINKING ABOUT CRIME, 1975

Robert L. Woodson (1937–)

*A*ctive in the civil rights movement and the NAACP in the 1960s, Robert L. Woodson came to dissent from the conventional forces of black advocacy in the latter part of that decade. In 1981, after leaving his position at the American Enterprise Institute, Woodson founded the National Center for Neighborhood Enterprise, a grass-roots organization dedicated to free enterprise and to efforts to help poor black people become self-reliant. Woodson has written a number of articles and books, including *A Summons to Life* (1981) and *On the Road to Economic Freedom* (1987).

People who are now "protected" by government aid programs need instead to be empowered by them. Policies should be geared toward maximizing independence, economic opportunity, and freedom-of-choice for those receiving government-funded services. Regulatory and procedural barriers that prevent a community from starting its own schools, day-care centers, and adoption agencies, should be done away with.

This less restricted policy approach will make it possible for greater numbers of low-income black citizens to participate in the mainstream of the American economy. A policy that will encourage the development of black enterprises will strengthen the economic base of black neighborhoods and put more money into the pockets of the black underclass.

ON THE ROAD TO ECONOMIC FREEDOM, 1987

With statistics available showing that many students enrolled in community-based schools are outperforming their public school counterparts, the groundwork has already been laid for future gen-erations to climb out of poverty and welfare dependency with relevant educations. For this reason alone, a voucher system should be established that would give money directly to impoverished parents who have been denied access to fee-charging private schools. Such a system would be a fair way of getting a return on the taxes spent to support public education.

An argument may also be made that the more educated our youth, the less likely their gravitation to crime and the unemployment rolls—two areas that cost governments dearly in social welfare and maintenance programs.

IBID.

[The] government-knows-best policy herded low-income families into high rise buildings that bred crime and frustration, discouraged the work ethic, fostered dependency on public assistance and stifled the initiative of small entrepreneurs with programmed-to-fail bureaucratic restrictions.

ORLANDO SENTINEL, JAN. 18, 1989

Anne Wortham (1941-)

A black sociologist, Anne Wortham is best known for

her book *The Other Side of Racism* (1981), in which she criticizes pressure exerted on black Americans to subordinate their individuality to "ethnorace consciousness."

We need to identify which aspects of the civil rights movement constitute a legitimate, moral quest for freedom in response to external discrimination and racism and which are but a revolt against freedom as a response to the internal dilemma of self-esteem.

THE OTHER SIDE OF RACISM, 1981

For the past four decades our response to civil rights activism has been to ask beleaguered minorities: "What do you want?" and to provide what is demanded whether or not it is necessary, just, or even feasible. But in our eagerness to satisfy—to content the discontented—to ease our own conscience—we have absolved them of the responsibility for their demands and sacrificed our own self-interest in the process.

IBID.

We have seen the concept "equal rights" transformed into yet another surrogate concept for social parasitism and it is now a euphemism for equality of results and equal conditions. We have seen "civil rights"—a valid concept deriving its objective meaning from the principle of human rights—stripped of all rational meaning and used as a legal weapon against the very principles of natural rights of which it is a subcategory. There is nothing figurative about "civil rights," but it has become a euphemism for political privileges forced into existence at the expense of the rights of others. It is employed by everyone, from storefront social workers to federal justices, in order to legitimate the transformation of personal desires into public policy.

IBID.

It is time to end the unprincipled, unjust compliance with the demands of the liberationist whose means of seeking liberation can only result in enslavement.

IBID.

A man without self-esteem cannot overcome socioeconomic and political limitations; he cannot respond rationally to prejudice, discrimination, and racism. If such injustice and hardships assume such great importance in his view of himself and reality, it is because he has no countervalues to offset them.

IBID.

Negroes are just as subject to the requirements of human nature as any other group of men. Being discriminated against, humiliated, and oppressed by laws abusive of their rights does not relegate them to the outer fringes of what defines the nature of the human being; such treatment does not render them *less* human. Neither does their "victimization" elevate them beyond the laws of reality entitling them to a special set of rules by which to function; they are not *more* human.

IBID.

Every man is his own creator—responsible for his own existence, the content of his consciousness, and the nature of his actions. He may surround himself by hundreds of thousands and march the streets of the Seat of Liberty, proclaiming his "dream" of an open community without prejudice, discrimination, and racism, but in the final analysis only he can create the personal sovereignty on which the establishment and maintenance of such a community must rest.

IBID.

If the plight of Negroes as a group continues to be a hardship, it is, to a large degree, because so many individuals in that group either do not know or refuse to accept the fact that self-determination and self-identity can be neither achieved nor destroyed by political means.

IBID.

To those . . . who would enslave us with . . . welfare statism, we must say: *No! The equality you urge on us is not a requirement of our existence as beings of volitional consciousness and we reject all your efforts to make it so. We reject your attempts to make us exceptions to the rules of human existence simply because of our skin color. We do not want the results of our action to be "equal" to everyone else's. We do not want any private doors opened for us by the force of government intervention. We do not want a guaranteed livelihood paid for by the expropriated resources of others. We do not want to be spared the responsibility and risks of surviving by our own means. We do not want "assistance" given as blackmail paid to silence a militant's gun or to prevent a looter's rampage. We do not want an education at universities we are not qualified to attend. We do not want positions of employment we are unqualified to hold. We do not want "preferential treatment" in order to be spared the risks of competition by achievement. We want no honors we do not deserve. We want no rewards we have not earned. We want only to be free! What you seek in our behalf and in the name of justice is unjust, immoral, and antihuman; it requires that some men exist at the expense of others; it requires the law of the jungle. But we will no longer participate in our own destruction. We will no longer help you pretend that what you do is right and just. We will not help you use freedom to destroy freedom.*

IBID.

While we must acknowledge the dark history . . . there is no reason to be bound by it as the reference point from which Negroes should fashion their present and future participation in American life. There is no more cause to base the free relations between contemporary blacks and whites on slavery and the Civil War than there is for basing relations between Great Britain and the United States on colonialism and the Revolutionary War. The voice of the past speaks to us, but it emits echoes of the deeds of men before us from whose tragedies and triumphs we can learn but can neither change nor claim as our own. There comes a time in the lives of individuals and in the history of groups of people when it is wise to take Shakespeare's advice: "Things without remedy, should be without regard; what is done, is done."

IBID.

In alliance with other ethnic and pressure groups, statist intellectuals and appeasing businessmen, he [the social metaphysician] has conned Americans into believing that in order to be moral they must sacrifice morality; that in order to achieve values, they must sacrifice virtues. In order for institutions of higher learning to be the mainstay of intellectual excellence, they must give up excellence. In order for employers to remain in business, they must give up standards of achievement, production, and free-market competition. In order for employees to enjoy the fruits of their labor, they must give up their wages to someone else's need. In order for government to protect equal opportunity, legislators, bureaucrats, and the courts must impose policies of "preferential treatment." And on it goes.

IBID.

He [the Negro] will have to accept the responsibility of standing alone—not behind the mask of ethnicity, but naked before the sunlight of truth and liberty.

IBID.

Zig Ziglar *(1926–)*

Since 1970, motivational speaker and entrepreneurial advisor Zig Ziglar has spoken around the world on platforms with Ronald Reagan, Norman Vincent Peale, Paul Harvey, Robert Schuller, congressmen and governors, and a host of others. He is the author of the best-selling *See You At the Top* (1974) as well as *Confessions of a Happy Christian* (1978), *Zig Ziglar's Secrets of Closing the Sale* (1984), *Raising Positive Kids in a Negative World* (1985), *Courtship After Marriage* (1990), and various other works. Ziglar's books, videos, and audiotapes are used by hundreds of corporations to train employees. In 1984, he was elected first vice president of the Southern Baptist Convention.

One look at the Post Office, Medicare, Medicaid, Social Security and the food stamp program will convince anyone that despite the efforts of tens of thousands of dedicated government employees, who have devoted a lifetime to conscientiously serving America and the general public, the government simply doesn't know how to run a business.

SEE YOU AT THE TOP, 1974

I'm especially concerned that American youth are not being sold on the American free enterprise system. According to the United States Chamber of Commerce and the Princeton Institute, 67% of our high school students do not believe a business needs a profit and nearly 50% of them cannot give you even one advantage that capital-ism has over communism. 63% of the American high school students feel the Federal Government should own the banks, railroads and the steel companies. 62% do not believe a worker should produce to the best of his ability . . . . These things are frightening but don't blame the kids. It's *our* fault. We write the books, build the schools and pay the educators. It is up to us to teach our sons and daughters.

IBID.

As Americans we must demand that our heroes and moral teaching be put back into the history books. According to the Thomas Jefferson Research Center, when America won its independence, religion and morals accounted for more than 90% of the content of school readers. By 1926 the figure was only 6% and today it is almost immeasurable. History proves that if we give our children heroes and moral principles to live up to—they will. We need to teach our children—from early childhood—about our heroes of yesteryear. We need to tell them the stories of America—its greatness and its goodness, because the spirit of America is caught—as it's taught.

IBID.

[W]e do have to sell America and the free enterprise system to our children, because only one generation stands between us and all the "Ism's" in the world. It's equally clear that we need to sell the free enterprise system to those teachers and professors who often belittle the very system that sustains them. We need to sell labor leaders and union members on the concept that a laborer should be free to work as hard and as enthusiastically as he wishes for the benefit of everyone. That *is* Free Enterprise. That *is* the American way . . . .

. . . We also need to sell government employees and officials on the fact that government doesn't produce income or prosperity. Instead, it exists and survives because free people working in a free land support the government. We need to sell elected officials on the simple fact

that the right to work and produce without undue government restraint is not only our right but our source of strength. One good look at any socialistic country will convince any clear thinker that *free enterprise is the only way to go.*

IBID.

What about you? Are you accepting your responsibility? If everyone in America was doing exactly the same thing you're doing, would our country be getting better, or worse? That's a question for you and your conscience. If you really love America, you will enthusiastically join the ever-increasing throng working to make a great America even greater.

IBID.

Index

This index of concepts allows the reader quickly to find the major concepts discussed in the quotations. (For a list of the names of the persons quoted in this book, along with their respective page numbers, refer to the table of contents.)

About the Compilers

*R*od Evans and Irwin Berent, the compilers of *The Quotable Conservative*, are also the coauthors of books on interpersonal communication (*The Right Words*, Warner Books, 1992) and word play (*Getting Your Words' Worth*, Warner Books, 1993), as well as the series of Putnam-Berkley dictionaries—*Weird Words* (1995), *More Weird Words* (1995), and *Word Circus* (1995)—and even *The ABC of Cat Trivia* (St. Martin's Press, 1996).

In addition, their scholarly works have included introductions and forewords from such persons as Linus Pauling, Hugh Downs, Isaac Asimov, and Steve Allen.

Evans and Berent also speak on words, writing, and getting published, as well as on conservatism, the war on drugs, and other social and political issues. For inquiries, call the Speaker's Agency at 1-800-577-3250.

Dr. Evans holds a doctorate in philosophy from the University of Virginia and is also the scriptwriter for the *Knowledge Products* audiotape, *Drugs and Alcohol*, a historical and philosophical analysis of drugs and drug laws.

Mr. Berent holds a master's in American history from East Carolina University and is also a co-creator of StoryCraft Software, the acclaimed computer program that uses stories with moral themes to teach the art of writing screenplays, novels, and short stories. The software is distributed by StoryCraft Corp. (1-800-97-STORY).